全国高等院校法律英语专业统编教材
法律英语证书（LEC）全国统一考试指定用书

英美法律
术语双解

Common Law Terms
You Need to Know

张法连　编著

北京大学出版社
PEKING UNIVERSITY PRESS

图书在版编目(CIP)数据

英美法律术语双解/张法连编著. —北京:北京大学出版社,2016.10
(全国高等院校法律英语专业统编教材)
ISBN 978-7-301-27614-3

Ⅰ.①英… Ⅱ.①张… Ⅲ.①法律—英语—名词术语—英国—高等学校—教材 ②法律—英语—名词术语—美国—高等学校—教材 Ⅳ.①D956.1-61②D971.2-61

中国版本图书馆 CIP 数据核字(2016)第 236303 号

书　　　名	英美法律术语双解 YING MEI FALÜ SHUYU SHUANGJIE
著作责任者	张法连　编著
策 划 编 辑	郭栋磊
责 任 编 辑	李　娜
标 准 书 号	ISBN 978-7-301-27614-3
出 版 发 行	北京大学出版社
地　　　址	北京市海淀区成府路 205 号　100871
网　　　址	http://www.pup.cn　新浪微博:@北京大学出版社
电 子 邮 箱	编辑部 pupwaiwen@pup.cn　总编室 zpup@pup.cn
电　　　话	邮购部 62752015　发行部 62750672　编辑部 62752027
印 刷 者	天津中印联印务有限公司
经 销 者	新华书店
	787 毫米×1092 毫米　16 开本　21.5 印张　375 千字 2016 年 10 月第 1 版　2024 年 12 月第 8 次印刷
定　　　价	68.00 元

未经许可,不得以任何方式复制或抄袭本书之部分或全部内容。
版权所有,侵权必究
举报电话: 010-62752024　电子信箱: fd@pup.cn
图书如有印装质量问题,请与出版部联系,电话: 010-62756370

前　言

法律英语是法律科学与英语语言学有机结合形成的一门实践性很强的交叉学科,是ESP(English for Specific Purpose)最重要的分支之一。法律英语是以普通英语为基础,在立法和司法等活动中形成和使用的具有法律专业特点的语言,是指表述法律科学概念以及诉讼或非诉讼法律事务时所使用的英语。当今世界的发展日新月异,经济全球化进程突飞猛进,国际交流合作日益加强,涉外法务活动空前频繁。中国共产党十八届四中全会提出要加强涉外法律工作,运用法律手段维护国家的发展利益。经济全球化过程中我们所面临的很多问题其实都是法律问题,而这些法律问题中的绝大多数又都属于涉外法律的工作范畴,所有这些工作都需要法律工作者通过专业外语完成。国家急需明晰国际法律规则、通晓英语语言的"精英明法"复合型人才,法律英语的重要性日益彰显,掌握专业外语已经成为法律人必备的职业素质。法律英语证书(LEC)全国统一考试的成功推出和中央政法委、教育部"卓越法律人才计划"的顺利启动无疑把法律英语的学习和研究推向了高潮。

法律英语是法律界通用的专业英语,包括书面法律英语和法律英语口语。法律英语是法律语言中的一种,它属于应用语言学的范畴,是一种具有法律职业技能特征的职业语言。词汇是语言的基本组成部分,它包括俚语、术语、行话等。英语词汇相当丰富,但不同的词汇有着不同的文体作用,不同的文体又要求用不同的词汇来表达。"法律语言部分地是由具有特定法律意义的词组成,部分地是由日常用语组成的。具有特定法律意义的词,在日常用语中即使有也很少使用"(戴维·沃克:《牛津法律大辞典》,光明日报出版社,1988:515)。除了具有特定法律意义的词之外,很多在日常生活中普遍应用的词汇,一旦到了法律语境中,便具有了法律意义。难怪很多学生抱怨说法律英语难学,阅读一篇判例,要么碰到一些非英语的词汇,使人摸不着头脑;要么碰到很多普通的英语单词却在文中肯定有着不普通的含义,令人无法猜测。其实法律术语已经成为学习法律英语的首要障碍。所以,对于广大的法律英语爱好者来说,了解和研究法律英语的术语特点,掌握一定量的法律英语术语是学好法律英语的前提,具有十分重要的意义。

要学好法律英语，首先从法律英语的词汇短语入手。本书收录的词条都是美国法学专业和美国法律实践中经常用到的术语。为了让读者更直观全面地理解术语含义，每个词条后面都有英语释义。词无定译，因为中美法律文化的差异和法律制度的不同，书中部分美国法术语的汉译颇费周折，其中的心酸只有译者自己知道；即使经过努力挣扎翻译出来的术语，译者也并非完全满意，所以有些术语翻译很值得商榷，希望广大读者不吝赐教。

和本书配套使用的教材共包括《法律英语精读教程》《法律英语泛读教程》《法律英语写作教程》《法律英语翻译教程》和《英美法律文化教程》，均由北京大学出版社出版发行。感谢法律英语证书（LEC）全国统一考试委员会（www.lectest.com）指定此书为LEC考试复习参考书。姜芳、唐丽玲、胡朝丽、贾小兰、赵钰伶等老师和同学参与了部分词条的修订工作。在编写此书的过程中，我们参阅了大量资料，恕不一一列出，在此谨对原作者表示衷心感谢。

书中不妥之处，敬请同仁指正。

张法连

2016年9月16日

CONTENTS 目录

英美法律术语双解

A	001
B	031
C	044
D	079
E	099
F	112
G	126
H	133
I	138
J	155
K	165
L	167
M	179
N	196
O	205
P	211
Q	244
R	247
S	267
T	289
U	299
V	305
W	310
X	317
Y	318
Z	320
附录一　常见美国法引证缩写	321
附录二　常用法律缩略语	324

A

ABA—American Bar Association is one of the world's largest voluntary professional organizations, with nearly 400,000 members and more than 3,500 entities. It is committed to doing what only a national association of attorneys can do: serving members, improving the legal profession, eliminating bias and enhancing diversity, and advancing the rule of law throughout the United States and around the world. Founded in 1878, the ABA is committed to supporting the legal profession with practical resources for legal professionals while improving the administration of justice, accrediting law schools, establishing model ethical codes, and more. Membership is open to lawyers, law students, and others interested in the law and the legal profession. The national headquarters are in Chicago, with a significant office presence in Washington DC.

美国律师协会

> ABA 是美国律师协会的英文全称缩写。ABA 成立于1878年，是美国律师的全国性组织。当时成立 ABA 的主要目的是为了改善法学教育，提高从业管理标准，并为了组织一些娱乐活动。该协会一直致力于推动法律科

ab initio

学发展、提高律师素质、完善司法管理、促进立法与裁判的统一,并加强会员之间的社会交流。经过一个多世纪的发展,ABA 已成为世界上最大的法律职业组织。ABA 制定了律师与法官职业准则,组建了美国法律研究机构,创建了统一各州法律的委员会大会,并负责全国范围内的会员的日常事务,但没有具体的管理职能。ABA 是自愿性组织,通过美国律师考试(BAR)的律师都可参加。美国律师协会的主席委员会执行行政管理职能,并设有常务委员会处理协会的日常事务和活动。来自各州和大地区的律师协会的代表组成的代表会议是美国律师协会的政策制定机构。美国律师协会还设有代表机构,协会的工作由代表机构的主管委员会及其他委员会监督、指导。律师协会下设许多分部,如法官会议、法律学生部、青年律师部、老年律师部以及其他一些分支机构,大量的专业领域里的论坛委员会等。每一分部负责法律的一个领域或法律事务的一个分支。注重保持律师职业行为的准则及提高法学教育水平,支持有助于完善司法管理与实现立法统一的措施。ABA 总部设在芝加哥。

ab initio—a Latin term meaning "from the beginning". For example, if something is said to be void ab initio, the thing was never created or valid to begin with. The term is often used in connection with contracts, estates, and marriages.

自始;从开始;说明事件由开始时的状态

abandon—to denote a complete giving up, especially of what one has previously been interested in or responsible for. In family law, it usually means to leave a spouse or child willfully and without an intention to return.

放弃或中止某项权利或义务,遗弃财产(永远不再主张);家庭法上指离弃配偶或家庭成员

abandonment—the act of leaving a spouse or child willfully and without an intent to return. In the context of contracts, it is merely the acceptance by one party of the situation that a nonperformance party has caused.

(永远)离弃配偶或子女;合同的撤销(仅指合同一方接受另一方当事人所造成的不予履行合同之情形)

abate—to lessen, reduce or remove (esp. a nuisance); to lower the price.

减轻或全部及部分废除(常用于降价及税收、遗产或骚扰的减少等)

abator—one who abates a nuisance.

排除妨害者

abdicate—to refuse or renounce a thing, a person in office to renounce it or give it up voluntarily.

放弃（某种权利或法定职位）

abduction—the action or an instance of forcibly taking a person or persons away against their will.

诱骗,绑架;挟持罪

abet—to encourage or assist (someone) to do something wrong, in particular, to commit a crime or other offense.

煽动;怂恿;教唆他人犯罪

abiding by plea—(*English law*) A defendant who pleads a frivolous plea, or a plea merely for the purpose of delaying the suit; or who for the same purpose, shall file a similar demurrer, may be compelled by rule in term time, or by a Judge's order in vacation, either to abide by that plea, or by that demurrer, or to plead peremptorily on the morrow; or if near the end of the term, and in order to afford time for notice of trial, the motion may be made in court for rule to abide or plead instanter; that is, within twenty-four hours after rule served, provided that the regular time for pleading be expired. If the defendant when ruled, do not abide, he can only plead the general issue; but he may add notice of set-off.

（英国法）紧急申辩规则（被告仅仅是为了拖延案件审理,也许会找出很牵强的借口提出申辩,在申辩期结束时向法庭提交抗辩,因为时间等关系,这种抗辩申请也许会被批准。被告只要在申辩期结束后的24小时内提出抗辩,便适用紧急申辩规则。）

abigeus—(*civ. law*) a particular kind of larceny, which is committed not by taking and carrying away the property from one place to another, but by driving a living thing away with an intention of feloniously appropriating the same.

家畜盗窃犯

ability—the capacity to perform an act or service, esp. the power to carry out a legal act.

法律行为能力

abjure—solemnly renounce (a belief, cause, or claim).
发誓放弃;公开放弃

abjuration—solemn repudiation, denial, abandonment, or renunciation by or upon oath. it is often the renunciation of citizenship or some other right or privilege.
发誓断绝;公开放弃

abolish—to do away with wholly, particularly to things of a permanent nature, such as institutions, usages, customs, etc.
(完全)废止、取消(制度、风俗、习惯等)

abortion—an intentionally-induced miscarriage as distinguished from one resulting naturally or by accident.
(人为的)堕胎;中止妊娠

abridge—(*usu. be abridged*) curtail (rights or privileges).
(权利、自由等)的剥夺

abrogate—formal repeal or do away with (a law, right or formal agreement).
(正式经授权)取消或废除(下级机关颁布的法律、法规等)

abscond—to leave hurriedly and secretly, typically to avoid detection of or arrest for an unlawful action such as theft.
潜逃(尤指逃避逮捕);逃跑

absentia—absent; proceeding without the defendant present.
(审判等的)缺席

absolve—to set free or release from some obligation or responsibility; to determine to be free of fault, guilt or liability.
免罪;免责;免除惩罚

absolute title—a guaranteed title to the ownership of a property or lease.
绝对所有权

absolution—a definite sentence whereby a man accused of any crime is acquitted.
宽恕;赦罪;(诺言或责任的)免除;解除

abstain—to hold oneself back voluntarily, especially from something regarded as improper or unhealthy.

自我约束以放弃某项权利或戒除某项不当或不健康行为

abstract of conviction—summary of the court's finding on a moving violation. It is simply a short-hand note of the plea and the sentence. It is issued instead of a formal certificate of a judgment of conviction in some states. The person has indeed been convicted and sentenced and the abstract shows that conviction.

判案简报

abstract of record—an abbreviated or partial record.

案卷摘录

abstract of title—a summary giving details of the title deeds and documents that prove an owner's right to dispose of land, together with any encumbrances that relate to the property.

（证明房地产所有权的）产权简史，产业契据摘要

abuse—(*general term*) covers all injurious use or treatment by word or act. it does not always connote a deliberate act.

虐待；滥用（泛指所有无意或有意的诽谤中伤行为、滥用的一切权利等）

abuse of discretion—it occurs when a court does not apply the correct law or if it bases its decision on a clearly erroneous finding of a material fact. a court may also abuse its discretion when the record contains no evidence to support its decision.

滥用自由裁量权

abuse of process—employment of the criminal or civil process for a use other than one which is intended by law; the improper use of process after it has been issued, that is, a perversion of it.

（刑事或民事）诉讼程序适用错误

abut—to adjoin; to cease at point of contact; to touch boundaries; to border on.

邻接；毗连

abuttals—the buttings and boundings of land, showing on what other lands, rivers, highways, or other places it does abut. More properly, it is said, the sides of land, are adjoining and the ends abutting to the thing contiguous.

地界；邻接，毗连（abuttal 的名词复数）

acceleration—the hastening of the time for enjoyment of an estate or a property right which would otherwise have been postponed to a later time.

财产权的提前享有

acceleration clause—a provision in a contract or document establishing that upon the happening of a certain event, a party's expected interest in the subject property will become prematurely vested.

提前偿付条款

acceptable use policy—regulations establishing who may use a network, website, or service's resources; the purposes allowed; and the privacy and security rules involved.

许可使用（网络、网址等）制度

acceptance—an unambiguous communication that the offer has been accepted.

（合同法）承诺；接受

acceptilation—In the civil law, it is a release made by a creditor to his debtor of his debt, without receiving any consideration. It is a species of donation, but not subject to the forms of the latter, and is valid, unless in fraud of creditors. Acceptilation may be defined as a certain arrangement of words by which on the question of the debtor, the creditor, wishing to dissolve the obligation, answers that he admits as received, what in fact, he has not received. The acceptilation is an imaginary payment.

（苏格兰法律）正式解除债务

acceptor—an individual or institution that assumes an obligation to pay by signing for or consenting to a check or draft. Also spelled "accepter".

承兑票据的人

accession—

1. the attainment or acquisition of a position of rank or power, typically that of monarch or president.

就职；就任；就位

2. the addition of something to personal property through the addition of labor.

财产的增附;添附

accessory—someone who gives assistance to the perpetrator of a crime, without directly committing it, sometimes without being present.

同谋;帮凶;从犯

access right—a right, granted in an order or agreement, of access to visitation of a child.

(家庭法上离婚父母对不属于其监护子女的)探视权,探望权

accomplice—a person who helps another commit a crime.

共犯;同谋;从犯

accord—agreement;an agreement whereby one of the parties undertakes to give or perform, and the others to accept, in satisfaction of a claim, liquidated (certain) or unliquidated (in dispute) and arising either from contract or from tort, something other than or different from what he is, or considers himself, entitled to.

和解协议;协定,协约

accord and satisfaction—compromise and settlement. A way to discharge a claim whereby the parties agree to give and accept something in settlement of the claim that will replace the terms of the parties' original agreement. Accord is the new agreement; satisfaction is performance of the new agreement.

和解与清偿(美国商法中的一个重要的法律程序)

account—a detailed statement of the mutual demand in the nature of debt and credit between parties, arising out of contracts or some fiduciary relation.

账目

account debtor—a person who is obligated on an account.

债务人

account-book—a book kept by a merchant, trader, mechanic, or other person, in which are entered from time to time the transactions of his trade or business.

账簿;账册;账本

account current—a running or open account between two persons.

往来账户;活期存款账户;流通账

account of sales—an account delivered by one merchant or tradesman to another, or by a factor to his principal, of the disposal, charges, commissions and net proceeds of certain merchandise consigned to such a merchant, tradesman or factor, to be sold.

承销清单;销售账;销货表

account payable—the amount owed by a business to its suppliers and other regular trading partners.

应付账款

account receivable—amounts owing on open account. Running accounts that are usually disclosed in the creditor's account books, representing unsettled claims and transactions not reduced to writing.

应收账款

account stated—The settlement of an account between the parties, by which a balance is struck in favor of one of them, is called an account stated.

确认账额;认可的结算、清账

accountant—This word has several significations: 1) One who is versed in accounts; 2) A person or officer appointed to keep the accounts of a public company; 3) He who renders to another or to a court a just and detailed statement of the administration of property which he holds as trustee, executor, admnistrator or guardian.

会计;会计师

accounting method—the method by which a business (corporation, partnership or sole proprietorship) keeps its books and records for purposes of computing income and deductions and determining taxable income. Generally, the method of accounting affects the timing of an item of income or deduction. The two major methods of accounting are accrual and cash.

会计方法;核算法

accouple—to marry.

结合;结婚

accredited investor—knowledgeable and sophisticated persons or institutions who qualify to purchase securities in transactions exempt from registration under the Securities Act of 1933.

官方认可或授权的投资者；授信投资者

accretion—the adding on or adhering of something to property; a means by which a property owner gains ownership of something additional. It is created by operation of natural causes.

（多指由自然原因引起的）财产的增加

accrue—generally, to accumulate, to happen, to come into fact or existence; as to a cause of action, to come into existence as an enforceable claim; as to a debt or bank account, the coming due of interest on principal sum. The point at which a cause of action is said to accrue also affects the length of time that a prospective plaintiff may wait to bring a suit under the statute of limitations.

（钱款、账目）积累、增长、生息；（诉讼）发生

accumulated depreciation—the total depreciation charged against all productive assets as stated on the balance sheet. The charge is made to allow realistic reduction in the value of productive assets and to allow taxfree recovery of the original investment in assets.

累积折旧

accumulative judgment—A second or additional judgment given against one, who has been convicted, the execution or effect of which is to commence after the first has expired; as, where a man is sentenced to an imprisonment for six months on conviction of larceny, and, afterwards he is convicted of burglary, he may be sentenced to undergo an imprisonment for the latter crime, to commence after the expiration of the first imprisonment.

累计判决

accusation—a charge against a person or corporation; in its broadest sense it includes indictment, presentment, information and any other forms in which a charge of crime or offense can be made against an individual.

指控；控告

accusatorial—(*esp. of a trial or legal procedure*) involving accusation by a prosecutor and a verdict reached by an impartial judge or jury. Often contrasted with *inquisitorial*.

控告者的;责问的

accusatory instrument—refers to the initial pleading or other paper which forms the procedural basis for a criminal charge. It may take the form of an indictment, information, or accusation. If the accusatory instrument is defective, the entire proceeding will be rendered null and void.

控告书;起诉书

accuse—to directly and formally institute legal proceedings against a person, charging that he or she has committed an offense cognizable at law; to prosecute; to charge with an offense judicially or by public process.

指控;控告

accused—a person against whom a criminal proceeding is initiated.

被告(accused 通常指刑事案件的被告,民事诉讼的被告称为 defendant;而申索案件中的被索偿的一方称为 respondent "答辩人")

accuser—one who makes an accusation.

原告

acknowledgment—

1. a statement of acceptance of responsibility.

承认(对自己的行为承担法律责任)

2. the short declaration at the end of a legal paper showing that the paper was duly executed and acknowledged.

确认书;确认声明

acquaintance rape—rape by a person who is known to the victim.

熟识者强暴;熟人强奸

acquiescence—the implied consent to do an act. it can also be a person's tacit or passive acceptance or agreement without protest.

默认;默许

acquire—to gain by any means; to obtain by any endeavor such as practice, purchase, or investment. In the law of contracts, it means to become the owner of property; to make something one's own. It implies some positive action as opposed to a more passive obtaining such as by an accrual.

获得;取得(acquire 强调通过各种人为的手段获得而不是被动的自然获得)

acquisition—In the corporate context, it refers to one firm buys majority interest in another, but both retain their identities.

收购;购并(多指一个公司以收购某较小公司股份的方式进行接管或达到控股的目的,两个法人实体地位在交易之后仍可同时存在。)

acquit—free (someone) from a criminal charge by a verdict of not guilty.

判决无罪;宣告无罪;开释

acquittal—a judgment that a person is not guilty of the crime with which the person has been charged.

无罪裁定;无罪判决

act—

1. (*often as criminal act*) a constituent element of a crime or tort.

(犯罪)行为

2. a written ordinance of Congress, or another legislative body; a statute.

法案;法令

Act of God—a natural catastrophe which no one can prevent such as an earthquake, a tidal wave, a volcanic eruption, a hurricane or a tornado.

不可抗力

action—a legal process; a lawsuit.

诉讼

actionable—giving sufficient reason to take legal action.

可控告的;可诉的

active case—pending case; not disposed of.

待审理案件

actual malice rule—In the United States law it is a condition required to establish libel against public officials or public figures and is defined as "knowledge that the information was false" or that it was published "with reckless disregard of whether it was false or not." Reckless disregard does not encompass mere neglect in following professional standards of fact checking.

actual malice rule

The publisher must entertain actual doubt as to the statement's truth. This is the definition only in the United States and came from the landmark 1964 lawsuit *New York Times Co. v. Sullivan*, which ruled that public officials needed to prove actual malice in order to recover damages for libel.

真实恶意原则

> 真实恶意原则起源于美国。1960年3月29日,一个民权组织在《纽约时报》刊登了题为《请倾听他们的呐喊》的政治宣传广告,广告描述了南部黑人正在进行的反种族歧视的非暴力抗争运动以及他们遭到地方警察残酷镇压的情形。事实上,广告中有个别细节是不够真实的。而L. B. Sullivan(沙利文)是一名警官并主管当地的警察局,他控告《纽约时报》严重损害了他的名誉,犯有诽谤罪。蒙哥马利市地方法院陪审团判沙利文胜诉。《纽约时报》不仅不服,把官司一直打到了联邦最高法院。1964年3月9日,联邦最高法院就《纽约时报》诉沙利文案做出裁决,9名大法官一致同意推翻阿拉巴马州最高法院关于沙利文胜诉的判决。最高法院指出:《纽约时报》虽然刊登了内容不实的广告,并且也的确对原告的名誉造成了一定的损害,但由于原告是一名"政府官员",他必须"明白无误地和令人信服地"证明《纽约时报》事先知道广告上的指控是假的但仍明知故犯,照登不误,或证明《纽约时报》严重失职,对于广告上的指控存有严重疑问,但未作任何努力去查核事实真相。在《纽约时报》诉沙利文案中,大法官William J. Brennan, Jr.指出:当公职官员因处理公众事务遭受批评和指责,致使其个人名誉受到可能的损害时,不能动辄以诽谤罪起诉或要求金钱赔偿,除非公职官员能拿出证据,证明这种指责是出于"真实恶意"。什么是"真实恶意"呢?最高法院解释说,那就是"明知其言虚假,或贸然不顾(reckless disregard)它是否虚假"。——因此"真实恶意"包括两层含义:一是当事人主观存在不友好的心态;二是这种不友好的主观状态表现出来并造成实质性的后果。美国最高法院把"真实恶意"定义为明知争论中的陈述为谬误或"毫不顾忌"陈述是否为谬误而公布于众。依此标准,当原告如是一个政府官员时,他要想打赢一场诽谤官司就必须向法庭证明被告含有恶意或是蓄意对他实施诽谤。含有恶意分为两种情况:一是明知故犯;二是严重失职。明知故犯意指被告明知消息与事实不符,仍不顾一切地将消息发表,换言之就是撒谎、造谣。严重失职则是反映记者、编辑在对消息的准确性有怀疑时不核实、不查证,照发不误。

> 真实恶意原则是美国现行诽谤法的最重要的原则。真实恶意原则规范了政府官员,或政治人物,只有在他们举证,证实新闻媒体具有"真实恶意"的前提下,才能对新闻媒体的报道提出诽谤诉讼。美国最高法院认为,所谓的真实恶意是指,明知这个资讯是不实的;或完全漠视,不去查证它是不是错误的。很多观点认为,真实恶意原则限制了公众人物以诽谤罪来阻止新闻媒体的报道自由,以防止寒蝉效应。同时,该原则也扩大了对新闻媒体的保障。

actus reus—a Latin term that refers to a guilty act.
犯罪行为

ad damnum—the amount of the plaintiff's claim of damages in a civil case.
(民事诉讼中的)索赔金额

additur—an increase by a judge in the amount of damages awarded by a jury.
增加赔偿金;增额命令

ademption—the act of revoking a gift mentioned in a will by destruction, or selling or giving away the gift before death.
撤销遗赠

adhesion contract—a contract balanced in favor of one party over the other that one can assume it was not entered into on equal bargaining grounds.
附意合同;附和合同;附加合同

ad idem—a Latin word of "meeting of the minds". If two parties to a contract understand the terms and conditions of a contract in the same manner, then it is said that the parties are "ad idem" on the terms and conditions.
法律(条件、意见等)契合;一致

adjourn—to suspend indefinitely, or until a later stated time.
使中止;使延期;拖延;推迟

adjournment—the postponing or putting-off of a case or session of court until another time or place.
延期审讯;休会待续;辩论中止待续

adjudicate—to determine judicially.
判决；宣判；裁定；审判

adjudication—

1. the act of a court in making an order, judgment, or decree.
（法院）宣告

2. a judicial decision or sentence.
判决；裁定

3. a court decree in bankruptcy.
破产之宣告

ad litem—(esp. of a guardian) appointed to act in a lawsuit on behalf of a child or other person who is not considered capable of representing themselves.
专为某一诉讼指定（诉讼监护人）

admiralty—(*maritime law*) the jurisdiction of courts of law over cases concerning ships or the sea and other navigable waters.
海事法

administration—the management and disposal of the property of an intestate, deceased person, debtor, or other individual, or of an insolvent company, by a legally appointed administrator.
遗产管理

administrator—

1. the chief administrative officer of a court (usually "court administrator").
法院的行政主管

2. a person appointed by a court to administer the estate of a deceased person. This person is referred to as a "personal representative" (if acting with court supervision), or an "independent personal representative" (if acting without court supervision). A female administrator is called an "administratrix."
法院指派的遗嘱执行人

administrator de bonis non—in cases where the administration of a decedent's estate is left unfinished due to the death, removal, or resignation of the personal representative, a court may appoint a new personal representative to complete the administration of the estate. In some jurisdictions, the new personal representative is called the "administrator de bonis non."
新指派的遗产管理人

administrative agency regulations—rules adopted by an administrative agency (such as the Department of State or the Department of Natural Resources) to govern matters under the jurisdiction of the agency.

行政规章；行政法规

administrative orders—orders issued by the State Supreme Court to regulate court procedures.

行政命令

administrative revocation—the taking of a driver's license by the Motor Vehicle Division, through law enforcement agents and administrative law judges without involvement by the courts.

吊销驾驶执照（由机动车管理部门或执法部门处理，不需要法院的介入。）

admissible evidence—evidence that can be legally and properly introduced in a civil or criminal trial.

可采纳的证据；可采信的证据

admission(s)—In criminal law, the voluntary acknowledgment that certain facts do exist or are true; but, of themselves, admissions are insufficient to be considered a confession of guilt, although they are generally admissible against a defendant.

坦白；认罪

admit—to permit into evidence. A judicial determination to admit some evidence and to exclude other evidence is a function of the perceived usefulness such evidence will have on the outcome of the case.

允许作为证据

admit to bail—permitting an accused person to be released from custody until trial upon posting of sufficient surety (bail).

允许保释

admit to practice—certification by a court that a lawyer possesses the required qualifications to practice law within that jurisdiction.

允许律师执业

admonish—to advise or caution. For example, the court may caution or admonish counsel or a witness for improper courtroom conduct.

警告;告诫

adoption—the act by which a person takes the child of another into his or her family and makes the child, for all legal purposes, his or her own child.

收养

ADR—alternative dispute resolution.

非诉讼程序

adult—a person who has reached the age of majority.

成年人

adultery—voluntary sexual intercourse between a married person and a person who is not his or her spouse.

通奸;通奸行为

ad valorem—(of the levying of tax or customs duties) in proportion to the estimated value of the goods or transaction concerned.

按价;从价

advance directive—a written statement of a person's wishes regarding medical treatment, often including a living will, made to ensure those wishes are carried out should they be unable to communicate them to a doctor.

预先指示(一份针对当当事人万一在生理上不能沟通的时候所希望或者不希望获得的治疗方式的法律文件。)

advancement—an irrevocable gift given by a parent in his or her lifetime to his or her child that is intended to represent all or part of the child's share of the estate which is to be deducted therefrom.

预付财产(父母生前给予子女不可撤销的继承财产,该部分财产应在最终的遗产继承中折算减除。)

adversarial—(of a trial or legal procedure) in which the parties in a dispute have the responsibility for finding and presenting evidence.

对抗性的;敌对的

adversary—opponent or litigant in a legal controversy or litigation.

对方当事人;对手

adversary proceedings—an action contested by opposing parties.

对抗诉讼制度

adversary system—the trial method used in the U. S. and some other countries. This system is based on the belief that truth can best be determined by giving opposing parties full opportunity to present and establish their evidence, and to test by cross-examination the evidence presented by their adversaries. This is done under the established rules of procedure before an impartial judge and/or jury.

对抗制(在对抗制模式下,被诉方首先被假定是无辜的,起诉方律师须举证证明自己的观点,被诉方对起诉方的证据进行反驳,法官在认定事实和证据时处于次要地位。)

adverse inference—unfavorable deduction that may be drawn by the fact-finder from the failure of a party to produce a normally expected witness or other evidence. It may be presumed that the failure to produce was because the testimony or other evidence would have been harmful to that party.

不利的推断

adverse interest—against the interest of some other person, usually so as to benefit one's own interest.

对自己有利而对对方不利的利益

adverse possession—the acquisition of property by a trespasser whose occupation of the property is exclusive, open, and continuous for a statutory period.

时效占有;无合法所有权之占有(取得财产所有权的一种方法,指无法律根据而占有他人财产者,根据法律规定的时间在一定条件下取得此项财产的所有权,财产所有人在法定的期限内不行使权利即被丧失收回其财产的诉讼权利。)

advocacy—the act of pleading for or arguing in favor of something or actively supporting a cause or proposal.

讼辩;辩护

advocate—a pleader in a court of law; a lawyer.

辩护人;律师

affiant—one who, being sworn, makes and signs an affidavit; a deponent.

宣誓者;口供人

affidavit—a written statement of fact that is verified by oath or affirmation. 宣誓书;(经陈述者宣誓在法律上可采作证据的)书面陈述

affiliates—business concerns, organizations, or individuals that control each other or that are controlled by a third party. Control may consist of shared management or ownership; common use of facilities, equipment, and employees; or family interest. 附属机构;分公司;关联公司

affinity—the relationship that exists as a result of a marriage, between a wife and her husband's relatives, or a husband and his wife's relatives, as distinguished from relationship by blood. 姻亲关系

affirmation—a solemn and formal declaration that a statement is true. In certain cases, an affirmation may be substituted for an oath. 严肃、正式的肯定证词;不经宣誓而作出的正式证词

affirmative defense—apart from denying a charge or claim, a defendant may assert affirmative defenses such as insanity, self-defense or entrapment to avoid criminal responsibility, or assert the statute of limitations or bankruptcy to avoid civil liability. 积极抗辩

affirmed—a decision by an appellate court stating that the decision of the trial court is correct. 维持原判的

affray—the fighting of two or more persons in a public place to the terror of ordinary people. 聚众斗殴;斗殴罪

aftermarket—refers to the sale of something after it is originally placed on the market for sale. For example, in securities transactions, aftermarket refers to the situation in which an investor purchases a security from another investor rather than the issuer, after its original issuance in the primary market. It is also called secondary market. 二级市场;售后市场;原始股上市后的市场

AG—attorney general.

首席检察官;司法部长

agent—someone authorized to act for another person. The other person is known as the "principal."

代理商;代理人

age of consent—the age at which a person's, typically a girl's, consent to sexual intercourse is valid in law.

法律认可年龄;法律承认年龄(一般指女子被认为可以发生性关系之年龄)

age of majority—the legally defined age at which a person is considered as an adult, with all the attendant rights and responsibilities of adulthood.

成年年龄;法定成年人年龄

aggravated—(of an offense) made more serious by attendant circumstances (such as frame of mind).

加重的

aggravated felony—a felony is a serious crime, usually punishable by more than one year in prison, as compared to a misdemeanor, which is a lesser offense.

恶性重罪

agreement—a typically legally binding arrangement between parties as to a course of action.

(当事人之间有法律约束力的)协议

aid and abet—to actively, knowingly or intentionally assist another person in the commission or attempted commission of a crime.

同谋;教唆(犯罪)

alias summons—a second or subsequent summons issued after the originally issued summons expires without being served.

第二传票;取代因无法送达或因其他原因失效的传票之传票

alibi—a Latin term meaning "in another place." It is an excuse supplied by a person suspected of or charged with a crime, supposedly explaining why they couldn't be guilty.

不在犯罪现场;犯罪发生时在其他地方

alien—a person born in a foreign country who owes his or her allegiance to that country; one not a citizen of the country in which one is living.

外国人；外籍人

alienable—able to be transferred to new ownership.

可转让的

alienate—transfer ownership of（property rights）to another person or group.

让与（财产或财产的任何权益）

alienation—the transfer of the ownership of property rights.

财产的转让

alimony—a financial benefit paid by one spouse to the other, upon divorce, which enables the second spouse to maintain himself or herself.

（离婚或分居后，常常是男方付给女方的）生活费；抚养费

aliunde—It means from another place or outside source. It is often used to refer to evidence given aliunde when meaning cannot be derived from a document or instrument itself.

来自其他方面；非由本文件引申而得

allegation—a declaration, assertion, or statement of a party to a lawsuit, made in a pleading, and setting out what the party intends to prove.

控诉主张；当事人在诉状中的肯定性陈述

allocution—the right of a convicted defendant to speak on his/her own behalf before sentencing is pronounced.

认罪供词

alternative pleading—refers to the legal practice of putting forth alternative theories of liability in a dispute.

选择性抗辩

amenable—(of a thing) capable of being acted upon in a particular way; susceptible.

遵守的；服从的

amendment—in a legal context it refers to a change made by a legislative or parliamentary process.

法律的修正；修正案

amicus curiae—one who is not a party to a case but who is interested in or affected by its outcome and is allowed by the court to introduce argument or evidence to assist the court in deciding the case.

法庭之友；法官的顾问（指案件当事人之外的个人、团体或政府机关对特定案件的事实或法律问题具有专业特长或独到见解，在法庭作出裁判〈一般限于二审程序〉之前就法院所面临的法律等问题向法院提供意见的制度。法庭之友向法庭提交意见的目的在于帮助法庭作出公正合理的判决，而提交的意见则表现为支持一方当事人的主张或完全从公共利益的角度出发而向法院提交法庭之友意见。）

amnesty—a pardon that is extended to a group of persons and that excuses them for criminal offenses. A grant of amnesty is usually motivated by political reasons, and may be limited or conditioned.

大赦；特赦

amortization—a gradual extinguishment of a debt, as the term is used for accounting purposes; the provision for the gradual extinction of a future obligation in advance of maturity, either by an annual charge against capital account, or, more specifically, by periodic contributions to a sinking fund which will be adequate to discharge a debt or make a replacement when it becomes necessary.

分期偿还；摊销

ampliation—(*civ. law*) a deferring of judgment until the cause is further examined. In this case, the judges pronounced the word amplius, or by writing the letters N.L. for non liquet, signifying that the cause was not clear.

（民事案件的事实不清需要）延期裁决

ancient demesne—manors that were in the actual possession of the Crown during the reign of William the Conqueror and that were recorded as such in the Domesday Book.

古时的领地

ancillary—that which is part of but subordinate to some other proceeding.

辅助的；附属的

ancillary administration—administration of an estate in another jurisdiction where a decedent had property but where the decedent did not live.

附加遗产管理权

ancillary proceeding—a proceeding which is subordinate to the primary action.

附带诉讼

ancillary suit—a lawsuit growing out of and supplementary to another suit, i.e., a suit seeking enforcement of a judgment.

附带起诉

annotations—brief summaries of cases interpreting statutes. These summaries are found in annotated compilations of statutes.

注释;评注

annul—to make void or of no effect. To annul a judgment or judicial proceeding is to deprive it of all force and authority.

废除;撤销;宣告无效

annulment—a court order declaring that a marriage or other agreement or a contract is invalid or not legal.

宣告无效;判决无效

answer—the legal paper in which the defendant answers the claims of the plaintiff in a lawsuit.

答辩书

antenuptial—made or done before marriage, usually an agreement regarding how property is to be distributed upon the death of one of the marriage partners.

婚前的

anticipatory breach(of contract)—a breach committed before the arrival of the actual time of required performance. It occurs when one party by declaration repudiates his contractual obligation before it is due. The repudiation required is a positive statement indicating that the promisor will not or cannot substantially perform his contractual duties.

预期违约(英美合同法中一个先进的概念,指在合同规定的履行期到来前,已有根据预示合同的一方当事人将不会履行其合同义务。)

antinomy—a term used in the civil law to signify the real or apparent contradiction between two laws or two decisions.

自相矛盾

antitrust laws—statutes aimed at promoting free competition in the marketplace. Any agreement or cooperative effort or intent by two or more entities that affects or restrains, or is likely to affect or restrain their competitors, is illegal under these statutes.

反垄断法

appeal—a request to a higher court to change the judgment of a lower court.

上诉；申诉

appeal by application or leave—an appeal where permission must be obtained from the higher court before the appeal may be filed.

上诉许可申请

appeal by right—an appeal to a higher court where permission does not first have to be obtained.

法定上诉权

appeal record—the record sent by the trial court of what happened at the trial court. It must be either a copy of the court record and transcripts or a settled record.

基层法院的庭审记录

appearance—

1. coming into court; the formal act by which a defendant submits to the jurisdiction of a court.

出庭；应诉

2. document identifying one who is representing himself or another. An attorney files an "appearance," making it known to the court and the other parties that (s)he is representing a specific individual.

应诉书

appellant—in a case on appeal, the party appealing a decision or judgment to a higher court.

上诉人

appellate court—a court which reviews lower court decisions, generally on the record of the lower court. Cases from the district courts are appealed to the circuit court. Cases from the circuit court are appealed to the Court of Appeals. Cases from the probate court are appealed to either the circuit court or the Court of Appeals depending upon the type of case.

上诉法院

appellee—in a case on appeal, the party who did not appeal the lower court's decision.

被上诉人

application—placing a request or petition before the court. The act of making the request.

(向法院提出)请求；申请

application for leave to appeal—a document requesting the appellate court to hear a party's appeal from a judgment when the party has no appeal of right or the time limit for an appeal of right has expired. An "application for leave to appeal" must be made if one wishes to have the court consider one's appeal where there is no appeal of right. The Court has final discretion to accept or reject an application.

上诉许可申请

appreciation—In a financial context, it refers to an increase in the value of property. It is used to distinguish between investments that are likely to provide profits because of increases in price and those that provide dividend payments.

(尤指土地或财产的)增值

appropriation—a legislative act authorizing the expenditure of a designated amount of public funds for a specific purpose.

拨款；批准支出

arbitral—relating to or resulting from the use of an arbitrator to settle a dispute.

仲裁的

arbitrary—based on unreasonable or capricious exercise of discretion.

任意的;专断的(自由裁量权)

arbitrate—(of an independent person or body) reach an authoritative judgment or settlement.

仲裁;公断

arbitration—a form of alternative dispute resolution under which the parties agree to have a neutral third party or a neutral panel resolve their dispute. The parties are generally bound by the arbitrator's decision.

仲裁(由中立的第三方就各方的争议做出决议,该决议对各争议方具有法律约束力。)

arbitrator—an independent person or body officially appointed to settle a dispute.

仲裁员

arraign—to bring a person charged with a crime before the court for the purpose of informing him or her of the charges, appointing counsel if necessary, setting bail, making pretrial motions, and taking a plea to the charges.

提审;传讯(刑事)被告

arraignment—

1. the act of arraigning, or the state of being arraigned; the act of calling and setting a prisoner before a court to answer to an indictment or complaint.

传讯;提审

2. In a criminal case, a pretrial court hearing at which the defendant is informed of the charges against him or her, is appointed counsel if necessary, and is permitted to plead to the charges. pretrial motions may be made, and bail is set.

提审;传讯刑事被告(刑事审讯中的法律程序,在该程序中,须向被控告人宣读公诉书,而他需对公诉书所载罪名做出答辩。)

array—a list of jurors empaneled.

陪审员名单

arrears—money that is owed and should have been paid earlier.

欠款;到期未付之债

arrest—seize (someone) by legal authority and take into custody.

拘捕;逮捕;缉捕

arrestee—a person who has been arrested.

被逮捕人

arrest of judgment—the withholding of judgment because of some error apparent from the face of the record; the method by which a court refuses to give judgment in a case, though it be regularly decided, where it appears on the face of the record, not including the evidence, either that intrinsically no cause of action exists, or that if judgment were rendered for the prevailing party it would be erroneous.

（因为发现法庭纪录上有明显错误）抑制判决;中止判决

arrest warrant—an order issued to a peace officer by a judge or magistrate, requiring the arrest of a named person.

逮捕证

arson—the criminal act of deliberately setting fire to property.

纵火罪（以火摧毁或毁坏他人财产的罪行）

article—a separate clause or paragraph of a legal document or agreement, typically one outlining a single rule or regulation.

法律条款

asportation—the felonious removal of goods from the place where they were deposited.

窃走;窃取;抢走

assault—make a physical attack on.

突袭;侵犯（人身）;威吓

> 在美国侵权法中,该词的法律定义是:希望引起他人对即将发生的殴打产生合理警觉的行为。也就是说,被告的行为,引起了他人对将要发生的伤害的警觉。至于他的行为是否伤害了原告,甚至是否碰到了原告,法律并没有要求。被告的行为只是让原告心理上感觉到将要受到伤害,使他的心智,而不是身体受到了触动。在很大程度上,这是一种扰乱他人安宁与和平的侵权行为。

assault and battery—the crime of threatening a person together with the act of making physical contact with them.

殴打罪；人身伤害

assets—

1. generally, all property belonging to a person, corporation, or estate that may be used to pay his/her/its debts.

资产

2. in probate matters, all of the property available to the personal representative for payments of debts, charges, and expenses, and for distribution to the parties who are entitled to it.

财产

assign—transfer (legal rights or liabilities).

转让（法律权利或义务）

assignee—a person to whom a right or liability is legally transferred.

受让人；承让人

assignment—

1. *assignment of Cases*: the system or method that a court used to assign cases to the judges of the court.

案件分配制度

2. *assignment of Counsel*: refers to the appointment of attorneys for indigent criminal defendants.

（刑事案件）指定辩护人

3. *assignment of Judges*: the function performed by the State Court Administrative Office in assigning judges to the various courts to handle vacancies caused by vacations, illness, etc., or to help reduce the number of cases pending in a court.

法官的合理分配使用

assignment of error—the appellant's declaration or complaint against the trial judge charging error in the acts of the lower court which assignments are the basic grounds for reversal.

错误归属或归因（上诉人申诉或控诉下级法院的错误）

assignment of income—an attempt by a taxpayer to have income earned by him or her taxed to another person by directing that such income be paid to such other person, or by entering into a transaction that will result in such income being paid to such other person.

收益分配

assignor—one who transfers property to another. Synonymous with grantor. The grantor of a trust is the creator of the trust.

出让人

assize—a court that formerly sat at intervals in each county of England and Wales to administer the civil and criminal law. In 1972 the civil jurisdiction of assizes was transferred to the High Court, and the criminal jurisdiction to the Crown Court.

巡回审判（源于中世纪的名词，指由武士或公民组成的立法或司法团体，负责指定法律及解决纷争，后来指巡回审判处理的诉讼。）

assumpsit—

1. an express or implied agreement to perform an oral contract.

口头契约

2. a legal action to enforce or recover damages for a breach of such an agreement.

损害赔偿之诉

assure—to give confidence; to make certain; to make safe or secure; to inform positively, as to remove doubt; to convince.

保证；保险

asylum state—the state holding a fugitive from justice in another state.

提供庇护的国家（州）

at issue—matters are "at issue" when the complaining party has stated his/her claim, the other side has responded with a denial, and the matter is ready to be tried.

有争议的；在审议中（在辩护过程中，原告、被告各执一词，待法庭裁决。）

attach—

1. include (a condition) as part of an agreement.

附加（条件）

2. seize (a person's property) by legal authority.
查封;扣押

attachment—the act of seizing a person or property under the authority of a judicial order so that the person or property is before the court, subject to its judgment.
财产保全;查封;扣押

attainder—the forfeiture of land and civil rights suffered as a consequence of a sentence of death for treason or felony.
剥夺民事权利(旧指被判死刑时,犯罪者放弃民事权利,后果包括没收或转让犯罪者的土地。)

attest/attestation—signing as a witness to the execution of a written document.
见证;鉴定书;证明书

attorney—a lawyer; a person admitted to legal practice in a state who is qualified to represent the legal interests of another person.
律师;代理人

attorney-client privilege—privilege that confidential communications between an attorney and a client in the course of the professional relationship cannot be disclosed without the consent of the client.
律师—当事人保密特权

attorney general—the chief law officer of the federal government or of each state government.
司法部长;首席检察官

attorney in fact—the attorney acting in a fiduciary capacity under a "power of attorney."
授权代理人;法律事务代理人(指接受委托人授权的法律事务代理人,不一定具有律师资格,主要从事非诉业务。)

attorney of record—the attorney named in the records or file of a case who bears the responsibility for the handling of the case on behalf of the party he or she represents.
记录在案的律师;经承认代表人

auction—a public sale in which property or items of merchandise are sold to the highest bidder.

拍卖

authenticated—certification of original or copy of recorded document.

认证;证明;鉴证

authority—the permission or power delegated to another. This may be expressed or implied.

授权

autopsy—the dissection of a body to determine the cause of death. It may involve inspection and exposure of important organs of a dead body in order to determine the nature of a disease or abnormality.

尸体检剖

aval—a shared common commitment of payment of an obligation in favor of the creditor or beneficiary. It is granted by a third party, in case the first party does not fulfill the obligation of the payment of a credit title.

(对于商业票据的)保障(第三方在票据上背书,以保证在债务人不履行债务时,债务能得到及时的清偿。)

aver—allege as a fact in support of a plea.

证明……属实;作为事实提出;证实

averment—a formal statement by a party in a case of a fact or circumstance that the party offers to prove or substantiate.

断言;主张;申辩;有实证的陈述

avoid—to annul, cancel, make void, or to destroy the efficacy of anything.

使无效;撤销,规避

avoidance of tax—the method by which a taxpayer reduces his or her tax liability without committing fraud.

避税

award—refers to a judgment or sentence. It could refer to the decision made by a panel of arbitrators or a jury in a controversy that has been presented for resolution. It could also refer to a judgment of money to a party to a lawsuit.

(仲裁)裁决;判决

automatic waiver—see *waiver of jurisdiction*.

B

back-bond—a bond given by one to a surety, to indemnify such surety in case of loss. In Scotland, a back-bond is an instrument which, in conjunction with another which gives an absolute disposition, constitutes a trust. A declaration of trust.

退还担保;退还担保保证书

backlog—total inventory of cases at issue (in civil cases) or defendants arraigned (in criminal cases) and awaiting trial.

案件积压量

bad debts—funds owing to a business which are determined to be uncollectible. The determination of when a debt is uncollectible, and therefore "bad", may be based on a discharge in bankruptcy, the running of the statute of limitations to bring a lawsuit, disappearance of the debtor, a pattern of avoiding debts or the destruction of the collateral security.

坏账;经认真核实,确认无法收回的贷款;不履行的债务

bad title—It is a title to property that does not confer distinct ownership. It is usually used in the context of real estate. A bad title will result when all interests in a real property are not properly transferred to the owner.

失效产权；无效所有权

bail—a method of pretrial release of an accused person by means of having the accused or someone on his or her behalf deposit money with the court or agree to pay a certain amount (post security) to insure his or her appearance at later proceedings, such as trial.

1. *n*. 保证金；保释金；保释人；保释（被控犯罪人获免被羁留的权利，条件是其承诺于指定时间返回，及遵守法院加诸的条件）；法院保释手续；保释保证人

2. *v*. 交保；准许保释，为……做保释人

bail bond—a financial obligation signed by the accused and those who serve as sureties to guarantee his or her future appearance in court.

保释保证书

bailee—a person who receives possession of a property or goods through a contract of bailment.

（财物的）受托保管人

bailiff—a court employee who maintains order in the courtroom and who is responsible for the custody of the jury, among other functions.

法警

bailment—the act of placing property in the custody and control of another, usually by agreement in which the holder (bailee) is responsible for the safekeeping and return of the property.

（财物的）寄托

bailor—a person who transfers possession of property or goods to the custody of another (bailee), usually under a contract of bailment.

（财物的）寄托人

balance sheet—a financial statement that gives an accounting picture of property owned by a company and of claims against the property on a specific date. Generally, a summation of assets is listed on one side and liabilities and equity are listed on the other side. Both sides are always in balance.

资产负债表

banker's lien—the authority enjoyed by a banker to appropriate a depositor's funds or securities that are in the banker's possession and are not dedicated to a special purpose (as a trust) in order to satisfy a debt owed by the depositor to the bank.

银行留置权

bankrupt—(of a person or organization) declared in law unable to pay outstanding debts.

破产人(经法庭判定无能力偿付债务的自然人或组织)

bankruptcy—refers to statutes and judicial proceedings involving persons or businesses that cannot pay their debts and seek the assistance of the court in getting a fresh start. Under the protection of the bankruptcy court, debtors may be released ("discharged") from their debts completely or allowed to repay them in whole or in part on a manageable schedule. Federal bankruptcy judges preside over these proceedings. The person with the debts is called the debtor and the people or companies to whom the debtor owes money are called creditors.

破产(无偿付能力、经营亏损迫使债务人进入的一种法律清偿程序)

bar—

1. the legal profession.

律师业

2. (*the bar*) a partition in a courtroom, now usually notional, beyond which most persons may not pass and at accused person stands.

法庭围栏(在法庭内,分隔法官坐席和律师席的虚拟分划)

bar examination—a state examination taken by prospective lawyers, qualifying them to be admitted to the bar and licensed to practice law.

美国律师资格考试

bargain—a mutual voluntary agreement between two parties for the exchange or purchase of some specified goods. An agreement of two or more persons to exchange promises or to exchange a promise for a performance or to exchange performances.

交易;契约

barratry—refers to the generation of profit for legal services by an attorney who stirs up a dispute and encourages lawsuits in order to file what is typically a groundless claim.

无理取闹的诉讼；(为谋利而进行)诉讼挑唆

barrister—a lawyer entitled to practice as an advocate, particularly in the higher courts.

出庭律师；大律师(在高级法院、高等法院及终审法院专享出庭发言权)

bar sinister—the fact or condition of being born out of wedlock.

私生；非婚生

battery—willful and unlawful use of force or violence upon the person of another; or actual, intentional and unlawful touching or striking of another person against the will of the other; or unlawfully and intentionally causing bodily harm to an individual.

殴打罪(在无合法理由及原告人同意之下，直接导致原告人身体遭受实质的干扰的蓄意行为。被告人必须意图对原告人使用武力，但无需有伤害原告人的意图。)；袭击、非法侵犯

bearer—a holder of a negotiable instrument such as a promissory note, check, bond, or bank draft.

持票人

belligerent—engaged in a war or conflict, as recognized by international law.

交战国

bench—the office of judge or magistrate.

法官、裁判官办公室；法官席

bencher—(*in the UK*) a senior member of any of the Inns of Court.

下议院议员

bench trial—trial of a case held before a judge sitting without a jury.

无陪审团员的审判

bench warrant—(*from the bench*) an order issued by the court, for the arrest of a person for violating a court order. See *capias*.

法院拘票；法院拘押令

beneficial—of or relating to rights, other than legal title.

受益的

beneficiary—

1. one who receives benefits under a trust or a will.

信托受益人;(遗嘱)受遗赠人

2. the person who is entitled to receive payments under an insurance policy.

保险受益人

bequeath—to give personal property by a will.

遗赠(一般指动产遗赠)

bequest—former term used for gift of personal property by a will.

遗赠物;遗产

best evidence rule—rule requiring parties to proffer the original writing, recording, or photograph when attempting to prove the contents thereof. However, a duplicate is admissible in place of an original unless there is a genuine question about the authenticity of the original or it would be unfair under the circumstances of the case to admit the duplicate instead of the original. Also, an original is not required if it is lost or destroyed, if it cannot be obtained through a subpoena, if it is in the possession of the opposing party, and if the original is not closely related to a controlling issue in the case.

美国诉讼法中最佳证据原则

> 对于待证事实的证明仅能提出最佳证据,如有最佳证据存在,就不能提出次要证据,在文书的情形下仅以原件为最佳证据,而具有证据能力,因此,仅在不可归责于举证人而不能取得原件时,才例外地允许提出影印件作为证据。在此等限制下,电磁记录、电子文件由于属非亲笔签名之书面文件,不符合原件之要求,不能作为证据提出。不过,随着电子信息时代的到来与发展,美国的法律也在进一步调整,现已经承认了电子文件的证据效力。

betterment—the enhanced value of real property arising from local improvements.

不动产增值;对不动产的改良升级

beyond reasonable doubt—the standard of proof that must be met in order to convict a criminal defendant of a crime.

排除合理怀疑原则(刑事诉讼证明标准)

bias—preconception; prejudice; taint; partiality
偏见;偏倚

bias crime—commission of an offense where the person acted, at least in part, with ill will, hatred, or bias toward, and with a purpose to intimidate, an individual or group because of race, color, religion, sexual orientation, or ethnicity.
仇恨犯罪(因对种族、宗教、性取向等问题生恨犯罪)

bicameral—(of a legislative body) having two branches or chambers.
两院制的

bid—an offer by an intending purchaser to buy goods or services at a stated price, or an offer by an intended seller to sell his goods or services for a stated price.
报价;投标

bid shopping—the practice of a general contractor who, before the award of the prime contract, discloses to interested subcontractors the current low subbids on certain subcontracts in an effort to obtain lower subbids.
出价竞买

bigamy—the condition of having two wives or two husbands at the same time.
重婚罪

bill of attainder—an item of legislation (prohibited by the US Constitution) that inflicts attainder without judicial process.
剥夺公权法案(美国旧时的一条法律,对于犯叛乱罪之人,不须经过审讯即可径行宣布死刑并剥夺其财产权和公民权。)

bill of indictment—a written accusation as presented to a grand jury.
刑事起诉书;公诉书;控告书

bill of lading—a receipt given by a shipper of goods from the carrier, such as a trucking company, railroad, ship or air freighter, for shipment to a particular buyer. It is a contract protecting the shipper by guaranteeing payment and ensures the carrier that the recipient has proof of the right to the goods.
(海运)提单

bill of particulars—the criminal law procedural equivalent of a civil action request for a "more definite statement".

索赔清单;明细单

bill of review—form of equitable proceedings brought to secure an explanation, alteration, or reversal of a final decree by the court which rendered it.

复审请求;复审函

bill of rights—a statement of the rights of a class of people in particular. The first ten amendments to the American Constitution.

权利法案;美国宪法前十条修正案

bind—to create a legal obligation upon one's self or upon another.

受约束;指定……作偿还债务之用

binding—as used in statute, commonly means obligatory.

有法律约束力的;强制性应尽义务

bind over—to hold for trial; a finding at a preliminary examination that sufficient evidence exists to require a trial on the charges made against the defendant.

具结候审;具结候讯

birth certificate—an official document issued to record a person's birth, including such identifying data as name, gender, date of birth, place of birth, and parentage.

出生证明

blackacre—a fictitious tract of land used in legal discourse to discuss real-property issues. When another tract of land is needed in a hypothetical, it is often termed whiteacre.

黑土地

> 这个术语在美国财产法的著作里经常看到,其实 blackacre 是一个虚构的概念,代表财产权的一种标的物:某一块土地或某一栋房屋。法学教授们在课堂上讨论与不动产有关的问题,需要假设一个案例时就会经常用到它。如果还想虚构另一块土地,那另一块土地就称之为 whiteacre 白土地。

blackmail—the crime of threatening to reveal embarrassing, disgraceful or damaging information about a person to the public, family, spouse or associates unless money is paid to purchase silence.

敲诈;勒索;恐吓(包含未遂的)

blank indorsement—it is made on a negotiable instrument and it does not specify any particular indorsee and is accomplished by merely writing the name of the indorser on the back of the instrument.

空白背书;无记名背书;不完全背书

blue laws—Sunday closing laws.

蓝法;严格的法律(美国旧时禁止星期日营业、饮酒、娱乐等的规定)

blue sky law—a popular name given to state statutes regulating the sales of corporate securities through investment companies, imposed to prevent the sale of securities of fraudulent enterprises.

防欺诈性转让公司股票法

board of directors—a group of persons elected by the shareholders of a corporation to govern and manage the affairs of the company.

董事会

bona fide—a Latin term meaning "good faith". In legal terms, it is often used to refer to a purchaser or holder who takes something without fraud, deceit, or knowledge of a lien or superior claim by another.

善意;诚意

bona fide purchaser—one who does not know of the seller's wrong doing but has a good faith that the seller has title, and in addition pays valuable consideration.

善意购买人

> 传统的普通法规则认为"没有人可以转让不属于他所有的商品",然而该原则已被众多的例外弄得千疮百孔,除了盗窃物等少数情形,其他所有的情形都有例外,从而最终确立了善意购买人原则:不知标的物的权利瑕疵并且为之付出了对价,善意购买人对于所购财产享有对抗一切先在物主的所有权。

bona vacantia—goods that are abandoned or unclaimed and without an apparent owner or property that is not disposed of and which belongs to those who died intestate.

无主货物；无主物

bond—a promise or contract to do or perform a specified act(s) or to pay a penalty for failure to perform, usually guaranteed by a "surety" who promises to pay if the "principal" defaults, or by deposit of money as a "cash bond". It means basically the same as "bail" on criminal cases; contract to pay; security. A contract to pay when another person defaults—a surety. A contract to act as surety and to pay where the principal defaults. It is given by public officers to guarantee honest and faithful performance of their official duties while in office. If the principal defaults, the surety has to pay, and the surety can then collect from the principal. It's not the same as insurance.

契约；保证金，保证券

bonded—

1. (of a person or company) bound by a legal agreement, in particular.

以债券作保证的；抵押的

2. (of dutiable goods) placed in bond.

保税仓库留置的（货物）

bondsman—a person who stands surety for a bond.

保证人

book value—in reference to corporations, the worth of the assets minus the cost of the liabilities.

账面价值

boycott—to refrain from commercial dealing with by concerted effort; refusal to work for, purchase from or handle the products of an employer.

联合抵制

breach—an act of breaking or failing to observe a law, agreement, or code of conduct.

违反法律；违约行为

breach of contract—means failing to perform any term of a contract

without a legitimate legal excuse.
违约;违反合同

breach of duty—a failure to perform a duty owed to another or to society; a failure to exercise that care which a reasonable man would exercise under similar circumstances.
失职;违反职责。
例如:Party B causes great loss to A due to its breach of duty and jobbery.
乙方严重失职,营私舞弊,给甲方利益造成重大损失。

breach of the peace—an offense embracing a great variety of conduct destroying or menacing public order and tranquility. It includes not only violent acts but acts and words likely to produce violence in others.
妨害治安

break—fail to observe (a law, regulation, or agreement).
违反(法律、规范、协议)

break-in—a forced or unconsented entry into a building, car, computer system, etc., typically to steal something.
未经许可闯入

breaking and entering—the crime of entering a building by force so as to commit burglary.
行为人以犯重罪或盗窃为目的破门窗闯入他人住宅的行为

breaking bulk—refers to a doctrine whereby a bailee could be charged with larceny by trespass if he opened a chest, parcel, or case containing goods entrusted to his care and converted some to his own use; the trespass necessary for larceny was complete even if the goods were not in a container but were themselves delivered in bulk provided that the bailee separated only a portion of the goods entrusted to him.
受托人义务原则(受托人应尽到对受托管财务的保管义务,如果受托人擅自开拆被托管的财物,部分或全部的挪作他用,均可以盗窃罪论处。)

breathalyzer—a chemical test of a person's breath to determine whether he or she is intoxicated, usually when he or she is suspected of drunken driving.
体内酒量测试;呼吸测醉器

例如:Policeman asked me to breathe into the breathalyzer. 警察要我对着测醉器呼气。

brethren—plural of brother, although its usage in wills can include sisters. Reference used among Justices of the United States Supreme Court to refer to fellow Justices. Since the appointment of female Justices the term has fallen from usage or been replaced with the awkward "brethren/sistern."

弟兄们(复数);同胞

bribery—in criminal law it refers to the improper acceptance by a public official, juror, or someone bound by a duty to act impartially, of any gain or advantage to the beneficiary, including any gain or advantage to a third person by the desire or consent of the beneficiary.

行贿;受贿;贿赂行为;贿赂罪

brief—a written argument submitted to the court by counsel setting forth facts and/or law supporting his or her client's case.

案件辩论书;辩护状

> 其实 brief 是诉讼双方律师撰写的向法院提交的一种重要的法律文书,包括 trial court brief 和 appellate court brief 两大类,有严格的格式要求。一般包括 statement of issue, statement of the case, statement of the facts, summary of the argument, argument, standard of review, discussion, conclusion 几部分。brief 也是在上诉法院控辩双方律师口头辩论的基础。有时,上诉法院根本不用开庭,法官会直接在双方律师提交的 brief 的基础上作出判决。

bring—initiate (legal action) against someone.

提起(诉讼)

broker—a person who buys and sells goods or assets for others.

经纪人(通常以主事人名义订立关于买卖不属于他管有货品的合约人)

burden of proof—the duty to prove a fact or facts in dispute. In criminal cases, the prosecution must prove its case "beyond a reasonable doubt." In most civil cases, the plaintiff must prove its case by a "preponderance of the evidence."

burglar

举证责任(刑法中为排除合理怀疑的证明标准,民法中采取的是最佳证据原则。)

burglar—a person who commits burglary.
入室行窃者;破门盗窃者

burglarize—enter (a building) illegally with intent to commit a crime, esp. theft.
闯入(楼房等建筑物)盗窃;行窃

burglary—entry into a building illegally with intent to commit a crime, esp. theft.
恶意侵入他人住宅罪

> 在英美法中,burglary 的定义曾是 the breaking and entering of the dwelling house of another person at night with the intention to commit a felony of larceny inside,即行为人以犯重罪或盗窃为目的在夜间破门窗闯入他人住宅的行为,译为"夜盗罪"。当今的刑法对 burglary 的定义已有了很大的修订,时间并不局限于夜间,住宅也可以包括其他建筑物,等等。美国《统一刑事案例汇编》(*Uniform Criminal Reports*, 1998)甚至对 burglary 的定义简单到"为犯重罪或偷窃而非法进入某一建筑内"。为了伤害、强奸甚至杀害某人而进入他人住宅或其他建筑物,同样也构成 burglary。

burgle—another term for *burglarize*.
偷窃;行窃

business judgment rule—deference given by courts to the good faith operations and transactions of a corporation by its executives. Reasonable decisions, even if not the most profitable, will not be disturbed by a court upon application by a disgruntled party such as a stockholder. The rationale behind the rule is that stockholders accept the risk that an informed business decision, honestly made and rationally thought to be in the corporation's best interests, may not be second-guessed. Therefore, courts afford business judgments special protection in order to limit litigation and avoid judicial intrusiveness in private sector business decision making.

商业判断规则(是由目前世界上较强大的国家法院在长期的公检法实践

中逐步形成的一项关于董事的注重义务的判例法规则。)

but for——in tort and in criminal law, a test of whether an individual's action caused a particular event. The test is applied by asking whether the event would have occurred "but for," or in the absence of, the individual's act. Since every event has several causes, the test can describe any and all of them, and therefore is widely regarded as being of little or no benefit in assigning civil or criminal, liability in many types of situations.

(侵权法与刑法中)是否是自然人的行为导致了特定事件的测试

buyout——in the corporate context, it refers to the purchase of a company or a controlling interest of a corporation's shares or a product line or some business.

收购;全部买下股份(权);出资购买

bylaw——rules that lay down the internal rules of a corporation. It typically states the rights, duties and liabilities of the members of the corporation, as well as the rules relating to transferring and selling shares.

内部章程,指社团或公司等为内部管理而制定的规章、命令、规则或制度;地方性法规

by virtue of——because of, in view of, on account of, by reason of, or owing to

凭借;依靠;由于;因为

C

cadaver—the body of a deceased person.
尸体

CAFC—Court of Appeals for the Federal Circuit
联邦上诉巡回法院

calendar—a list of all pending cases, or all pending issues ready for trial in court. A court's complete trial schedule. Often used interchangeably, but improperly, with "docket."
案审日程表

calendar audit—review of status of all cases on active lists. The audit might result in the removal of cases from the calendar and identification of cases which have been delayed excessively.
案审日程表的审查

call—in property law, an identifiable natural object serving to mark the boundary of the land conveyed and designated as a landmark in an instrument of conveyance.
（在土地转让中视为土地界限的可辨认的）自然标志

case

callable bond—a bond which the issuer may retire at any time before its maturity. Usually the issuer must pay a premium (an amount more than the face value of the bond) to call the bond.

可提前兑付债券

calumny—slander, defamation; false prosecution or accusation; a word once used in civil law which signified an unjust prosecution or defense of a suit, and the word is still said to be used in the courts of Scotland and the ecclesiastical and admiralty courts of England.

诽谤;中伤;诬蔑

cancellation—the annulling of a legal document.

(法律文书的)无效或废止

canons of ethics—a document outlining the professional responsibilities and goals of doctors, lawyers, judges, etc.

(职业)道德守则;道德准则

capias—a bench warrant, issued when a defendant does not appear in court when required to do so; court-issued warrant for arrest.

拘票;逮捕证;传票

capital crime—a crime possibly punishable by death.

死刑

capital stock—the amount of money or property contributed by shareholders to be used as the financial foundation from which the business of incorporation is to be carried on.

股本;股金总额

caption—a title or brief explanation appended to a pleading document or judicial opinion.

(法律文件等的)标题;提要;说明

capture—acquiring ownership where no prior ownership existed as with wild animals, mining, and water. Also refers to a taking by a military group.

获得所有权;捕获

case—a legal dispute brought before a court. A "case" is also referred to as an "action", "lawsuit", "cause of action", or "cause".

045

诉讼;案件;判例

casebook—a book containing a selection of source materials on a particular subject, esp. one used as a reference work or in teaching.

(法学院等供教学或参考用的)案例教科书

caseflow—the management of cases through the court; the passage of cases through the court system. (Ideally cases are to "flow" through the judicial process in a smooth, orderly manner, hence the name "caseflow".)

案件审理流程

case law—published decisions issued by appellate courts in particular cases. the legal principles announced in these decisions are binding authority for lower courts.

判例法;案例法;法官制定法

caseload—the number of cases a judge handles in a specific time period.

(法官在特定时间段内)承办案件量

casualty—a person killed or injured in a war or accident.

受害者;伤亡者

causation—in tort law, the requirement of factual connection between the defendant's conduct and the plaintiff's harm.

原因;因果关系

cause—

1. a person or thing that gives rise to an action, phenomenon, or condition.

起因;原因

2. a matter to be resolved in a court of law.

案件

cause of action/cause—

1. a legal dispute brought before a court, also referred to as an "action", "lawsuit", or "case".

诉讼事由;案由

2. the right to judicial relief, also referred to as a "claim".

主张;诉求

caveat—a notice, esp. in a probate, that certain actions temporarily may not be taken.

中止诉讼的申请

caveat emptor—the principle that the buyer alone is responsible for checking the quality and suitability of goods before a purchase is made.

货物出门概不退换原则;买受人自负其责原则

censure—the official reprimand by a legislative or other formal body of one of its own members.

谴责;责备

certificate—an official document attesting a certain fact, in particular.

证明文书;证明文件

certificate of deposit /CD—an acknowledgment by a bank of receipt of money with an engagement to repay it.

存款单

certificate of occupancy—a document by a local government agency signifying that a building or dwelling conforms to local building code regulations. Generally, entry or transfer of title requires a valid certificate of occupancy.

符合使用标准证书;准用证

certificate of title—a document indicating ownership, similar to a bill of sale and usually associated with the sale of motor vehicles.

所有权证书

certification—as pertains to mental health; the written conclusion and statements of a physician that an individual is a person requiring treatment together with the information and opinions in reasonable detail which underlie the conclusion.

证明;证明书

certified copy—a copy of a document, order or record of the court, or other public office, signed and certified as an exact duplicate by the officer of the court having custody of the original.

证明无误的副本;经核证的副本

certify—to vouch for something in writing; to put in writing a statement.

To attest in writing to the authenticity and accuracy of a written instrument or document, or a copy of it.

有签字盖章的、符合法律程序的书面证明

certiorari—an order by an appellate court directing a lower court to certify and forward the record of a case for judicial review for legal error. This term is obsolete in Michigan.

移审令;诉讼文件移送命令

challenge—

1. to ask that a member of the jury panel be excused.

要求陪审员回避

2. to question or dispute an action.

质问

challenge for cause—to ask that a member of the jury panel be excused because there appears to be a specific reason, set out in the court rule, that one is not legally qualified to act as a juror in this case.

有因回避

challenge to the array—to question the qualifications of an entire panel summoned for jury duty, usually because of alleged partiality or some deficiency in the manner by which the panel was selected and summoned.

对陪审团的组成表示反对或提出异议;要求全体陪审员回避或更换

chamber—

1. a hall used by a legislative or judicial body.

立法或司法机关办公场所

2. (*chambers*) a judge's office.

法官办公室

champerty—an illegal agreement in which a person with no previous interest in a lawsuit finances it with a view to sharing the disputed property if the suit succeeds.

帮诉行为;帮诉罪(诉讼一方与另一方在争议中毫无利益的人之间存在某种协定,若胜诉的话,双方瓜分在诉讼中的财物,代价为另一个人自费进行该诉讼。)

chancery—

1. a court of equity.

衡平法院

2. a public records office.

大法官法庭

change of venue—a transfer or removal of a case to a court of another territorial location and jurisdiction, either because it should have been commenced there in the first place, or for the convenience of the parties or witnesses, or because a fair trial cannot be had in the original court location.

变更审判地点

charge—

1. accuse (someone) of an offense under law.

指控(某人触犯法律)

2. instruct (a jury) as to the law.

对陪审团适用法律的指导

charges—(*multiple*) a case with more than one count or offense listed on the court file.

多项指控

charge to the jury—a judge's instructions to the jury which contain information about the laws which relate to the issues to be decided in a case.

(在陪审团未就案件的裁决商议前,法官给予陪审团的)指示

charging document—a citation, information, indictment or notice to appear, indicating that the named person committed a specific criminal offense or civil infraction.

诉讼卷宗;起诉文书

charter—a written grant by a country's legislative or sovereign power, by which an institution such as a company, university, or city is created and its rights and privileges defined.

许可证;特许设立状;纲领;宪章

chattel mortgage—a conveyance of some present legal or equitable right in personal property, as security for the payment of money, or for the performance of some other act. Most commonly used in buying high-priced consumer goods on credit, such as automobiles and large appliances.

动产抵押;动产质押

chattel paper—a writing or writings which evidence both a monetary obligation and a security interest in or a lease of specific goods.

动产文据;动产契据

chattels—personal property as opposed to real property.

动产

chief judge—in all trial courts one judge is selected as chief judge. The chief judge represents the court in its relations with other agencies and the public. In addition the chief judge is the director of the administration of the court.

审判长;法庭庭长

chief justice—(the title of) the presiding judge in a supreme court.

首席大法官

child abuse—mistreatment of a minor by an adult legally responsible for the minor.

虐待儿童

child born out of wedlock—

1. a child born to a woman who was not married from the date of conception to the date of birth

私生子

2. a child who the court has determined to be born or conceived during a marriage but who is not a child of the marriage.

非婚生子女

child care fund—state funds used to reimburse counties for part of the expenses incurred in providing foster care and other services to children under the jurisdiction of the family division of the circuit court.

儿童保育专款;儿童保育基金

child care rules—the administrative rules for the care of children in foster care.

保育条例

child custody—the responsibility to care for and exercise control over a child. Child custody may be awarded incident to a domestic relations proceeding.
儿童监护

child neglect—the failure of a parent, guardian, or custodian of a minor to provide the minor with proper or necessary support, education, medical care, or physical care; also, the failure to provide a fit home environment for the minor.
疏忽儿童;忽略看顾儿童

child protective proceedings—proceedings in the family division of the circuit court regarding children under age 18 who are abused or neglected.
保护儿童程序

Children'S Protective Services /CPS—a division in the Office of Children's Services in the Family Independence Agency. Children's Protective Services workers investigate reports of suspected child abuse or neglect. They can also provide services to families in an effort to prevent abuse or neglect.
儿童保护中心

child support—in domestic relations cases, ongoing payments made by a parent to meet the financial needs of that parent's child, including medical, dental, educational, and child care expenses. See also *support order*.
子女抚养费

child support formula—factors used by the Friend of the Court and the Prosecuting Attorney when recommending an appropriate amount of child support. Both the non-custodial and custodial parent's income are factors considered in the determination of child support under the formula.
儿童抚养费计算公式;儿童抚养费计算原则

circuit—a regular journey made by a judge around a particular district to hear cases in court.
(法官的)巡回审判

circuit court—a specific tribunal that possesses the legal authority to hear cases within its own geographical territory. The following cases are heard in circuit court: felony trials; civil lawsuits seeking injunctions, equitable relief, or damages in excess of $25,000; domestic relations matters; adoptions; child protection proceedings; juvenile delinquency proceedings; emancipation of minors; waiver of parental consent to an abortion; personal protection orders; name changes; and, guardianships or conservatorships arising out of protective proceedings, delinquency proceedings, or domestic relations custody cases. Each circuit court has superintending control over the district and probate courts in its circuit.

巡回法院

> 巡回法院是根据地理位置，为方便管理和诉讼分设在不同区域内的法院。巡回法院也称上诉法院，相当于我国的中级法院，但不直接审理一审案件。美国联邦法院将全国50个州划分为13个审判区域，设有13个巡回法院，一个巡回法院往往下辖数个地区法院。

circumstantial—(of evidence or a legal case) pointing indirectly toward someone's guilt but not conclusively proving it.

（指证据）有充分细节却无法证实的

circumstantial evidence—all evidence except eyewitness testimony. Evidence from which an inference must be drawn. Examples include documents, photographs, and physical evidence, such as fingerprints.

旁证；间接证据

citation—

1. the court copy (original) of the "traffic ticket" is the citation, and also serves as the original complaint in the case.

传讯；传票；交通罚单

2. also can be reference to an authority (such as case or statute), that supports a statement of law or from which a quotation is taken. Citations occur most frequently in briefs.

引证；引用；引文

citator—books or services which provide, through letter form abbreviations or words, the judicial history and interpretation of reported decisions, and information as to cases and legislative enactments construing, applying or affecting statutes.

引证(文)索引

cite—

1. induce a former tried case as a guide to deciding a comparable case or in support of an argument.

引证;援引(先例)

2. summon (someone) to appear in a court of law.

传唤;传讯

citizen's arrest—an arrest by an ordinary person without a warrant, allowable in certain cases.

公民的逮捕(权)

civil—relating to private relations between members of a community; noncriminal.

民事的

civil action/lawswit—generally, a non-criminal case concerning the claim of one private individual against another.

民事诉讼;非刑事案件

civil contempt—see *contempt of court*.

(不遵守法院命令的)藐视法庭罪

civil court—a court dealing with non-criminal cases.

民事法庭;民事审判庭

civil death—In common law, civil death was the status given to a person who, though alive, had been convicted of a felony and sentenced to life imprisonment. It referred to the fact that the convict had lost all civil rights and was thus thought to be dead as regards any participation in society.

法律上的死亡(如褫夺公权、宣告失踪人死亡等)

civil disobedience—the refusal to comply with certain laws or to pay taxes and fines, as a peaceful form of political protest.

不合作;温和抵抗;公民抗命

civil infraction—an act or omission prohibited by law which is not a crime, for which civil sanctions may be ordered. Many traffic violations are classified as civil infractions.

民事违规行为

civil infraction determination—a decision whether a person is responsible for a civil infraction by one of the following:

1) An admission of responsibility for the civil infraction.

2) An admission of responsibility for the civil infraction with an explanation.

3) An informal hearing or formal hearing.

4) A default judgment, for failing to appear at a scheduled informal or formal hearing.

民事违规认定

civil infraction formal hearing—a hearing conducted only by a district court judge involving the police officer, defendant and all witnesses. Defendant may be represented by an attorney and a prosecutor must be present.

民事违规行为正式听证

civil infraction informal hearing—a hearing conducted by a district court magistrate or judge involving the police officer, the defendant and any witnesses, held without a prosecutor or defense attorney. The determination may be appealed to a formal hearing.

民事违规行为非正式听证

civil infraction sanction—the penalty imposed upon a person found responsible for a civil infraction; such as the assessment of fine and costs, mandatory attendance at a corrective program such as driver's training program, drug or alcohol abuse program.

民事违规制裁、处罚

civil law—laws regarding the establishment, recovery, or redress of private and civil rights.

民法

civil liberty—the state of being subject only to laws established for the good of the community, esp. with regard to freedom of action and speech.

（法律规定的）公民自由权

civil penalties—generally, fines or money damages imposed by a regulatory scheme.

民事罚款;民事处罚

civil rights—rights given, defined, and circumscribed by positive laws enacted by civilized communities.

民事权利

civil wrong—an infringement of a person's rights, such as a tort or breach of contract.

民事过错行为

claim—

1. the right to judicial relief, also referred to as a "cause of action." See *cause of action*.

诉讼请求权

2. a creditor's right to payment from a decedent's estate that arises at or before the decedent's death, including the decedent's funeral and burial expenses.

从死者遗产中得到偿款的权利(包括丧葬费等花费)

3. a creditor's right to payment from the estate of a minor, legally incapacitated person, disappeared person, or ward.

从未成年人、无民事行为能力人、失踪或病人的遗产中得到偿款的权利

a. *Contingent Claim*—a claim for expenses not yet incurred that is dependent on some future event that may or may not happen.

附带要求

b. *Tardy Claim*—a claim filed after the date for the final presentation of claims.

延迟申请的权利主张

claim and delivery—a civil action to recover: 1) property unlawfully taken or held by another; and, 2) damages sustained by the unlawful taking or retention.

追回被非法扣押的财物的诉讼;取得不当扣押赔偿的诉讼

claimant—one who has a claim to or makes a claim to something.

提出权利主张人;提出要求人;索赔人;起诉人

claim of appeal—the form or paper that is filed indicating an appeal is being taken. The original is filed with court where appeal is going to take place and copy with trial court.

上诉请求书

class action—a lawsuit filed or defended by an individual or small group acting on behalf of a large group.

集体诉讼(一个人或几个人为原告,代表一个更大的团体的诉讼类型。)

clause—a particular and separate article, stipulation, or provision in a treaty, bill, or contract.

条款;条文

clear and convincing evidence—standard of proof commonly used in civil lawsuits and in regulatory agency appeals. It governs the amount of proof that must be offered in order for the plaintiff to win the case. It imposes a greater burden than the preponderance of evidence standard, but less than the criminal standard "beyond a reasonable doubt."

明确而令人信服的证据

clearinghouse—an association, usually formed voluntarily by banks, to exchange checks, drafts, or other forms of indebtedness held by one member and owed to another.

票据交易所

clear title—title free from any encumbrance, obstruction, burden or limitation that presents a doubtful or even a reasonable question of law or fact.

完全所有权

clemency or executive clemency—act of grace or mercy by the president or governor to ease the consequences of a criminal act, accusation, or conviction. It may take the form of commutation or pardon.

行政赦免

clerk—an official in charge of the records of a local council or court.

书记员

clerkship—the position or status of a clerk, esp. in the legal profession.

书记员职位

closing argument—the closing statement, by counsel, to the trier of facts after all parties have concluded their presentation of evidence.

结束辩论；收场辩论

cloture—in legislative assemblies that permit unlimited debate, a procedure or rule by which debate is ended so that a vote may be taken on the matter.

讨论终结（结束辩论而付诸表决，以表决的方法结束辩论。）

cloud on title—any matter appearing in the record of a title to real estate that on its face appears to reflect the existence of an outstanding claim or encumbrance that, if valid, would defeat or impair title, but that might be proven invalid by evidence outside the title record.

影响不动产所有权的障碍

code—a grouping of statutes, relating to a particular subject matter and arranged in classified order. Usually created by enactment of a new statute by the legislature embodying all the old statutes relating to the subject and including changes necessitated by court decisions. In some cases, the change would result in a new statutory concept.

法典（表明悉数涵盖当时某个法律体系或某方面法律的立法）

codefendant—a joint defendant.

共同被告

codicil—a legal document made after a will that modifies the will.

遗嘱附录

codify—arrange (laws or rules) into a systematic code.

将……编成法典

cognizable—within the jurisdiction of a court.

审判权限内；可以审理的

cognizance—knowledge, awareness, or notice.

法官常识；认定；认识

collateral—money or goods given to secure payments of a debt (*civil law*) or to insure appearance in court (*criminal law*).

抵押物；担保物

collateral estoppel—rule that bars relitigation between the same parties of a particular issue or determinative fact when there is a prior judgment.

间接禁止反言（要求在前后不同案件中，当事人对于相同案件事实应当做出一致的主张。）

collateral matters—matters related to but not legally relevant to the question before the court.

枝节问题；旁系问题

collateral source rule—benefits or compensation received by an injured person from a separate source such as insurance do not serve to reduce the damages owed by a tort-feasor.

间接来源规则

collation—the bringing into the estate of an intestate person who dies without a will an estimate of the value of advancements made by the intestate to his or her children, in order that the whole may be divided in accordance with the Statute of Descents.

对未留遗嘱者的遗产进行评估分配

collective bargaining—in labor law, the negotiation of employment matters between employers and employees through the use of a bargaining agent designated by an uncoerced majority of the employees within the bargaining unit.

劳资双方就工资等问题谈判

collusion—secret or illegal cooperation or conspiracy, esp. between ostensible opponents in a lawsuit.

通谋；串通；共谋

color—an apparent right or ground.

立场

colorable—that which presents an appearance which does not correspond with the reality, or an appearance intended to conceal or to deceive.

伪装的；似是而非的

color of title—lending the appearance of title, when in reality there is no title at all; an instrument which appears to pass title, and which one relies on as passing title but which fails to do so; an instrument which, on its face, professes to pass title, but which fails to do so either because title is lacking in the person conveying or because the conveyance itself is defective.

有名无实的所有权

comakers—two (or more) persons who sign a note. Upon such signature, each assumes full liability in the event of default by the other person(s).

联署者;共同签字者

commercial paper—a negotiable instrument, i.e., a writing indorsed by the maker or drawee, containing an unconditional promise or order to pay a certain sum on demand or at a specified time, made payable to order or to bearer.

票据

commission—in contracts, a form of payment for services performed. The ordinary understanding of the word is compensation based on a percentage of an amount collected, received, or agreed to be paid for results accomplished, as distinguished from "salary" which is a fixed and periodic amount payable without regard to actual results achieved.

佣金

commit—

1. to do, perform, or perpetrate: commit a murder.

犯罪

2. the act of sending a person to a prison, reformatory, mental hospital or other facility, pursuant to a court order.

(根据法院命令)押解到……;遣送到……

commitment—the order by which the court directs:

1. the sending of a person to a prison or jail in execution of sentence.

下狱;收监

2. the sending of a person to a hospital because of a mental disorder.

关进精神病院

common law—a system of laws which has evolved from early days to the present consisting of old and accepted customs, precedents and court decisions, old English statutes and other unwritten but accepted standards. Common law is the foundation for the legal system in every state of the United States except

Louisiana.

共同法；普遍法

common pleas court—This court was abolished in 1981 and merged into the 36th District Court. It was a court in the City of Detroit that had exclusive jurisdiction over civil cases involving claims up to $5,000 and concurrent jurisdiction with Wayne County Circuit Court over civil cases involving claims up to $10,000.

民诉法院

community property—(*in certain US states*) property that is owned jointly by a husband and wife, and which is distributed equally on termination of the marriage.

夫妻共有财产

community service—unpaid work, intended to be of social use, that an offender is required to do instead of going to prison.

社区劳动

> 这是法庭可以作出的要求罪犯从事一定时间的无偿劳动,以替代对罪犯的其他处置方式的命令。该命令需要罪犯的同意并在其要工作的社区提供相应的准备。该罪犯必须完成特定小时数的劳动,期间他可能受到相关官员的指导。如果该罪犯未遵守命令或不能令人满意地完成被要求从事的劳动,则他可以被带到地方法庭并处以罚金或受到他本来应该受到的处理。这类命令可以被改正或撤销,并用其他方式来选择处理罪犯。

commute—reduce (a judicial sentence, esp. a sentence of death) to one less severe.

减轻刑罚（特别是死刑）；改判

comparative negligence—failure of an injured plaintiff to act with reasonable care, thereby reducing the amount recovered from the defendant or preventing the plaintiff from receiving any compensation.

比较过失

> 比较过失指通过比较原、被告双方的过错在整体过失责任中所占的比例来分配损害赔偿责任。如果原告的过错比较小，那么被告就要多赔，而如果原、被告过错相当，或原告的过错比较大，就要根据每一个州所采用的比较过失原则的具体种类来决定是否要赔，因为不同的州很可能采用的是不同类型的比较过失原则。

compensable—(of a loss or hardship) for which compensation can be obtained.

可补（赔）偿的

compensatory damages—damages awarded to compensate the non-breaching or injured party.

赔（补）偿金

competence—the legal authority of a court or other body to deal with a particular matter.

（法院的）权限；管辖权；资格

competency—the presence of those characteristics, which make a witness legally fit and qualified to give testimony in court—applied, in the same sense, to documents or other written evidence.

（证据法上的）作证资格

competency to stand trial—In order to be competent to stand trial, a person must have the capacity to understand the nature and object of the proceedings, to consult with counsel, and to assist in preparing his/her defense. Due process prohibits the government from prosecuting a defendant who is not competent to stand trial.

受审能力

competency witness—Every person is considered competent to be a witness. When a party questions the competency of a witness, the judge must determine the witness's capacity to observe, recall, and communicate what he or she witnessed, and that the witness understands the duty to be truthful.

法律上适格的证人

competent—legally sufficient, relating primarily to evidence and witnesses in a court action, i.e., competent to stand trial.

有法定资格的

complainant—in a civil case, one who makes a complaint, often referred to as the "plaintiff". In a criminal case, the one who instigates the prosecution, also referred to as the "complaining witness".

申诉人；原告

complaint—in a civil lawsuit, the first paper filed with the court in which the plaintiff gives the reasons for the suit. A complaint in a criminal action is a written accusation (under oath or upon affirmation) that a felony, misdemeanor, or ordinance violation has been committed and probable cause exists that the named person is guilty of the offense.

（民事）起诉书；（刑事）控告书

composition—a legal agreement to pay an amount of money in lieu of a larger debt or other obligation.

和解协议

compound—forbear from prosecuting (a felony) in exchange for money or other consideration.

（为了金钱或其他利益）私下和解；私了

compurgation—acquittal from a charge or accusation, obtained by statements of innocence given by witnesses under oath.

根据他人的保证宣告被告无罪

compurgator—a sworn witness to the innocence or good character of an accused person.

辩护者；为他人作证者

concert—agreement, accordance, or coordination.

一致；协调；协同安排

conciliation—a form of alternative dispute resolution in which a "conciliator" uses mediation principles to assist the disputing parties in reaching an agreement. A conciliator may prepare a recommendation for the court if the parties are not able to agree; this recommendation may become the court's order unless one of the parties objects. See *mediation*.

调解；当庭和解

conclusive evidence—evidence which is incontrovertible, that is to say, either not open or not able to be questioned, as where it is said that a thing is conclusively proved. It means that such result follows from the facts shown as the only one possible.

决定性证据；确证；结论性证据

concur—to agree. A concurring opinion states agreement with the conclusion of the majority, but may state different reasons why such conclusion is reached. An opinion "concurring in the result only" is one which implies no agreement with the reasoning of the prevailing opinion, but which fails to state reasons of its own.

同意；赞成

concurrent—to run together, in conjunction with; to exist together

同时进行的；与之共同的；并存的

concurrent jurisdiction—the authority of multiple courts to hear the same type of case at the choice of the litigants.

共同管辖权

concurrent sentences—sentences of imprisonment served simultaneously in cases where a criminal defendant is convicted of more than one offense and sentenced to separate terms of imprisonment for each offense. The defendant is entitled to release from prison at the expiration of the longest term specified. See also *consecutive sentence*.

合并服刑（刑事案中的被告犯了两项或以上的罪名同时成立，但各项罪名的判刑同时执行。）

concurring opinion—an opinion written by an appellate judge who agrees with the decision reached in a case on appeal, but who would base this decision on reasons different from those expressed by the majority of judges considering the case. See also *dissenting opinion*, *majority opinion*.

附和意见；同意意见（指一名或少数法官的单独意见。同意多数法官做出的判决，但对判决依据提出不同理由。）

condemn—sentence (someone) to a particular punishment, esp. death.

判定有罪；宣告有罪

condemnation—the process by which private real estate is taken for public use without the owner's consent but with just compensation, pursuant to a court order—a forced sale for public use. Destruction ordered for public health or safety. In such cases, there is no taking for a public use and thus there is no compensation.

判决没收（财产）

condominium—

1. a building or complex of buildings containing a number of individually owned apartments or houses.

各户有独立产权的公寓

2. the joint control of a country's or territory's affairs by other countries.

国际共管

confession—a statement by person, either oral or written, admitting that he committed a certain offense. The statement must include all of the elements of the offense, or it is not a confession but an admission. An oral or written statement is not necessarily a confession.

（认罪）供词；供认；自首

confiscate—to take private property without just compensation; to transfer property from a private use to a public use.

没收；充公；（战时）没收地方财产

conflict of interest(s)—a situation in which regard for one duty leads to disregard of another, or might reasonably be expected to do so.

利益冲突

conformed copy—an exact copy of a document, often certified to be so by a clerk of a court, with handwritten notations duplicating those on the original document. Thus, an order may have the date, precise terms, and signature of the judge written by hand on another copy of a proposed order which had not been signed. This then becomes a conformed copy of the order which was completed and signed by the court.

（内容）一致的副本

conforming—goods or conduct including any part of a performance are "conforming" or conform to the contract when they are in accordance with the obligations under the contract.

一致的;符合的;相符的

conforming use—a term for those property uses which are permitted because they are in compliance with current zoning requirements.

符合要求的使用

confrontation clause—Under the Sixth Amendment of the Constitution, the accused in a criminal prosecution is entitled "to confront the witnesses against him or her". This right also entitles the accused to be present at the trial, and to hear and cross-examine the witnesses.

对质条款

confusion of goods—results when personal property belonging to two or more owners becomes intermixed to the point when the property of any of them no longer can be identified except as part of a mass of like goods.

物的混合;混合财产

conglomerate—a group of corporations engaged in unrelated businesses which are controlled by a single corporate entity.

联合大企业;集团公司

conjugal rights—the rights, especially to sexual relations, regarded as exercisable in law by each partner in a marriage.

(夫妻)同居权

conjugal visit—a visit by the spouse of a prisoner, especially for sexual relations.

配偶探视

consanguinity—a relationship created by blood; persons who descend from a common ancestor.

血亲关系;血缘关系

conscience clause—a clause that makes concessions to the consciences of those affected by a law.

道德条款(说明因其宗教或道德的原则不能遵守某一规定时,可不受处分的法律条款)

conscience of the court—refers to the power of the court of equity to resolve a controversy by applying common standards of decency and fairness. The term does not refer to the private opinion of a particular judge but to uniformly held judgment of the community. The proper application of the doctrine rests upon general principles of equitable law and to established precedent.

法庭良知(指法庭有衡平法上的权力,根据公平和公正原则作出裁决;指法庭在决定当事人或陪审团是否依法从事诉讼活动时所适用的准则,如在某些案件中,法庭否定了陪审团对损害赔偿的裁断,因为这种裁断"使法庭的良知受到震惊"。)

consecutive sentence—In cases where a criminal defendant is sentenced to separate terms of imprisonment for multiple offenses, a consecutive sentence is one that will be served after another sentence has expired. See also *concurrent sentences*.

连续刑罚;分期执行的刑罚(刑事案中的被告所犯的不同罪行,判处不同刑期,则被告需要分别服刑。)

consent calendar—a schedule of informal hearings involving a child in which it appears it will serve the best interests of the child and society, with the consent of the child and all interested parties, to hear the case informally. The schedule or calendar upon which such informal hearings are placed is called the "consent calendar".

无争议案件审理日程表(因为对案件的主要问题都已达成共识,所以不需要讨论,非常节约时间。)

consequential—resulting from an act, but not immediately and directly.
间接因果关系

conservator—a person with the legal duty and power to manage and protect the estate of another individual who:
1) is under age 18;
2) is a legally incapacitated person.
保护者;(公共福利的)监督人

conservatorship—legal right given to a person to manage the property and financial affairs of a person deemed incapable of doing that for himself/herself. (See also *guardianship*. Conservators have somewhat less responsibility than guardians.）

托管或管理委员的职位（法庭对无自主能力者个人事务和/或个人护理的管理进行监督的法律程序）

consideration—

1. （in a contractual agreement）anything given or promised or forborne by one party in exchange for the promise or undertaking of another.

对价

2. archaic importance; consequence.

重要性；结果；后果

consolidate—combine（two or more legal actions involving similar or related questions）into one for action by a court.

合并审理

consortium—the right of association and companionship with one's husband or wife.

配偶权利

conspiracy—an unlawful agreement to commit a crime or do a lawful act in an illegal manner.

阴谋；同谋；串通；共谋

constable—a peace officer with limited policing authority, typically in a small town.

警官；巡警

constabulary—the constables of a district, collectively.

地方警察部队；保安队

constituent—being a voting member of a community or organization and having the power to appoint or elect.

选民

constitute—give legal or constitutional form to（an institution）; establish by law.

（根据法律）设立机构等

constitutionalize—make subject to explicit provisions of a country's constitution.

使宪法化

constructionist—a person who puts a particular construction upon a legal document, esp. the US Constitution.

宪法解释者;法令解释者

constructive—derived by inference; implied by operation of law; not obvious or explicit.

（法律）推定的

consul—

1. an official appointed by a government to live in a foreign city and protect and promote the government's citizens and interests there.

领事

2. (*in ancient Rome*) one of the two annually elected chief magistrates who jointly rule the republic.

（古罗马的）执政官

consulate—

1. the place or building in which a consul's duties are carried out.

领事馆

2. the period of office of a Roman consul.

领事任期

contemnor—one who commits an act in contempt of court.

藐视法庭者

contemplation—the state of being thought about or planned; anticipation.

深思熟虑;沉思

contempt of court—an act or failure to act that violates a court order, impedes the functioning of the court, or impairs the authority of the court. Contempt may be "direct" (i.e., in the immediate view and presence of the court), or "indirect" (i.e., outside the immediate view and presence of the court). Contempt of court is subject to civil or criminal contempt sanctions, both of which can involve fines and/or jail terms. Civil contempt sanctions are generally imposed to compel a contemnor to comply with the court's directives. Criminal contempt sanctions are generally imposed to punish past misconduct.

藐视法庭

contest—the act of disputing or challenging the validity of a will.
对遗嘱有效性的异议

contestant—a person who takes part in a legal contest.
（在法庭上）对遗嘱有效性提出异议的人

contiguous—near or in close proximity to.
邻接的；毗邻的；相邻的；毗连的

contingent beneficiary—one who will receive the benefit or proceeds of an estate, trust, life insurance policy or the like but only if some particular event or circumstance, whose happening or outcome is not presently known or assured, does in fact occur.
潜在收益人

continuance—postponement of an action pending in court. See *adjournment*.
诉讼延期；延期审理

contract—an agreement between two or more parties to do or not do a particular thing. The agreement may be stated in an oral or written exchange of promises or implied by the parties' actions.
合同；有法律约束力的承诺或协议

contra proferentem—(of the interpretation of a contract) against the party that proposed (or, more usually, drafted) the contract or a provision in the contract; The rule that a contract must be construed most strictly against the drafter.
逆向利益合同解释原则；反意居先合同解释原则（对书面文件的词句应当按照对提出词句的当事人尤为不利的原则来解释。）

contributory—(of or relating to a pension or insurance plan) operated by means of a fund into which people pay.
贡献的；捐献的

contributory negligence—failure of an injured plaintiff to act with reasonable care, considered to be a contributory factor in the injury suffered, thereby barring the plaintiff from compensation by the defendant.
混合过错；过失竞合（意外中的伤者对意外的造成及他自己的受伤程度，

需要分担部分疏忽的责任,他所获得的赔偿额也会相对地减少。)

contumacious—(*esp. of a defendant's behavior*) stubbornly or willfully disobedient to authority; in contempt.
(对法庭命令)抗拒的

contumacy—stubborn refusal to obey or comply with authority,esp. a court order or summons.
拒不服从法庭命令

conversion—the wrongful exercise of the right of ownership or control over goods which belong to another.
变换;侵占(他人财物)

convert—wrongfully deal with (goods or money) in a manner inconsistent with the owner's rights.
转换;非法挪用(物资或财产)

convey—to transfer title to property.
转让财产

conveyance—
1. the transfer of a title to property from one person to another.
财产转让
2. the instruments in writing (documents) which effect the transfer of title.
财产转让书

conveyancing—the branch of law concerned with the preparation of documents for the transferring of property.
关于(不动产等的)转让证书的制作业务的法律

convict—
1. to find or adjudge guilty of a criminal offense.
宣判……有罪
2. one who has been convicted of a criminal offense.
囚犯;被定罪人

conviction—a formal declaration that someone is guilty of a criminal offense,made by the verdict of a jury or the decision of a judge in a court of law.

判决有罪；刑事定罪

corespondent—

1. a joint defendant in a lawsuit, esp. one on appeal.

答辩人；被告

2. a person cited in a divorce case as having committed adultery with the respondent.

离婚诉讼中(被列明)的与被告通奸的人

corporate—(of a company or group of people) authorized to act as a single entity and recognized as such in law.

法人；公司

corporation—a company or group of people authorized to act as a single entity (legally a person) in which the individuals who make up the corporation have limited liability.

股份有限公司

corporeal—consisting of material objects.

有形的；物质的

corpus delicti—the body of the crime. That which the prosecutors must prove (that a crime was committed) before introducing a confession or admission into evidence.

犯罪事实

corroborating evidence—supplementary evidence that tends to strengthen or confirm the initial evidence.

佐证；确证的证据(也是一种附加的证据，这种证据使得提供的证据更为有利。)

corrupt practice—a fraudulent activity, especially an attempt to rig an election or bribe an official.

政治行贿

Cosa Nostra—a US criminal organization resembling and related to the Mafia.

黑手党

costs—legal expenses, esp. those allowed in favor of the winning party or against the losing party in a suit.
诉讼费用

counsel—an attorney; one who gives advice, especially legal advice.
律师;辩护人;法律顾问

count—a separate charge in an indictment.
一项指控;一项罪名

counterclaim—in a civil lawsuit, a claim that the defendant asserts against the plaintiff.
反诉

countermand—revoke (an order).
收回;撤回;取消(命令)

counter offer—an offer made by someone who has rejected a prior offer
(买方)还价,还盘

counterpart—one of two or more copies of a legal document.
契约文本等的副本

county agent—an officer of the juvenile court who serves under the supervision of a family division judge to organize, direct and develop the child welfare work of the court. Also known as a "juvenile officer".
主管少年犯罪的警官

county court—a court in some states with civil and criminal jurisdiction for a given county.
地方法院

court—a tribunal presided over by a judge, judges, or a magistrate.
法院;裁判所;审判庭

court congestion—an accumulation of cases impeding the timely movement of those cases through the judicial process.
法院案件拥塞

courthouse—
1. a building in which a judicial court is held.
法院大楼

2. a building containing the administrative offices of a county.
县行政办公楼

court martial—a judicial court for trying members of the armed services accused of offenses against military law.
军事法庭

court of appeals—the court in which appeals from the probate courts, court of claims, and circuit courts are heard and decided.
上诉法院

court of claims—a U.S. federal court that determines claims brought by individuals against the government.
联邦行政法院；索赔法院

court of record—a court whose proceedings are by law permanently recorded by a public officer other than the judge. They have the power to fine or imprison for contempt. Courts not of record have less authority and their proceedings are not permanently recorded.
记录法院（永久保存诉讼记录的法院）

court order—a direction issued by a court or a judge requiring a person to do or not do something.
法院命令；法院指令

court recorder—a court official who records the activities of a court using an electronic recording device, usually for the purpose of preparing a verbatim transcript.
法庭记录器；记录员

court reporter—a person who records the activities of a court using manual shorthand, a stenotype machine or a steno mask.
书记员

court reporting and recording board of review—a board appointed by the Supreme Court to administer the certification of court reporters and recorders.
法院记录审查委员会

court rules—rules adopted by the Supreme Court to govern procedure in all the state's courts.

法庭规则

court system—consists of State Supreme Court, Court of Appeals, Circuit Court, District Court, Probate Court, Municipal Court, Court of Claims. See the name of each court for descriptions of individual courts.

法院系统；法院体系

covenant—a contract drawn up by deed.

盖印合同；契约条款

covenantee—the person to whom a promise by covenant is made.

合同受约方；订约人

covert—(of a woman) married and under the authority and protection of her husband.

在丈夫保护下的；秘密的

coverture—the legal status of a married woman, considered to be under her husband's protection and authority.

有夫之妇的法律身份

credibility—whether or not a witness is being truthful.

（证人的）可信性；可靠性

creditor—one to whom money is owed by the debtor; one to whom an obligation exists.

债权人；贷方；贷项

crier—an officer who makes public announcements in a court of justice.

传布公告者；法庭发言人

crime—an act in violation of criminal law; an offense against the State of Michigan punishable by imprisonment or a fine other than a civil fine.

刑事犯罪

crime against nature—sexual deviations which were considered crimes at common law and have been carried over by statute, including sodomy and bestiality.

鸡奸；兽奸

crime of passion—a crime committed under the influence of sudden or extreme passion. For instance, a man's attack on another person with an axe after that person insulted the attacker's wife might be considered a crime committed in the heat of passion.

激情犯罪(指在绝望、暴怒等剧烈情绪状态下实施的犯罪行为。它缺乏明显的犯罪预谋,是在强烈的情绪冲动支配下迅速暴发的犯罪行为,犯罪人缺乏自制力,不能正确地评价自己的行为的意义及其法律后果。激情犯罪的破坏性大,容易造成严重的危害结果,而且难以预防。)

criminal—one who has committed a criminal offense; one who has been legally convicted of a crime; one adjudged guilty of a crime.

刑事罪犯;犯罪分子

criminal case—a lawsuit is called a criminal case when it is between the people of the State on one side as plaintiff, and a person or corporation on the other as defendant and involves a question of whether the defendant has violated one of the laws defining crimes.

刑事案件

criminal contempt—see *contempt of court*.

严重的藐视法庭行为

criminal conversation—adultery, esp. as formerly constituting grounds for the recovery of legal damages by a husband from his adulterous wife's partner.

通奸行为(之诉)

criminalistics—another term for forensics. See *forensic*.

刑事学

criminal law—the statutes that forbid certain actions or conduct as detrimental to the welfare of the state and that provide punishment. Criminal acts are prosecuted by the Prosecuting Attorney.

刑法

criminal libel—a malicious, defamatory statement in a permanent form, rendering the maker liable to criminal prosecution.

刑事诽谤罪

criminal record—a history of being convicted for crime.

犯罪记录

criminology—the scientific study of crime and criminals.

刑事学；犯罪学

cross appeal—in a case on appeal, the appellee's request that the court review aspects of the lower court's decision that were not raised in the appellant's papers.

交叉上诉；交互上诉

> 英美法系大都规定了交叉上诉制度，即被上诉人可在一定时间内对上诉人的上诉提出反请求。而美国的被上诉人在绝大多数情况下都会提出交叉上诉，从而为加重单方上诉人的责任留下极小的空间。

cross-claim—in a civil lawsuit involving multiple plaintiffs or multiple defendants, a claim brought by one plaintiff against another plaintiff, or by one defendant against another defendant.

交叉诉讼

cross examination—the questioning of a witness by the opposing party to test the truthfulness of the witness's testimony, to further develop it or to otherwise expand on it.

交叉讯问

> 按照英美法系的审判制度，起诉方和被告方均可要求法院传唤证人出庭作证，在庭上先由要求传证人的一方向证人提问，然后再由对方向证人提问，也就是起诉方讯问被告方的证人或被告方讯问起诉方的证人，即双方交叉讯问证人。

cross-examine—question (a witness called by the other party) in a court of law to discredit or undercut testimony already given.

交叉讯问证人

cruelty—behavior that causes physical or mental harm to another, esp. a spouse, whether intentionally or not.

（家庭）虐待

cuckold—a man whose wife is unfaithful; the husband of an adulteress. It is explained that the word alludes to the habit of the female cuckold, which lays her eggs in the nests of other birds to be hatched by them. To make a cuckold of a man is to seduce his wife.

妻子有外遇的人

cui bono—who stands, or stood, to gain (from a crime, and so might have been responsible for it)

谁人获益;为何目的

culpa—a term from the civil law meaning fault, neglect, or negligence. Compare *dolus*, also from the civil law meaning fraud, guile, or deceit.

过失

culpable—deserving of moral blame; implies fault rather than guilt; criminal, reckless, gross disregarding of the consequence which may ensue from the act, and indifference to the rights of others.

犯罪的;应受处罚的

curtesy—a tenure by which a husband, after his wife's death, held certain kinds of property that she had inherited.

鳏夫产业(丈夫继承亡妻财产的权利)

curtilage—an area of land attached to a house and forming one enclosure with it.

庭院;宅地

custodial parent—the parent having custody of a child. See *child custody*.

监护家长

custody—

1. care and control of a thing or person. See also *child custody*.

监护

2. a person who is "in custody" is imprisoned or otherwise physically detained.

监禁;羁押

custody statement—in some circumstances a child in custody is not released to his/her parent(s), guardian, etc., but is detained by the court. When this occurs, the officer taking the child in custody must prepare a statement setting forth the grounds for detention and submit this report to the court.

监护陈述;监护声明

cy-pres—as near as possible to the testator's or donor's intentions when these cannot be precisely followed.

力求近似的;力求达意(解释)原则

D

DA—district attorney.
地方检察官

damages—money paid to a person who has been injured by the actions of another person.
损害赔偿金

date rape—rape committed by the victim's escort.
约会男友强奸

DDP—see *developmentally disabled person*.
智能障碍者

dead hand—an undesirable persisting influence, especially concerning property after the death of a prior owner.
难以消除的不利影响

death certificate—an official statement, signed by a physician, of the cause, date, and place of a person's death.
死亡证明书

death penalty—the punishment of execution, administered to someone convicted of a capital crime.
死刑

death tax—
1. another term for *estate tax*.
房地产遗产税
2. another term for *inheritance tax*.
遗产税;继承税

death warrant—an official order for the execution of a condemned person.
死刑执行令

de bonis non—see *administrator de bonis non*.
未指定管理人的财产;尚未管理的财产

de bonis non administratis—see *administrator de bonis non*.
遗产管理人的后继人

decease—death.
死亡

deceased—(*the deceased*) a person who has died.
死者

decedent—a person who has died.
死者;被继承人

decedent's estate—the real and personal property that an individual owns upon his or her death.
被继承人财产;遗产

decision—a formal judgment.
法律判决

declarant—a person or party who makes a formal declaration.
申诉者;声明者

declaratory judgment—A declaratory judgment, also called a declaration, is the legal determination of a court that resolves legal uncertainty for the litigants. It is a form of legally binding preventive adjudication by which a party involved in an actual or possible legal matter can ask a court to conclusively rule on and affirm the rights, duties, or obligations of one or more parties in a civil dispute (subject to any appeal).

宣告式判决;确认判决;确认之诉;确认诉讼

declaration—statement asserting or protecting a legal right.

(原告的)申诉;(证人的)证言

decree—a court judgment. A final decree is one fully and finally disposing of a case; an interlocutory decree is preliminary in nature, determining some issue in the case but not the ultimate question involved.

判决;裁定

decriminalize—cease to treat (something) as illegal, typically by legislation.

使(原属非法的东西)合法化

deed—a legal document that is signed and delivered, esp. one regarding the ownership of property or legal rights. See also *title deed*.

地契;土地证

deed of trust—another term for *trust deed*.

信托契约

de facto—in fact, whether by right or not.

事实上;实际存在的;执行上(而法律上并未宣告)

de facto segregation—segregation that exists as a consequence of social, economic, and political circumstances, and not as the result of legislation.

事实上的种族隔离

defalcate—misappropriate or fail to turn over (funds with which one has been entrusted).

侵吞公款;盗用公款

defamation—the modern form of the action for slander or libel.

诽谤(向遭诽谤的人以外的人士发布贬损该人言辞的侵权行为,其影响是在整体公众人士的眼中降低遭诽谤人的名誉。)

defame—damage the good reputation of (someone); slander or libel.

破坏名誉;诋毁;诽谤

default—a failure to do what ought to be done, i. e., when a defendant does not plead within the time allowed or fails to appear for trial.

不履行义务;拖欠;对……处以缺席判决

default judgment—action taken by the court when a person fails to appear in court in answer to a summons in a civil case.

缺席判决

defeasance—the action or process of rendering something null and void.

使无效;废止

defeasible—(especially of an interest in land) subject to being defeated or extinguished.

可废除的;可取消的(尤其指土地权利)

defeat—reject or block (a motion or proposal).

使(申请、提案)无效;废除

defective—something that is wanting as to an essential; incomplete, deficient, faulty, also, not reasonably safe for a use which can be reasonably anticipated or for which reason it was purchased.

有缺陷的;有毛病的;欠缺法律要件的;(产品)有瑕疵的

defend—conduct the case for (the party being accused or sued) in a lawsuit.

辩护;抗辩

defendant—the person against whom a lawsuit is started or a crime charged.

被告;被告人

defense—

1. the case presented by or on behalf of the party being accused or sued in a lawsuit.

辩护方

2. one or more defendants in a trial.

被告方

defense attorney—the attorney representing the accused (defendant).

辩护人;辩护律师

deferment—postponing or putting off to a future time. It may apply to the vesting or enjoyment of an estate, or to the calling of a person to serve in the armed forces.

推迟；延期；（军事法）缓役；暂缓服刑

deferred payments—payments extended over a period of time or put off to a future date. Installment payments are usually a series of equal deferred payments made over a course of time.

延期付款；延付贷款；分期付款

deferred sentence—a sentence that is postponed to a future time. After conviction, the judge does not announce or impose a sentence, but defers sentencing to a future date so that the defendant will complete certain conditions, such as attending driving school or completing a probationary period. If the person completes the requirements, the case will be dismissed and will not be part of the defendant's criminal record.

暂缓宣判

deficit—want or insufficiency in an account or number.

逆差；赤字；亏损（额）；亏空（额）；缺乏；不足（额）

defraud—to deprive a person of property or interest, estate or right by fraud, deceit, or artifice; to misrepresent some fact knowing it to be false and intending that another person be deceived as a consequence.

骗取；诈取

degree—a legal grade of crime or offense, esp. murder.

等级（根据轻重程度对罪行的分类）

de jure—according to rightful entitlement or law.

按照法律的

delay—time periods between phases in the processing of cases through the judicial system.

延迟；延缓

delayed appeal—an appeal after the time for taking an appeal has run out and the higher court has granted permission to appeal because of some special circumstances.

延迟上诉（仅限于法律规定的特殊情况）

deliberate—

1. in criminal cases, as applied to a jury, the weighing of evidence relating to the law, for the purpose of determining the guilt or innocence of a defendant.

在刑事案件中用以确定被告人的罪与非罪

2. in civil cases, as applied to a jury, the weighing of evidence for the purpose of determining relevant facts.

在民事案件中用来认定相关事实

delict—a violation of the law.

违法行为

delinquency proceedings—see *juvenile delinquency proceedings*.

未成年人犯罪特别诉讼程序

delinquent—in a monetary context, something which has been made payable and is overdue and unpaid; implies a previous opportunity to make payment. With reference to persons, implies carelessness, recklessness.

犯罪（尤指少年犯）；（债务等）到期未付的；有过错的；违法的

deliver—

1. transfer (property), acknowledging that one intends to be bound by a deed, either explicitly by declaration or implicitly by formal handover.

交付（财产）；送货；递交

2. (of a judge or court) give (a judgment or verdict).

宣判

delivery—the formal or symbolic handing over of property, esp. by deed, to a grantee or third party.

交付

demand—a formal request, as a right.

（正式的）要求

demise—convey or grant (an estate) by will or lease.

转让；遗赠（房产）

demonstrative evidence—evidence that makes use of a demonstration or display or an addition to testimony.

示意证据；确证

demur—to respond to a civil complaint by filing a demurrer. See *demurrer*.
抗辩

demurrage—a charge payable to the owner of a chartered ship in the event of failure to load or discharge the ship within the time agreed.
（车、船等）停留过久的滞留费

demurrer—in some states, a response to a civil complaint alleging that even if the facts alleged in the complaint are true, they do not create any legal liability and therefore do not warrant any further proceedings in the matter.
妨诉抗辩；抗诉

denial—
1. a refusal by a court to grant a request presented by petition or motion.
2. in pleadings, an assertion that the allegations of the opposing party are untrue.
否认；否定

de novo—Latin words means "anew". For example, a trial de novo is a trial anew or a new trial, as opposed to a mere review of the record of the first trial. It means to start over from beginning. For example, appeals from the probate court are not de novo, but rather on the record of what happened in the probate court.
重新开始；再一次

department of social services—see *family independence agency*.
社会服务部

dependency—a territory or possession not within the boundaries of the country which has jurisdiction to govern it.
附属国；附属地

dependent—one who looks to another for support in whole or in part; unable to exist or sustain oneself without support or aid.
被抚养的；被赡养的；非独立生活的人

deponent—one who gives a deposition.
证人；提供口供者

deport—expel (a foreigner) from a country, typically on the grounds of illegal status or for having committed a crime.

驱逐出境

depose—

1. remove from office suddenly and forcefully.

免职

2. testify to or give (evidence) on oath, typically in a written statement.

宣誓作证

3. question (a witness) in deposition.

讯问证人

deposition—a method of pretrial discovery in civil cases. During a deposition, a party or witness (the "deponent") is placed under oath and required to give oral answers to questions. Most depositions are taken without court supervision; the deponent is usually questioned by an attorney for one of the parties. At the deposition, a transcript or videotape is made of the deponent's testimony. The transcript or videotape may be used to support various pretrial motions, or admitted into evidence at trial in cases where the deponent is unable to be present in court. See also *discovery*.

庭外采证（英美诉讼法上特有的制度，可以由双方当事人在审判前互相询问对方或其证人进行采证，发生在审判前，而且是在庭外进行的，通常在一方律师的办公室举行，所以不同于中国法律制度中的"证词"或"法庭作证"。）

derelict—in a very poor condition as a result of disuse and neglect.

被抛弃的；被遗弃的

dereliction—the state of having been abandoned and become dilapidated.

无主；抛弃；废弃

derestrict—remove restrictions from.

取消对……的限制

dermatoglyphics—the study of skin markings or patterns on fingers, hands, and feet, and its application, esp. in criminology.

（犯罪学上的）皮纹、肤纹等研究

derogation—partial taking away of the effectiveness of a law; to partially repeal or abolish a law.

（法律、合同、条约等的）背离；部分废除

descendible—able to be inherited by a descendant.

可遗传的

descent—

there are two types of descent: lineal and collateral.

1. lineal descent is descent in a direct line, as from father or grandfather to son or grandson.

直系血亲

2. collateral descent is descent in a collateral or oblique line; that is, up to the common ancestor and then down from him, as from brother to brother, or between cousins.

旁系血亲

descent and distribution statutes—state laws that provide for the distribution of estate property of a person who dies without a will. Same as intestacy laws.

血缘及分配遗产法律

designated proceedings—proceedings in which a juvenile under age 17 is tried in criminal proceedings that occur within the family division of the circuit court. The juvenile is afforded all the legal and procedural protections that an adult would be given if charged with the same offense in a court of general criminal jurisdiction.

指定程序

detain—keep (someone) in official custody, typically for questioning about a crime or in politically sensitive.

羁押；拘留

detainer—

1. the action of detaining or withholding property.

扣押（财产）

2. a person who detains someone or something.

扣留者

detention—the action of detaining someone or the state of being detained in official custody.

拘留;扣留;收押

detention center—an institution where people are held in detention, usually for short periods, in particular illegal immigrants, refugees, people awaiting trial or sentence, or young offenders.

拘留所;青少年感化中心

determinable—capable of being brought to an end under given conditions; terminable.

可中止的;可终结的

determination—

1. the settlement of a dispute by the authoritative decision of a judge or arbitrator.

法律责任的认定

2. the cessation of an estate or interest.

(权利的)消失;终止

detinue—common-law claim or action to recover wrongfully detained goods or possessions.

收回被非法占有的动产的诉讼

Developmentally Disabled Person /DDP—

Under the Mental Health Code, a person with either of the following characteristics:

1) The person is older than five years of age and has a severe, chronic condition attributable to a mental and/or physical impairment. This condition manifested before the individual's 22nd birthday, is likely to continue indefinitely, and results in substantial functional limitations in three or more areas of major life activity, including self-care, language, learning, mobility, self-direction, capacity for independent living, or economic self-sufficiency. Because of his or her condition, the person needs individually planned services that are of lifelong or extended duration.

2) The person is age five or younger and has a substantial developmental delay or a specific congenital or acquired condition with a high probability of resulting in a developmental disability as defined in 1) above if services are not

provided.

伤残人士；老幼病残人

devise—

1. *n*. a gift of personal or real property or both, made in a will.

遗赠的财产

2. *v*. to give real or personal property or both in a will.

遗赠

devisee—a person given real or personal property under a will.

接受遗赠者

devolution—the transfer or delegation of power to a lower level, esp. by central government to local or regional administration.

(政府或个人的)权利转移；授权代理

devolve—transfer or delegate (power) to a lower level, esp. from central government to local or regional administration.

(中央对地方的)权力的移交、转移

dies non—a day on which no court is in session or which does not count for legal or other purposes.

休庭日；停审日

digest—a methodical summary of a body of laws, decided cases, legal rules, etc.

法规汇编；法律汇编

dilatory defenses—defenses made solely for purposes of delay.

延期答辩

dilatory fiduciary—a fiduciary (trustee) who causes undue delays in administering an estate.

拖沓、延迟的受托人

dilatory motion—a motion made only for purposes of delay.

延期申请

dilatory plea—a response to a lawsuit which has the object of delaying the action, without responding to the merits of the lawsuit.

延期答辩

diminished capacity—an unbalanced mental state that is considered to make a person unable to act with the intent necessary for a particular crime and is recognized as grounds to reduce the charge.

行为能力减退；能力减弱标准（该标准允许被告人提交精神病学专家证据，以证明他缺乏指控犯罪所需的犯罪心态。如果辩护成功，那么患精神病的被告人将被无罪释放或被定较轻的罪并受到减轻的处罚。）

direct examination—a witness by the party that has called that witness to give evidence, in the questioning of order to support the case that is being made.

（由同一方律师进行的）直接询问

directed verdict—verdict returned by the jury at the direction of the trial judge, by whose direction the jury is bound.

指示裁判（陪审团不用审查证据而直接按照法官的指示作出裁判。）

directed verdict of acquittal—a verdict issued by a judge at the conclusion of a criminal jury trial when the prosecutor has not presented sufficient evidence to convict the defendant. A directed verdict may not be granted to the prosecutor in criminal cases.

无罪裁定

disability—a disadvantage or handicap, esp. one imposed or recognized by the law.

无（法律）资格；无能力

disaffirm—repudiate; declare void.

否认（以前的判决）；宣告无效

disappeared person—absent from place of residence for at least seven continuous years; whereabouts unknown by person most likely to know whereabouts (for seven years as above); has not communicated with person above.

被宣告失踪人

disbar—expel (a lawyer) from the Bar, so that they no longer have the right to practice law.

取消律师资格

discharge—

1. (*often be discharged*) tell (someone) officially that they can or must leave, in particular.

释放

2. pay off (a debt or other financial claim).

清偿债务

3. dated (of a judge or court) cancel (an order of a court).

撤销法院命令

disclaim—renounce a legal claim to (a property or title).

放弃某人的权利；宣布弃权

disclaimer—a statement that denies something, esp. responsibility.

否认（责任的）声明

disclosure—the action of making new or secret information known.

（信息）披露

discontinuance—the termination of a civil case by withdrawal or failure to continue it by the plaintiff. A voluntary dismissal by the plaintiff.

撤销（诉讼）

discovery—the process of gathering and preserving evidence prior to trial in a civil or criminal case.

证据开示；证据发现（程序）

discretion—the reasonable exercise of a power or right to act in an official capacity; involves the idea of choice, of an exercise of the will, so that abuse of discretion involves more than a difference in judicial opinion between the trial and appellate courts, and in order to constitute an "abuse" of discretion, the judgment must demonstrate a perversity of will, a defiance of good judgment, or bias.

裁量权；斟酌决定的自由；（刑法）判断能力；辨别能力

discrimination—the unequal treatment of parties who are similarly situated. Federal law prohibits discrimination on the basis of race, sex, nationality, religion, and age in matters of employment, housing, education, voting rights, and access to public facilities.

区别对待;歧视

disenfranchise—deprive (someone) of the right to vote.
剥夺公民选举权

dismiss—to order a cause or prosecution to be terminated; to refuse to hear further.
(诉讼)驳回;不予受理

dismissal—an order or judgment deciding a particular lawsuit in favor of the defendant by sending it out of court without trial. Dismissal "with prejudice" forever bars the right to bring a lawsuit on the same claim or cause; dismissal "without prejudice" disposes of the particular lawsuit before the court but permits a new lawsuit to be brought based on the same claim or cause.
驳回诉讼;撤销诉讼

disorderly—involving or contributing to a breakdown of peaceful and law-abiding behavior.
妨害治安的

disorderly conduct—unruly behavior constituting a minor offense.
扰乱治安的行为

disorderly house—(*archaic*) a brothel.
妓院

dispose—(*dispose of*) make a final resolution of.
最终处理;最后决定

disposed case—not pending, decided, closed case.
已决案件

disposition—determination of a case, whether by dismissal, plea and sentence, settlement and dismissal, verdict and judgment.
处置;支配;处理

dispositive—relating to or bringing about the settlement of an issue or the disposition especially of property.
(事件、行为等)决定性的

disqualification—refers to the disqualification of judges from hearing a case. Any interest which may impair the ability of a judge to decide the case in a fair and impartial manner. Disqualification maybe voluntary or it may be done on the motion of a party to the case.

（法律上）丧失资格；取消资格

disqualify—pronounce (someone) ineligible for an office or activity because of an offense, infringement, or conflict of interest.

使无资格；剥夺……的法定权力；使失去资格

dissenting opinion—an opinion written by an appellate judge explaining why he or she disagrees with the decision reached by the majority of judges considering the case.

异议；反对意见（上诉法院的法官对多数法官作出的相同判决所持的不同观点）

dissolution—in the law of corporations, the end of the legal existence of a corporation. It is a termination in any manner, whether by expiration of charter, decree of count, act of legislature or other means.

解散；终止；结束

distrain—seize(someone's property) to obtain payment of rent or other money owed.

为抵债而扣押（财产）

distraint—the seizure of someone's property in order to obtain payment of money owed, esp. rent.

扣押财物；强制执行

distress—

1. (*esp. as emotional distress*) extreme anxiety, sorrow, or pain.

极度焦虑；悲伤；苦恼

2. another term for *distraint*.

扣押财务

distributee—one who receives property from a personal representative (but not a creditor or purchaser); a testamentary trustee to the extent of assets remaining in his/her hands; a beneficiary taking through a trustee.

被分配到（财产等）之人；分配遗产受益人

distribution—the division of the residue of an estate among the parties entitled thereto by the order of the court, after the payment of the debts and charges. It also includes the division of the residue of an estate by the Independent Personal Representative.

分配;分发

district court—A trial court that hears the following types of cases: civil suits involving $25,000 or less; adult criminal misdemeanor offenses punishable by up to one year's imprisonment; civil infractions; landlord/tenant disputes; small claims (civil suits involving $1,750 or less); and, land contract forfeitures. Additionally, the district court is the court in which all adult criminal proceedings begin, regardless of the nature of the offense. In carrying out this function, the district court issues arrest and search warrants, sets bail, conducts arraignments, and presides over preliminary examinations. See also *arraignment*, *bail*, *civil infraction*, *land contract*, *preliminary examination*, *small claims court*, *warrant*.

地方法院;地区法院

disturbance—the interruption of a settled and peaceful condition, specifically.

侵犯(权利);妨害(治安)

divestiture—a remedy, by virtue of which the court orders the offending party to rid itself of property or assets before the party would normally have done so.

剥夺财产;取消称号(职位等);放弃财产令

dividend—profits appropriated for division among stockholders.

股息;红利;破产偿金;清偿金额

divorce—the termination of the legal relationship between a husband and wife.

离婚

dock—the enclosure in a criminal court where a defendant is placed.

被告席

docket—a written list of all important acts done in court in the conduct of an individual case from beginning to end. This is properly called a "case docket". The docket (for acts done), the case file (for documents filed) and any transcript of proceedings together form the "record" or a court of record. This word is often improperly used interchangeably with "calendar".

备审案件目录表;待判决的案件目录

doctrine—a rule or standard of law; the body of such rule.

（法律）原则

documentary evidence—a document having legal effect which is offered as evidence. For instance, a contract or a deed.

书证;书面证据

domain—ownership of land; immediate or absolute ownership; paramount or ultimate ownership; an estate or patrimony which one has in his own right; land of which one is absolute owner.

对土地绝对和完全的所有权;土地领有权;国家领土;领地;版图;领域

domestic abuse—a pattern of sexual, physical, emotional and/or financial abuse, perpetrated with the intent and result of establishing and maintaining control over an intimate partner. Domestic abuse may include both criminal and non-criminal acts, such as hitting, choking, kicking, shoving, scratching, biting, raping, kidnapping, threatening violence, stalking, destroying property, or attacking pets. The abuse may be directed at persons other than the intimate partner (e.g., children) for the purpose of controlling the partner.

家庭暴力;家庭虐待

domestic relations action—a case involving divorce, separate maintenance, annulment of marriage, affirmation of marriage, paternity, child or spousal support, custody of a minor, parenting time, or grandparenting time.

家庭关系诉讼

domestic violence—see *domestic abuse*.

家庭暴力

domicile—the permanent home to which a person, when absent, always intends to return. See *residence*.

法定住所

donee—a person who receives a gift.

受赠人

double jeopardy—The Double Jeopardy Clause of the Fifth Amendment states: "nor shall any person be subject for the same offence to be twice put in jeopardy of life or limb." The principle is one of the oldest in Western civilization, having roots in ancient Greek and Roman law. Nevertheless, the clause is one of the least understood in the Bill of Rights, and the Supreme Court has done little to remove the confusion.

一事不再理原则(美国宪法第五条修正案具体规定了这一原则,即任何人不因同一罪行而受两次审判。任何已被释放或已被宣判无罪的人,均不能因同一罪行而再次被置于"生命或肢体的危险"之中。)

dower—that part of a man's real property which his widow is entitled to use for her lifetime after her husband's death, as a result of her status as wife, as opposed to property devised or inherited.

亡夫遗产

dowry—money and personalty which the wife brings to the husband to support the expenses of marriage; a donation to the maintenance and support of the marriage.

聘礼;嫁妆

draft—an order in writing directing a person other than the maker to pay a specified sum of money to a named person.

汇票

drug abuse—the repeated or uncontrolled use of controlled substances. While possession or use of controlled substances may be a crime, addiction to drugs is a disease which cannot be made a crime under the due process clause of the Constitution.

滥用毒品

drunk driving—the crime of driving a vehicle with an excess of alcohol in the blood.

醉酒驾车(罪)

duces tecum—a Latin term meaning "bring with you". On a subpoena it means that the person subpoenaed must bring records or other specified material into court.

(携带文件及其他材料)出庭传票;文件传票

due care—a concept used in tort law to indicate the standard of care or the legal duty one owes to others.

应有的注意;适当的注意;具体情况所要求的正当、合适和充分的注意

due diligence—reasonable steps taken by a person in order to satisfy a legal requirement, esp. in performing a professional duty.

应有的注意

due process (of law)—the fundamental procedural rules that guarantee "fair play" in the conduct of legal proceedings; e.g., the right to notice and a hearing, the right to an impartial judge and jury, the right to present evidence on one's own behalf, the right to confront one's accuser, the right to be represented by counsel, etc.

正当法律程序

> 美国联邦宪法第五和第十四条修正案规定,"非经正当法律程序,不得剥夺任何人的生命、自由和财产",这便是著名的正当法律程序条款。正当程序是英美法上重要的宪政和法治原则。正当程序的本质是一种对政府行为和权力的检验和审查,美国的正当程序制度是法院运用司法权力对政府行为和权力进行广泛干预的重要手段,其目的是保障个人权利,是一项重要的司法审查制度。它虽然是美国宪法中最难理解的部分,却又被认为是美国法律的本质所在;它虽然引起了前所未有的论争,对什么是正当法律程序至今未达成一致意见,却在上诉到联邦最高法院的案件中有40%与正当法律程序有关,在联邦最高法院适用于各个案件的次数远远超过美国宪法其他条款的规定,而成为美国公民权利的最重要的宪法保障。正当法律程序的理论和实践已经成为美国宪政的基石并正在超越英美法系的传统文化藩篱,而逐渐为世界其他法律文化所认同。

DUI—driving under the influence (of drugs or alcohol).

醉酒驾车

duplicitous—(of a charge or plea) containing more than one allegation.

双重辩解、陈述;狡辩

duress—constraint illegally exercised to force someone to perform an act. 强迫；胁迫；威胁

dwelling house—a house used as a residence and not for business purposes. 住宅

E

earnest money—money paid to confirm a contract.
定金

easement—the right to use another's land for a specific limited purpose. One common type of easement arises when one parcel of land is separated from any access to a road by a second parcel. In this case, the owner of the first parcel might obtain access to the road by way of an easement across the second parcel.
地役权;在他人土地上的通行权

eject—dispossess (a tenant or occupant) by legal process.
依法剥夺;依法逐出

ejectment—the action or process of evicting a tenant from property.
(依法从房屋或土地上)驱逐、赶出

elements of a crime—specific factors that define a crime and which the prosecution must prove beyond a reasonable doubt in order to obtain a conviction.
犯罪要件;犯罪要素

emancipate—set free, esp. from legal, social, or political restrictions.
解放;(从法律、社会或政治限制中)解脱

emancipation—the process by which a minor between the ages of 16 and 18 can be freed from his or her parents' control.
解脱;解放(16—18岁未成年人挣脱父母的控制过程)

embezzlement—the fraudulent appropriation by a person to his own use or benefit of property or money entrusted to him by another.
盗用;挪用

eminent domain—the power of the government to take private property for public use through condemnation.
支配权;征用权

emolument—profit derived from office, employment, or labor, including salary, wages, fees, rank, and other compensation.
报酬;薪水

emotional distress—extreme personal suffering caused by the intentional or negligent actions of another.
精神上的极度痛苦

empanel—variant spelling of *impanel*.
选任(陪审员)

enabling act—a statute empowering a person or body to take certain action, esp. to make regulations, rules, or orders.
授权法

enactment—the process of passing legislation.
制定(法律);通过(法案)

en banc—all the judges of a court sitting together. Appellate courts can consist of a dozen or more judges, but often they hear cases in panels of three judges. If a case is heard or reheard by the full court, it is heard en banc.
全体法官出庭审案

encumbrance—a charge or claim levied on property, such as unpaid taxes or assessments.
承担债务

endorsed—stamped with the seal of the court indicating the date and time of filing with the court.

背书

enforce—compel observance of or compliance with (a law, rule, or obligation).

实施;执行

engross—produce (a legal document) in its final or definitive form.

正式写成(议案、条约、决议等)

enjoin—to forbid; restrain.

限制;禁止;阻止

enjoyment—substantial present economic benefit. It refers to beneficial use, interest, and purpose to which real or personal property may be put and implies rights, profits, and income therefrom, rather than a technical vesting of title.

享有;行使权力

en masse—all together, as a group.

全体地;一同地

entail—to create a fee tail; to create a fee tail from a fee simple.

先嗣继承;先嗣继承的地产

enter—submit (a statement) in an official capacity, usually in a court of law.

进入程序

entrapment—a defense to criminal charges alleging that agents of the government induced a person to commit a crime he/she otherwise would not have committed.

诱人犯罪;诱捕

entry—the action of taking up the legal right to property.

取得财产权的行为

entry of judgment or order—the filing of a written, dated and signed judgment or order.

裁决或法庭命令归档

equal

equal—(of people) having the same status, rights, or opportunities.
平等

Equal Protection of the Law—the guarantee in the Fourteenth Amendment to the U.S. Constitution Article III, and Article II, Section 18, of the NM Constitution, that the law treat all persons equally. Court decisions have established that this guarantee requires that courts be open to all persons on the same conditions, with like rules of evidence and modes of procedure; that persons be subject to no restrictions in the acquisition of property, the enjoyment of personal liberty, and the pursuit of happiness, which do not generally affect others; that persons are liable to no other or greater burdens than those are laid upon others; and that no different or greater punishment is enforced against them for a violation of the laws.
平等保护(权);同等保护

> 该条款是在美国南北战争后增补到宪法中去的。在批准的时候,平等保护条款原本是要对先前的努力按照法律和公民的一定的基本权利予以平等保护。最高法院曾在黑人适用该条款时尽力将其内容作了限制,认为在州法律"严重非正义地和残酷地歧视新近解放的黑人"时,才能适用该条款。只有在种族歧视导源于州的行为时,方得使用联邦权利;因为该条款的目的仅仅是要防止"种族歧视和非常事变"。对适用于各类种族的条款加以限制后,最高法院在随后的几年里又对按照该条款给黑人提供的平等保护的性质作了规定。最高法院根据平等保护条款要求采取积极步骤消除那些具有违宪性的种族隔离。多少年来,宪法增补的平等保护条款对公共政策仅具有限的影响力。它是专门针对种族歧视制定的,但并非总是得到积极的应用,即使在发生种族歧视的情况之下,第十四条的正当法律程序条款最为审查州法律的合理性的工具,已被证明具有更大意义。

equal rights amendment /ERA—a proposed amendment hoping to eliminate sex as a basis for any decisions made by a state of the United States. This amendment was never ratified by a sufficient number of states to qualify as a constitutional amendment, but the basic premise underlying the proposal has become an accepted standard in many statutes and court decisions.

男女平等权修正案

equitable action—an action that may be brought for the purpose of restraining the threatened infliction of wrongs or injuries, and the prevention of threatened illegal action. (Remedies not available at common law.)

预防性诉讼

equitable remedy—when a plaintiff seeks injunction, restitution, rescission and/or specific performance (as opposed to legal remedy).

衡平法上的留置权；衡平法上的救济

equity—

1. the amount or value of property above the total liens, charges or encumbrances.

财产超过其负债的剩余价额

2. a system of legal principles and remedies in civil cases that originated in England and survives in modern U.S. jurisprudence. Historically, there were two distinct courts in England—courts of law and courts of equity. Courts of law could award monetary damages in civil cases, but could give no other relief. If a party sought relief other than monetary damages, he or she had to turn to a court of equity, which could grant injunctions, grant divorces, afford relief from creditors in bankruptcy, etc. There are no longer separate courts of law and equity in the U.S; most trial courts can now issue both monetary and non-monetary relief. Different legal principles still apply to law and equity actions, however, and a few procedural distinctions survive, most notably the absence of a right to a jury trial in cases seeking equitable relief.

衡平法

Erie doctrine—In United States law, the Erie doctrine is a fundamental legal doctrine of civil procedure mandating that a federal court in diversity jurisdiction (and some allied state-law claims in federal-law actions) must apply state substantive law.

伊利原则

equity of redemption

> 尽管在美国并不存在区别于各州自己采纳并作为当地的法律适用的国家普通法,不过就美国宪法、条约和法律可依普通法原则来解释而言,的确存在联邦普通法。进言之,在有关实质上涉及联邦政府或部门的利益或责任事务中实体问题的案件里,联邦法院也可以适用普通法原则。但联邦普通法的适用受到伊利原则和《判决规则法》*Rules of Decision Act* 的限制,即除宪法、美国所订立的条约及国会所制定的法律支配的案件外,联邦法院须适用各州的法律。联邦普通法的适用范围包括联邦专利利益、海事及对外关系。

equity of redemption—the right of one who has mortgaged property to redeem that property upon payment of the sum due within a reasonable amount of time after the due date.

抵押人依法赎回抵押品的权利;抵押人对抵押品所保留的权益

error—a mistake of fact or of law in a court's opinion, judgment or order.

错误

escape clause—a clause in a contract that specifies the conditions under which one party can be freed from an obligation.

例外条款

escheat—the reversion of property to the State when a person dies leaving no heirs.

(土地或财产)归还国家;充公

escrow—money or a written instrument such as a deed that, by agreement between two parties, is held by a neutral third party (held in escrow) until all conditions of the agreement are met.

有待完成条件的契据(或合同等);暂交第三者保管的款项(或保证金等)

esquire—a title appended to a lawyer's surname.

先生;绅士(古时称呼律师用语)

estate—

1. the interest a person has in real or personal property. Examples: Property that was owned by a person who has died is referred to as a *decedent's estate*. Property held in trust for the benefit of another is a *trust estate*. The

property of a person or corporation that has declared bankruptcy is an *estate in bankruptcy* or *bankrupt estate*.

不动产；财产

2. the assets of a decedent or other person subject to be administered under the authority of a court.

遗产

estate in bankruptcy—the estate is all of the legal and equitable interests of the debtor as of the commencement of the case.

破产财产

estate tax—generally, a tax on the privilege of transferring property to others after a person's death. In addition to federal estate taxes, many states, including New Mexico, have their own estate taxes.

遗产税；地产税

estop—bar or preclude by estoppels

禁止反言；禁止翻供

estoppel—a prohibition against a claim or position which is inconsistent with the claimant's prior conduct, e.g., one who sells land representing that he/she is authorized to do so may not claim in a later lawsuit against him or her that he or she had no authority to sell.

禁止翻供

et al.—and others.

以及其他人；等人

et seq.—and the following.

以下及下列等等

et ux—an abbreviation for *et uxor*, literally "and wife." Used when a grantor's or grantee's wife joins in a transaction.

及妻子

European Commission for Human Rights—an institution of the Council of Europe, set up to examine complaints of alleged breaches of the European Convention on Human Rights (an international agreement set up by the Council of Europe in 1950 to protect human rights). It is based in Strasbourg, France.

European Court of Justice

欧洲人权委员会(现已被欧洲人权法院所替代)

European Court of Justice—an institution of the European Union, with thirteen judges appointed by its member governments, meeting in Luxembourg. Established in 1958, it exists to safeguard the law in the interpretation and application of Community treaties.

欧洲法院

> 欧洲法院是欧洲联盟法院的简称,所在地是卢森堡。它是欧洲联盟的一个机关。"欧盟法院应当审查由欧盟议会和欧盟理事会共同制定的法令的合法性;审查由欧盟理事会、欧盟委员会、欧盟中央银行以及欧盟议会制定的旨在对第三方直接产生法律效力的法令的合法性,但对于他们所作的建议和意见除外。"为了减轻欧洲法院的负担,1989年建立了一个初审法院。从此个人或企业单位直接上诉时都由初审法院解决。欧洲法院只是复审法院。欧盟委员会以及成员国的上诉依然由欧洲法院负责。欧洲法院的法庭语言可以是欧洲联盟成员国的任何一种官方语言以及爱尔兰语。法官及当事人的陈述被同步翻译。法庭的内部工作语言是法语。

euthanasia—the painless killing of a patient suffering from an incurable and painful disease or in an irreversible coma. The practice is illegal in most countries.

安乐死

evade—escape or avoid, in particular.

逃避;规避

even date—of the same date.

同一日期(签发的)

evict—expel (someone, usually a tenant) from a property, esp. with the support of the law.

(依法从房屋或土地上)驱逐,赶出

evidence—testimony, documents, physical objects, or other things presented at a trial or court hearing for the purpose of proving or disproving facts relevant to a case.

证据;证词

evidentiary motion hearing—hearings at which evidence is presented (a "speaking motion") as opposed to a hearing at which lawyers argue matters of law.

证据听证

examination—an inspection or investigation. As pertains to court action, the term is used to describe a preliminary hearing before the district court to determine whether there is sufficient cause to hold a person to answer a felony charge before the circuit court.

讯问;调查

examine—formally question (a defendant or witness) in court. Compare with *cross-examine*.

审问;询问;审查

exceptions—declarations by either side in a civil or criminal case reserving the right to appeal a judge's ruling upon a motion or objection. These are no longer required to preserve error in New Mexico courts. Also, in regulatory cases, objections by either side to points made by the other side or to rulings by the agency or one of its hearing officers.

反对;抗辩;除外条件

exclude—prevent the occurrence of.

排除;不包括在内

exclusion—the process or state of excluding or being excluded.

拒绝;排除

exclusionary rule—the rule preventing illegally obtained evidence, such as property found during an illegal search, from being used in any trial.

证据排除原则(禁止任何法庭使用非法采集的证据)

ex contractu—In both civil and common law, rights and causes of action are divided into two classes: those arising *ex contractu* (from a contract) and *ex delicto* (from a wrong or tort).

由契约引起的

exculpate—show or declare that (someone) is not guilty of wrongdoing.

开脱;使无罪

ex delicto—rights and causes of action arising from a wrong or "tort".
根据侵权行为提起的诉讼；根据损害赔偿提起的诉讼

execute—to carry out, complete or dispose of according to law.
实行；实施；执行；使生效

execution—
1. a post judgment remedy to collect a money judgment; a writ issued by the court to authorize the process server to seize or take possession of real or personal property to be sold to satisfy the judgment.
判决后补救；判决后赔偿
2. the carrying out of some act or course of conduct to its completion; i.e., execution of a civil judgment is the putting into effect of the final judgment of the court by obtaining possession of that which the judgment has awarded.
执行；实行

executioner—an official who carries out a sentence of death on a legally condemned person.
行刑者；死刑执行者

execution of an instrument—the signing, sealing and delivery of a written instrument or document.
签字使文件生效（合法化）

executive session—a private meeting of a legislative body.
（立法机关的）秘密会议

executor/executrix—executor (male)/executrix (female); a person named in a will to carry out its terms, that is, to execute the will.
遗嘱执行人

exemplary—(of a punishment) serving as a warning or deterrent.
警戒性的；惩戒性的

exempt property—
1. personal property that the surviving spouse of a decedent is automatically entitled to receive from the decedent's estate.
存活配偶继承的个人财产

2. property of a judgment debtor that is exempt from executions under either state law or federal bankruptcy law.

免税财产;豁免财产(根据各州或联邦破产法债权人可以保留的财产)

exhibits—a document or item which is formally introduced in court and which, when accepted, is made part of the case file.

物证

exigent circumstances—an emergency, demand, or need calling for immediate action or remedy that, for instance, would justify a warrantless search.

紧急情况

exonerate—removal of a charge, responsibility or duty.

使免罪;免除

ex parte—involving only one party to a lawsuit, without prior notice to any other party.

单方;单方面;片面的

ex parte communication—a communication between the court and one party to a lawsuit, made without prior notice to any other party.

一方当事人与法院单方面联系或协商

ex parte injunction—an injunction issued upon the request of one party to a lawsuit, without prior notice to any other party.

单方禁(制)令

ex parte motion—a motion made to the court by one party to a lawsuit without prior notice to any other party.

当事人单方面向法院提出的申请

ex parte order—an order made by the court upon the application of one of the parties to a lawsuit, without prior notice to any other party.

根据单方或一方当事人的要求,法院做出的决议

expert witness—a person who is permitted to testify at a trial because of their special knowledge or proficiency in a particular field that is relevant to the case.

专家证人

ex post facto—legislation made applicable to an act after the act was committed. Statutes making a prior legal act illegal.

有追溯力的法律

express easement—an express easement arises when the owner of land expressly agrees to allow another person to use the land.

明示地役权(土地所有人以明示同意准许他人使用其土地者为明示的地役权)

express warranty—an affirmation of fact or promise made by the seller to the buyer that is relied upon by the buyer in agreeing to the contract.

明示质量保证

expropriate—(*esp. of the state*) take away (property) from its owner.

没收(财产);剥夺(所有权)

expunge—to legally void records—including criminal records—in files, computers or other depositories.

合法销毁;合法删除

extinguish—render (a right or obligation) void.

使无效;取消;废除(权利、义务等)

extraditable—(of a crime) making a criminal liable to extradition.

可引渡的;该引渡的

extradite—hand over (a person accused or convicted of a crime) to the jurisdiction of another state or country.

引渡

extradition—the formal process of delivering a person found in one state to the authorities of another state where that person has been accused or convicted of a crime.

(根据法令或条约对逃犯等的)引渡

extrajudicial—(of a sentence) not legally authorized.

违反通常法律(司法)程序的;非经法律许可的

extralegal—(of an action or situation) beyond the authority of the law; not regulated by the law.

不受法律支配的;未经法律制定的

extraterritorial—(of a law or decree) valid outside a country's territory.
治外法权的;境外有效的

extrinsic—foreign, from outside sources.
外来的;外部的

eyewitness—a person who has personally seen something happen and so can give a firsthand description of it.
目击者

F

FAC case—stands for "Failure to Answer Citation". When a person fails to answer a traffic citation (ticket) the court concerned notifies the Department of State, which enters this information into its computer system. When this occurs it is called a "FAC Case", and the defendant's license is suspended until the FAC is set aside after the case is disposed of, and a fee is paid.

漠视交通处罚案（如果被告漠视交通处罚罚单，法庭就会通知美国国务院记录在案，暂时吊销被告驾照直到缴费接受处罚。）

face value—the stated value expressed in the language of the instrument.

票面价值

facilitation—in criminal law, a statutory offense rendering one guilt when, believing it probable that one is aiding a person who intends to commit a crime, one engages in conduct which assists that person in obtaining the means or opportunity to commit the crime and in fact one's conduct does aid the person to so commit it.

胁从犯罪

fact—the truth about events as opposed to interpretation.

事实

fair comment—a term used in the law of libel, applying to statements made by a writer in an honest belief of their truth, relating to official act, even though the statements are not true in fact.

公平评论;正当的批评

fair preponderance—evidence sufficient to create in the minds of the triers of fact the belief that the party that bears the burden of proof has established its case.

合理的证据优势

fair use—the doctrine that, under certain conditions, copyright material may be quoted verbatim without need for permission from or payment to the copyright holder.

正当使用(法律允许在不影响作者利益的情况下有限引用他人的作品。)

false arrest—any unlawful physical restraint of another's liberty, whether in prison or elsewhere.

非法拘留

false pretenses—designed misrepresentation of existing fact or condition whereby a person obtains another's money or goods.

欺诈;诈骗

family allowance—a small amount of money set aside from the estate of the deceased. Its purpose is to provide for the surviving family members during the administration of the estate.

(工资以外的)家庭津贴

family division of the circuit court—A division of the circuit court devoted to the following proceedings: divorce; paternity; child or spousal support; parenting time; child custody; adoptions; juvenile delinquency; child protective proceedings; name changes; personal protection orders; emancipation of minors; waiver of parental consent to an abortion; and, guardianships or conservatorships for persons under 18 where the matter arises out of a child protective proceeding, delinquency proceeding, or a domestic relations custody case. See also *adoption*, *conservator*, *domestic relations action*, *child protective* *proceedings*, *emancipation*, *guardian*, *juvenile delinquency proceedings*, *personal protection order*.

巡回法庭家事庭,专司离婚,儿童监护、收养,青少年犯罪等家庭案件的审理。

Family Independence Agency /FIA—the state agency responsible for administering a broad range of social services programs, including financial aid to families and elderly persons, foster care services, and adoption services. The Family Independence Agency was formerly known as the Department of Social Services. See also *children's protective services*.

家庭事务服务局(州政府机构,主要负责管理社会服务项目,包括资助困难家庭和老龄人口,收养服务等。)

family law—(also called matrimonial law) is an area of the law that deals with family matters and domestic relations, including:
• marriage, civil unions, and domestic partnerships
• adoption and surrogacy
• child abuse and child abduction
• the termination of relationships and ancillary matters, including divorce, annulment, property settlements, alimony, child custody and visitation, child support and alimony awards.
• juvenile adjudication
• paternity testing and paternity fraud

This list is not exhaustive and varies depending on jurisdiction. In many jurisdictions in the United States, the family courts see the most crowded dockets. Litigants representative of all social and economic classes are parties within the system.

家庭法

在美国,家庭法亦可称为家庭关系法。它涉及婚姻、夫妻关系、离婚、分局、父母子女关系、收养、监护和供养等问题。美国的家庭法完全属于州法律的范畴,联邦政府无权在这一领域制定法律。不过,联邦宪法可以从保护公民自由权利的角度影响各州家庭法的制定和实施。从历史上来看,美国的家庭法受英国普通法的影响很大。由于各州的传统不同,所以各州的家庭法也有较大差异。例如,有些州要求结婚不仅要有结婚证书,而且还要有正式的婚礼;还有些州则仍然承认普通法婚姻,即无需结婚证或婚礼的婚姻。在美国的有些州有专门的家庭法院。虽然这些家庭法院的权限也是因州而已,但多数都具有以下几类诉讼案件的管辖权:1.虐待儿童的案件;2.供养诉讼;3.确定亲子关系和供养婚外生子女的诉讼;4.终止监护权的诉讼;5.未成年人违法案件;6.家庭罪案件等。

fault—responsibility for an accident or misfortune.

过失;过错

FCJ case—means "Failure to Comply with Judgment" imposed for violations that are civil infractions that are issued on traffic violations and follows the same procedure as FAC cases.

漠视交通处置案(被告违犯交通法规,但对有关判决置之不理。此类案件的处理程序同漠视交通处罚案。)

FCPV case—means "Failure to Comply with Parking Violation" entries. The Secretary of State will prohibit individuals from obtaining or renewing licenses when they have six or more unpaid parking tickets within a court. The court concerned notifies the Department of State in the same procedure as in FAC and FCJ cases.

漠视违规停车处罚案

在美国有些州,如果违规停车罚款单累计超过6次不缴纳罚款的话,州务卿将禁止违规者获得或更新驾照。

fees—

1. a charge fixed by law for services of public officers or for use of a privilege under government control; a charge or wages for services given to one for the services performed, such as fiduciary or attorney fees.

服务费;酬金

2. an inheritable estate of land, either absolute or conditional.

可继承的地产

fee simple—absolute ownership of real property.
无条件继承的不动产（权）

fee tail—a former type of tenure of an estate in land with restrictions or entailment regarding the line of heirs to whom it may be willed.
指定继承人的不动产

felon—a person who has been convicted of a felony.
重罪犯

felonious—of, relating to, or involved in a felony or felonies.
重罪的；穷凶极恶的

felony—a crime punishable by more than a year in the state prison, unless it is specifically stated to be a misdemeanor. Felonies are tried in circuit court.
重罪（一般判刑入狱1年以上或死刑，由巡回法庭审理。）

feme covert—a married woman.
已婚女子

feme sole—a woman without a husband, esp. one who is divorced.
单身女子（多指已离婚）

fiduciary—a fiduciary is someone who has undertaken to act for and on behalf of another in a particular matter in circumstances which give rise to a relationship of trust and confidence. For examples of fiduciaries, see *attorney in fact*, *conservator*, *guardian*, *independent personal representative*, *personal representative*, *trustee*.
基于信用的，受托的；受托人，被信托者

1. *successor fiduciary*: one who is appointed to take the place of a prior fiduciary.
继承受托人

2. *temporary fiduciary*: one appointed by the court to act as a fiduciary until a permanent fiduciary is appointed.
临时受托人

fiduciary duty—a fiduciary duty is a legal or ethical relationship of confidence or trust between two or more parties, most commonly a *fiduciary* or *trustee* and a *principal* or *beneficiary*. A fiduciary duty is the highest standard of care at either equity or law.

信托责任；诚信义务

fieri facias—a writ commanding a sheriff to seize and sell a debtor's goods in executing a judgment.

扣押债务人财产令；强制执行令

Fifth—the Fifth Amendment to the US Constitution, used in particular reference to the amendment's provision that no person "shall be compelled in any criminal case to be a witness against himself".

美国宪法第五修正案禁止自证其罪原则

> 美国宪法第五修正案规定："任何人……于任何刑事案件中，不得被强迫成为对自己不利的证人。"根据该项规定，在刑事诉讼中，对于任何人，无论他是本案的被追诉人还是证人，司法机关不得强迫其提供不利于自己的证据。

fighting words—informal words, such as those expressing an insult, esp. of an ethnic, racial, or sexist nature, which are considered likely to provoke a violent response.

侮辱、挑衅、挑逗语言

file—to submit (a legal document, application, or charge) to be placed on record by the appropriate authority.

提起（申请等）；提起（诉讼等）；把……登记备案

filed in open court—court documents entered into the file in court during legal proceedings.

公开法庭审理

filing—the act of recording the various legal documents pertaining to a suit with the clerk of the court. "Filing" also specifically refers to the original warrant, complaint, or other document which initiates the action.

法律文件的归档；有时也指法律行动的开始、起诉

filing fees—sums of money which must be paid to the court clerk before a civil action or an estate proceeding may start.

诉讼费

final judgment—refers to a court's last action that settles the rights of the parties and disposes of all issues in controversy, except for the award of costs (and, sometimes, attorney's fees) and enforcement of the judgment. This is also termed as final appealable judgment or final decision or final decree or definitive judgment or determinative judgment or final appealable order.

最后判决

final order—an order that ends the lawsuit between the parties, resolves the merits of the case, and leaves nothing to be done but enforcement.

终审裁定

find—(of a court) officially declare to be the case.

判决;裁决

finding—formal conclusion by a judge or regulatory agency on issues of fact. Also, a conclusion by a jury regarding a fact.

结论;(陪审团)裁决

fine—sum of money exacted as a penalty by a court of law or other authority.

罚款;罚金

fine print—inconspicuous details or conditions printed in an agreement or contract, esp. ones that may prove unfavorable.

(故意弄的模糊的)文字;(尤指合同中用小字载明的)附属细则

first appearance—the initial appearance of an arrested person before a judge to determine whether or not there is probable cause for his/her arrest. Generally, the person comes before a judge within hours of the arrest. Also called initial appearance.

首次出庭

first-degree—denoting the most serious category of a crime, esp. murder.

一级（最严重的犯罪等级）

first offender—a person who is convicted of a criminal offense for the first time.

初犯

fixtures—articles attached to a house or land and considered legally part of it so that they normally remain in place when an owner moves.

固定物;(不动产的)附着物

floating charge—a security (i. e. mortgage, lien, etc.) that has an underlying asset or group of assets which is subject to change in quantity and value. Corporations can use floating charges and it does not affect their ability to use the underlying asset as normal. Only if the company fails to repay the loan and/or goes into liquidation, does the floating charge become "crystallized" or frozen into a fixed charge. At that point the lender becomes the first-in-line creditor to be able to draw against the underlying asset and/or its value to recoup its loss on the loan.

浮动抵押

> 浮动抵押是一种特别抵押,指抵押人在其现在和将来所有的全部财产或者部分财产上设定的担保,在行使抵押权之前,抵押人对抵押财产保留在正常经营过程中的处分权。浮动抵押的概念来源于英国衡平法院在司法实践中发展出来的一种特殊的抵押制度。

force majeure—unforeseeable circumstances that prevent someone from fulfilling a contract.

不可抗力

forcible entry and detainer—a summary proceeding for restoring possession of land to one who has been wrongfully deprived of possession.

强行占有他人土地者;强行占有

foreclose—take possession of a mortgaged property as a result of someone's failure to keep up their mortgage payments.

取消(抵押品)赎回权;取消(抵押人的)赎回抵押品的权利

foreclosure—a legal proceeding to enforce payment of a debt through the sale of property on which the creditor holds lien.

丧失抵押品收回权;(抵押人)回赎权的取消

foreign judgment—a judgment issued by a court having jurisdiction in Indian territory, a foreign state, or a state other than the home state. See also *judgment*.

异州(国)互惠执行判决(一般通过和外州或外国的双边条约或多边协议确定,互相承认某项判决。)

foreign support order—a support order issued by a court having jurisdiction in Indian territory, a foreign state, or a state other than home state. See also *support order*.

异州(国)互惠有效的法庭命令

foreman—(in a court of law) a person, esp. a man, who presides over a jury and speaks on its behalf.

陪审团的领班;陪审团的领头

forensic—of, relating to, or denoting the application of scientific methods and techniques to the investigation of crime.

法庭的;法律的

forensic center—another name for the Center for Forensic Psychiatry operated by the Department of Mental Health. Criminal defendants are often sent there by trial courts to determine if they are competent to stand trial.

法医鉴定中心

forensic medicine—the application of medical knowledge to the investigation of crime, particularly in establishing the causes of injury or death.

法医学

foreperson—(in a court of law) a person who presides over a jury and speaks on its behalf (used as a neutral alternative to *foeman*).

陪审团的领头

forfeit—lose or be deprived of (property or a right or privilege) as a penalty for wrongdoing.

丧失;没收

forge—produce a copy or imitation of (a document, signature, banknote, or work or art) for the purpose of deception.

伪造;仿造

forgery—the false making or material altering with intent to defraud, of any writing which, if genuine, might be the foundation of a legal liability.

伪造；伪造的文件、签名等

formal calendar—If it appears that formal jurisdiction is required in juvenile matters, a petition shall be filed. Further hearings shall be scheduled on the "formal calendar".

庭审安排表

forum—a court or the jurisdiction where a court sits.

法庭

forum non conveniens—a court's power to decline to exercise its jurisdiction in a case because the convenience of the parties and/or the interests of justice would be better served if the case were tried in another court.

法院不便审理权；法院不便原则

> 这是英美法院拒绝管辖权的原则，它反映了立法管辖权和司法管辖权相分离的平行主义，使其成为解决涉外民商事诉讼管辖权冲突的一个有效途径。

foster home—a licensed home for the temporary board and care of abused and neglected or delinquent children.

抚养受虐或问题儿童的家庭

foundation—preliminary questions to a witness to establish admissibility of evidence; i.e., "laying a foundation" for admissibility.

（证据）采信基础

franchise—

1. an authorization granted by a government or company to an individual or group enabling them to carry out specified commercial activities, e.g., providing a broadcasting service or acting as an agent for a company's products.

特许经营权；给予特许权

2. the right to vote.

选举权；参政权

fraud—the intentional communication of an untruth to deceive another to deprive one of property or to induce one to surrender a legal right, or to injure him or her in some other way.

欺诈;欺骗行为

fraudulent—obtained, done by, or involving deception, esp. criminal deception.

欺骗的;不诚实的

freedom of contract—the liberty or ability to enter into agreements with others. Freedom of contract is a basic and fundamental right reserved to the people by the Fifth and Fourteenth Amendments to the Constitution which prohibit the deprivation of liberty without due process of law. Freedom of contract is the core and essence of modern contract law.

合同自由(合同自由原则是近代契约法的核心和精髓。)

free exercise clause—provision in First Amendment to the United States Constitution providing that "Congress shall make no law... prohibiting the free exercise" of religion. It is applicable to both the federal and state governments through the due process clause of the Fourteenth Amendment.

自由行使条款

freehold—permanent and absolute tenure of land or property with freedom to dispose of it at will. Often contrasted with *leasehold*.

自由保有不动产

friend of the court—

1. the office connected with the family division of the circuit court that investigates and advises the court in domestic relations cases involving minor children. The Friend of the Court Office is also responsible for enforcement of court orders in those cases.

未成年人法律援助办公室

2. the person responsible for directing the Friend of the Court Office.

未成年人法庭之友

fruit of the crime—property acquired by means and in consequence of the commission of a crime, and sometimes constituting the subject matter of the crime.

违法所得;犯罪所获

fruit of the poisonous tree—a legal metaphor in the United States used to describe evidence gathered with the aid of information obtained illegally. The logic of the terminology is that if the source of the evidence (the "tree") is tainted, then anything gained from it (the "fruit") is as well. Fruit of the poisonous tree is generally not admissible in evidence because it is tainted by the illegal search or interrogation.

毒树之果理论

> 若证据是通过非法行为获得，则法庭不予采信。所谓"毒树之果"，是美国刑事诉讼中对某种证据所作的一个形象化的概括，意指"根据以刑讯逼供等非法手段所获得的犯罪嫌疑人、刑事被告人的口供，并获得的第二手证据（派生性证据）"。以非法手段所获得的口供是毒树，而以此所获得的第二手证据是毒树之果。简而言之，笔者认为毒树即非法获取的刑事证据，毒树之果指从毒树线索中获取的其他证据。

Frye Standard—In order to amend the Constitution, the amendment must be proposed by both houses of Congress. A proposal is achieved by passing the amendment with a two-thirds majority vote. Following the proposal, three-fourths of the state's legislatures must also approve the amendment by a two-thirds vote. As of 1919, there is a seven-year time limit on proposal and ratification.

佛赖伊标准

> 佛赖伊法则（Frye Rule）是1923年一项联邦法院判决所确立的证据法先例。1923年美国哥伦比亚巡回法庭，判决不接受一起谋杀案中由测谎得出的结论，理由是测谎技术尚未被有关的科学界所接受。此判决确立了科学证据（scientific evidence）的佛赖伊法则（Frye Rule），该规则规定："一个科学原理或新发现越过实验和论证之间的界线是很难的，在这一交叉点上，必须认识到该科学原理的证据力量，当法庭采取主动去承认从那些已得到普遍认可的科学原理或发现演绎出来的专家证明时，必须有足够的事实证明供演绎用的科学原理或发现在其所属的领域里获得普遍的承认。"按照佛赖伊规则，确定一个具体的科学技术是否获得普遍承认需要两个步骤：首先，

确定科学原理或新发现所属的特殊的科学领域以及相关的科学领域;其次,确定该技术或原理是该领域接受的技术、原理以及新发现。"若使用的技术是由该领域绝大部分成员明显支持,则该项检验是可行的。"

  赞成佛赖伊法则的人认为,它一方面可以确保科学证据审查认定的统一性,防止陪审团轻率地将新颖的专家证言识别为可靠证据之危险出现。另一方面,它阻止新颖的专家证言在对抗审判中被过早地提出,直到可以找到一批专家来评估该专业性证言时为止。这样做可以有效地保障专家证言的可采性和可靠性。反对该规则的人认为其存在两个严重的缺陷:第一,该法则实际上将法律上的证据判断认定权完全交给了科学家,有将专家证人变质为"科学法官"的嫌疑;第二,对该法则的适用造成原告方举证负担沉重,不利于平等保护双方当事人的权益。自20世纪70年代以来,佛赖伊法则一直受到有关学者、法官的批判,最终被废弃了。

fugitive—one who flees; always used in law with the implication of a flight, evasion, or escape from some duty or penalty or from the consequences of a misdeed.

逃跑者;逃避(责任、处罚等)者

fugitive warrant—a warrant authorizing the taking into custody of a person who has fled from one state to another to avoid prosecution or punishment for crime.

收留证;庇护证

full faith and credit—a court's constitutional obligation to recognize and enforce orders, decrees, and judgments issued by the courts of other U. S. states or Indian tribes(*U. S. Const. Art. IV, Sec. 1*).

法庭信用保证责任(根据美国宪法,法庭有责任承认并执行异州法院的命令、裁决或判决等。)

fungible—(of goods contracted for without an individual specimen being specified) able to replace or be replaced by another identical item; mutually interchangeable.

可互换的;可代替的

future interest—an interest in presently existing real or personal property, or in a gift or trust, which may commence in use, possession, and/or enjoyment at a time in the future.

远期权益;长远利益

futures—agreements whereby one person agrees to sell a commodity at a certain time in the future for a certain price. The buyer agrees to pay that price, knowing that the person will have nothing to deliver at the time. Instead, the buyer understands that at the delivery date, he will pay the seller the difference between the market value of that commodity and the price agreed upon if the commodity's value declines; if its value advances, the seller is to pay to the buyer the difference between the agreed upon price and the market price.

期货

G

gag order—a court-imposed order to restrict information or comment about a case. The ostensible purpose of such an order is to protect the interests of all parties and preserve the right to a fair trial by curbing publicity likely to prejudice a jury. A gag order cannot be directly imposed on members of the press because this constitutes an impermissible prior restraint and violates the First Amendment.

禁评案情令;噤声令;禁止公开评论令

> 这是美国法院的一种禁制令。在一些小的民事纠纷中,特别是在离婚前的纠纷中,法官可以发布禁制令,限制一方不得以任何方式接近另一方。这种禁制令甚至可以详尽到被限制一方不得靠近另一方 200 码之内。该禁止令一般是在比较重要的、媒体特别重视的案件中,法官下令当事各方(包括律师)不得公开谈论案情,以免误导舆论,影响陪审团的判断。在言论自由原则下,此禁令不适用于媒体。

gambling—a play for value against an uncertain event in the hope of gaining something for value, whose elements include the payment of a price for a chance to gain a prize.

赌博

game laws—laws whose general aim is to protect from unauthorized pursuit and killing certain birds and animals.

野生动物保护法;狩猎法

garnishee—
1. *n*. the person upon whom a garnishment is served, usually a debtor of the defendant in the action.

第三债务人;接到扣押债权通知的人;出庭令

2. *v*. to institute garnishment proceedings.

扣押

garnishment—a court order to take part of a person's wages or other money owed to him or her before he or she receives the money, because of an unpaid debt owed to a creditor who has obtained a judgment against the debtor.

法院扣押财产(或欠款)令

general assignment—the voluntary transfer, by a debtor of all his property to a trustee for the benefit of all his creditors.

全部转让(他的利益)给他的债权人

general damages—compensation for the loss directly and necessarily incurred by a breach of contract.

违约赔偿金

general demurrer—a demurrer that raises the question whether the pleading against which it is directed lacks the definite allegations essential to a cause of action, or defense.

全面抗辩

general jurisdiction—refers to courts that have no limit on the types of criminal and civil cases they may hear.

普通管辖权(指法院无限制审理刑事或民事案件。)

Geneva Conventions—a set of treaties and protocols that apply during periods of armed conflict and which set forth the expectations under international law for humanitarian treatment of prisoners of war, those wounded in war, war zone civilians, and medical and religious personnel.

日内瓦公约

gift—a present transfer of property by one person to another without any consideration or compensation.

赠与

> 某人自愿将其财产转让给另一个人,并不附加任何条件和补偿。要使赠与行为有效,须符合以下三个要素:一、必须正式移交所赠与的财产;二、必须是赠与人的主观意愿;三、必须被接受。

golden parachute—a financial package with extremely generous terms received by an executive who loses his or her job or resigns due to a corporate merger or takeover.

黄金降落伞(按照聘用合同中公司控制权变动条款对高层管理人员进行补偿的规定)

good faith—honest intent to act without taking an unfair advantage over another person. This term is applied to many kinds of transactions.

诚实信用;诚信原则

goods and chattels—all kinds of personal possessions.

私有财物;全部动产

good time—a reduction in sentenced time in prison as a reward for good behavior. It usually is one-third to one-half off the maximum sentence.

减刑(常指因表现良好而减掉刑期的 1/3—1/2)

good title—a title free present litigation, obvious defects and grave doubts concerning its validity or merchantability.

有效所有权;有效权利凭证

good will/goodwill—an intangible but recognized business asset which is the result of such features of an ongoing enterprise as the production or sale of reputable brand name products, a good relationship with customers and suppliers, and the standing of the business in its community.

善意;良好心愿的;慈善性质的

grace—a period officially allowed for payment of a sum due or for compliance with a law or condition, esp. an extended period granted as a special favor.

宽限期

grand—(of a crime) involving money or items with a value over a statutorily defined amount; serious.

重大的;严重的

grandfather clause—a clause exempting certain classes of people or things from the requirements of a piece of legislation affecting their previous rights, privileges, or practices.

保留条款;不追索条款

grand jury—a jury of inquiry which receives complaints and accusations in criminal cases. It hears the prosecutor's evidence and issues indictments when satisfied that there is probable cause to believe that a crime was committed, and that the accused committed that crime. Grand juries are rarely used in Michigan, but are very common in the federal judicial system.

大陪审团(通常由 12—23 人组成,其选任必须通过中立的或非歧视性程序。)

grand larceny—(*in many US states and formerly in Britain*) theft of personal property having a value above a legally specified amount.

重大盗窃案

grandparenting time—the time a child spends with a grandparent. A grandparent may seek a court order for grandparenting time in America.

(外)祖父母探视时间

grant—

1. to transfer property to another, especially real property.

转让(财产等)

2. to give (a right, power, property, etc.) formally or legally.

正式、合法的给予(权利、财产等)

grantee—the person to whom a grant is made, e. g., the person who receives title to real property by deed.

被授予者;受让人

grantor—the person who makes a grant.

授予者;让与人

gratuitous guest—in automobile law, a person riding at the invitation of the owner of a vehicle or his authorized agent, without payment of a consideration or a fare.

免票乘客

gravamen—the essence or most serious part of a complaint or accusation.

起诉或控诉要旨

gravitas—seriousness or weightiness in conduct or speech.

郑重;庄严

grievance—one's allegation that something imposes an illegal obligation or burden, or denies some equitable or legal right, or causes injustice.

冤屈

grievous bodily harm—serious physical injury inflicted on a person by the deliberate action of another.

严重的人身伤害

group home—a licensed home for the temporary board and care of abused and neglected or delinquent children.

儿童救助之家(一般位于美国社区,专门为受虐待、被遗弃、有残疾或问题少年提供服务。)

guarantee—a formal promise or assurance (typically in writing) that certain conditions will be fulfilled, esp. that a product will be repaired or replaced if not of a specified quality and durability.

保证书;保用期;保修期

guarantor—a person who is liable to fulfill another person's financial obligation in the event the other person fails to fulfill it. The other person is known as the "principal". A guarantor's obligation typically arises from a different contract than the one binding the principal. See also *principal*, *surety*.

保证人

guaranty—a formal pledge to pay another person's debt or to perform another person's obligation in the case of default.

担保；保证

guardian—

1. a person with the legal duty and power to care for the person of another individual who is: a) under age 18; or, b) a legally incapacitated person. A guardian may be appointed by a court or designated in a will.

监护人

2. under the Mental Health Code, a person with the legal duty and power to care for the person and/or the estate of a developmentally disabled person. See *developmentally disabled person*, *estate*, *mental health code*.

保护人；维护者

guardian ad litem—someone appointed by the court during the course of litigation to promote and protect the interests of a person affected by the litigation. Examples:

1) A guardian ad litem may be appointed to protect the interests of a minor orincompetent person who is a defendant in a civil action.

2) If necessary, a guardian ad litem may be appointed to appear for and represent the interests of any person in any proceeding in probate court. Sometimes a court appoints a guardian ad litem to protect the interests of an unascertained, unknown, unborn, or disappeared person.

3) A court sometimes appoints a guardian ad litem to protect the interests of a minor in a domestic relations or juvenile proceeding.

法定监护人（一般在诉讼过程中由法庭指定）

guest statute—law which provides that a special standard of care is owed by an automobile owner or driver toward his gratuitous passenger. These statutes differ from state to state in their particulars, but all require more than just ordinary negligence on the part of an owner or driver in order for a "guest" to recover damages in a civil suit.

乘客法则

guilty—responsible for a crime.

有罪的

gun control law—a law restricting or regulating the sale, purchase or possession of firearms, or establishing a system of licensing, registration or identification of firearms or their owners or users.

枪支管理法

H

habeas corpus—"You have the body", the name of a writ used to bring a person before a court or judge. Generally, the writ is addressed to an official or person who holds another. It commands him or her to produce the detained person in court so that the court may determine whether that person is being denied his or her freedom lawfully.

人身保护权(对被拘禁者的关押予以限制)

habeas corpus ad respondenum—to bring in a prisoner for trial on another charge.

(因另一指控)解叫被拘押者出庭答辩

habeas corpus ad testificandum—to bring a prisoner in to testify.

解叫被拘押者出庭作证

habendum—the part of a deed or conveyance that states the estate or quantity of interest to be granted.

(契据或转让证书中的)物权条款;转让条款

halfway house—a center for helping former drug addicts, prisoners, psychiatric patients, or others to adjust to life in general society.

harmless error

重返社会训练所（为协助出院之精神病患者、吸毒者或即将出狱之受刑人等重新适应社会而施以自力更生训练之观护所、戒护所、职训中心等。）

harmless error—an error committed in the course of a trial which does not justify reversal of the verdict on appeal.

无害过错（在刑事审判中产生的过错，其严重性不足以影响审判结果。）

headnote—a summary of a decided case prefixed to the case report, setting out the principles behind the decision and an outline of the facts.

批注；注释

hear—listen to and judge (a case, appeal, etc.)

听审；听证

hearing—

1. a court proceeding on the record. Hearings are often used to determine issues arising before or after the full trial of a case, and may be less formal than the trial.

听证；申辩的机会

2. an act of listening to evidence or arguments in a court of law or before an official, esp. a trial before a judge without a jury.

听证会

hearsay—second-hand evidence not arising from personal knowledge of the witness but generally from repetition of what the witness has heard others say. The repetition of a statement, that was made outside of court, by a witness in a trial, intended to prove the truth of the statement. Hearsay is generally inadmissible, but if there is no objection it is admitted into evidence.

传闻证据；道听途说

heir—

1. someone who is entitled by statute to inherit the property of another person in the event that person dies without a valid will.

继承人（根据有关法规有权继承且死者无有效遗嘱。）

2. a person who inherits the property of another, whether by will or by intestate succession.

继承人（根据遗嘱或无遗嘱继承。）

heiress—a female heir, esp. to vast wealth.
女继承人;嗣女

hereditament—any item of inheritable property, either a corporeal hereditament (such as land or a building) or an incorporeal hereditament (such as a rent or a right of way).
可继承的财产;世袭财产

hereinafter—further on in this document.
以下;在下文中

hereinbefore—before this point in this document.
以上;在上文中

heritable—(of property) capable of being inherited.
可继承的

high court—the court of final appeal in a state or national judicial system.
高等法院;最高法院

higher court—a count that can overrule the decision of another.
高级法院;上一级法院

high seas—(*the high seas*) the open ocean, esp. that not within any country's territorial jurisdiction but governed by maritime law.
公海

hijacking—the commandeering or seizure of a mode of transportation such as an airplane, truck, or train by force or threat of force for illegal purposes. Such purposes may include theft of the cargo or other contents; redirection of the destination to suit the hijacker's specific purposes; or kidnapping or hostage taking for monetary or political demands.
劫持

hit-and-run statutes—statutes requiring that a motorist involved in an accident stop and identify himself and give certain information about himself to the other motorist and to the police.
肇事逃逸法则

hold—
1. keep or detain (someone).
拘留;扣留

2. have in one's possession.
拥有；占有

holding company—a corporation organized to hold the stock of other corporations; any company, incorporated or unincorporated, which is in a position to control or materially influence the management of one or more other companies by virtue, in part at least, of its ownership of securities in the other company or companies.
控股公司

holdup suit—a lawsuit that has no legal basis and is instituted solely to prevent or block something from occurring. A party harmed by such a suit may have an action for malicious prosecution.
预防诉讼

holographic will—an unwitnessed will where the dispositionary portions are in the handwriting of the decedent, signed at the end and dated.
（无证人且手写的）遗嘱

homestead—an artificial estate in land, devised to protect the possession and enjoyment of the owner against the claims of creditors.
家宅；农庄

homicide—the killing of one person by another.
杀人行为

honor—(*His*, *Your*, etc., *Honor*) a title of respect given to or used in addressing a judge or a mayor.
阁下；先生（对法官的尊称）

hornbook—a one-volume treatise summarizing the law in a specific field.
法律专题概论

hornbook law—those principles of law which are known generally to all and are free from doubt and ambiguity. They are therefore such as would probably be enunciated in a hornbook. Such basic and accepted legal principles were formerly called *black letter law*.
基本法

hostage—a person delivered into the possession of a public enemy in the time of war, as a security for the performance of a contract entered into between the belligerents. Hostages are frequently given as a security for the payment of a ransom bill, and if they should die, their death would not discharge the contract.

人质;抵押品

hostile possession—actual occupation or possession of real estate without the permission of anyone claiming paramount title, coupled with a claim, express or implied, of ownership.

恶意占有

hostile witness—a witness who exhibits such antagonism toward the party who called the witness to testify that cross-examination of that witness by that party is permitted by the court.

恶意证人

house arrest—confinement to one's home as a condition of bail or even as one's sentence. May include the use of electronic devices to monitor compliance. Exceptions may be granted by the judge to allow the person to have a specified curfew, work, or attend religious services or medical appointments.

保释在家;软禁

housebreaking—the action of breaking into a building, esp. in daytime, to commit a felony.

入室盗窃

hung jury—jury unable to reach a verdict. A trial ending in a hung jury results in a retrial with a new jury.

悬而不决的陪审团

hypothecate—pledge (money) by law to a specific purpose.

抵押;担保

hypothetical question—a combination of facts and circumstances, assumed or proved, stated in such a form as to constitute a coherent state of facts upon which the opinion of an expert can be asked by way of evidence in a trial.

假设的问题

I

ib./ibid.—in the same place, at the same time, in the same manner; abbreviated from of the word "ibidem". It is used to mean "in the same book" or "on the same page". It functions to avoid repetition of source data contained in the reference immediately preceding.

出处同上

id.—the same, the very same, exactly this, likewise; abbreviated form of the word "idem". This term is used in citation to avoid repetition of the author's name and title when a reference to an item immediately follows another to the same item.

同前；同上

identity theft/fraud—illegal use of another's personal data (name, driver's license, social security number, medical information, credit cards, or bank accounts) for one's own gain.

身份盗窃；身份盗用

i.e.—"id est", meaning, "that is".

也就是；即

ignorantia legis non excusat—ignorance of the law is no excuse, i.e., the fact that defendant did not think his act was against the law does not prevent the law from punishing the prohibited act.

不懂法律不是借口

illegal—contrary to or forbidden by law, esp. criminal law.

不合法的;违法的

illegitimate—not authorized by the law; not in accordance with accepted standards or rules.

非婚生的;法律不容的

illegitimate child—a child born to parties who are not married to each other.

非婚生孩子;私生子

immigration—the action of coming to live permanently in a country of which one is not a native or citizen.

移民

immovable—(of property) consisting of land, buildings, or other permanent items.

固定的;不可移动的

immunity—a grant by the court assuring someone that they will not face prosecution in return for their providing criminal evidence.

免除;豁免

impanel—(as pertains to juries) to select a jury and enroll their names.

挑选陪审团员

impeach—call into question the integrity or validity of (a judgment, etc.)

怀疑;提出异议;弹劾

impeachment of witness—questioning of a witness by an adverse party that attempts to cast doubt on the credibility (believability) of the witness.

质疑证人(指通过提出证据对证人的一般可信性或在特定案件中的可信性进行攻击。)

impediment—an obstruction to a legal right or power.

障碍;妨碍

imperfect obligation—obligations are not binding on us as of charity or gratitude, which can not be enforced by law.

不受法律约束的责任(债务);不完全义务

implied consent—knowing indirectly(through conduct or inaction) that a person would agree or give permission. For example, in New Mexico a person who gets a driver's license has given implied consent to allow a police officer to conduct an alcohol breath or blood test, when the police suspects the person is driving while intoxicated.

默示同意

implied contract—a contract in which the promise made by the obligor is not express, but inferred by his conduct or implied in law.

默示契约、合同

implied easement—An implied easement is a type of ownership interest in land. An easement occurs when an individual is granted the right-of-use of someone else's land. An implied easement, specifically, occurs when the grant of the right of use is implied and not formally written or deeded. An easement is the legal term used to grant the person a partial right to do certain things on someone else's land. For example, in the situation in which a person needs to run sewer lines on his neighbors property, his neighbor could grant him an easement. That easement means he has the right to run those sewer lines. Easements are a limited type of property ownership. The person who is granted an easement can only do the things that the easement grants. This means if a person is granted an easement to walk on a driveway to get to a beach, the person can walk on that driveway only and he may not do other things on it.

默示地役权

> 美国法律中普通法上的地役权是指使用他人土地或限制他人使用土地的权利。从概念上看,这里的地役权制度指的是:在他人的土地中所享有的一项权益,其主要特征在于为了某一特定的、有限的目的,该权益构成对该土地,以及该土地之上或其下某区域的使用或控制权。默示型的地役权是由于法律以及当事人默示承认地役权合同中包含这样的条款而产生的;即是说,当地役权契约中所约定的内容虽没有明示地役权的存在和归属,但是

> 法律上规定依据合同内容可以取得地役权的,或者当事人没有明示但是合同中规定默认的情况,合同当事人一方就默认随土地取得地役权。

implied warranty of merchantability—an assumption in law that the goods are fit for the ordinary purposes for which such goods are used. This implied warranty applies to every sale by a merchant who deals in goods of the kind sold. However, if there is a warning that the goods are sold "as is", the implied warranty does not apply.

(产品质量的)默示保证;默示担保

impound—seize and take legal custody of (something, esp. a vehicle, goods, or documents) because of an infringement of a law or regulation.

依法没收;扣押

imputed negligence—negligence that is not directly attributable to the person himself, but which is the negligence of a person who is privity with him, and with whose fault he is chargeable.

关系人受牵连的过失

inactive case—a pending case over which the court has no effective control; a case which is filed in the court, but for some reason cannot be processed by the court.

Examples: non-service, no progress (*civil*); defendant absconded or never arraigned (*criminal*).

悬案(已经起诉的案子,但法庭因为某种原因而无法控制或进行审理。)

inadmissible—that which, under the rules of evidence, cannot be admitted or received as evidence.

不能被采纳的(证据)

inalienable—unable to be given away or transferred by the possessor.

不能转让的;不可分割的

in banc—on the bench; all judges of the court sitting together to hear a cause.

开庭中;在法庭上;全体法官出庭

in camera—in chambers or in private. A hearing in camera takes place in

the judge's office outside of the presence of the jury and the public.
秘密听证(一般在法官的办公室进行)

incapacitate—deprive (someone) of their legal capacity.
使无能力；使不适合；剥夺合法身份

incapacity—legal disqualification.
(法律上)无行为能力；无资格

incarceration—commitment to jail or prison.
监禁；禁闭

incest—sexual relations between people classed as being too closely related to marry each other.
近亲乱伦

incestuous—involving or guilty of incest.
近亲相奸的；乱伦的

inchoate—(of an offense, such as incitement or conspiracy) a further criminal act.
尚未完成的；尚未生效的

incident—attaching to.
附带条件；附属于财产的权利和义务

income withholding order—an order entered by the circuit court providing for the withholding of a person's income to enforce a child support order.
扣薪命令(法院发出的定期扣交薪水用来抚养儿童的命令)

incompetent—not qualified to act in a particular capacity.
无能力的；不称职的

incompetent evidence—inadmissible evidence.
无效证据；不能采纳的证据；非法证据

inconvenient forum—see *forum non conveniens*.
法庭不便原则

incorporate—constitute (a company, city, or other organization) as a legal corporation.
合并组成；成立公司

incorporeal—(often of a property interest) having no material existence.
无实体的；无形的；非物质的

incriminate—make (someone) appear guilty of a crime or wrongdoing.
使(某人)显得有罪；牵连；归罪于

indecency—indecent behavior.
下流；不适当；猥亵

indecent assault—see *sexual harassment*.
强暴猥亵罪；性侵犯

indecent exposure—the crime of intentionally showing one's sexual organs in public.
露阴罪

indefeasible—not able to be lost, annulled, or overturned.
难使无效的；不能废弃的

indemnify—to compensate another for loss or damage that already has occurred or to give security against future loss.
赔偿；使免于受罚

indenture—a formal legal agreement, contract, or document, in particular.
契约；合同

independent personal representative—person administering a decedent's estate or an independent personal representative administers the estate without the court's supervision.
(执行遗产事宜的)私人代表、个人代表

indeterminate—
1. (of a judicial sentence) not fixed in length, typically so that the convicted person's conduct determines the date of release.
不定刑期
2. (of rules) not capable of mechanical application.
不确定的；模糊的

indeterminate sentence—a sentence of imprisonment to a specified minimum and maximum period of time, specifically authorized by statute, subject to termination by a parole board or other authorized agency after the prisoner has served the minimum term.

模糊判决；不确定刑期

indicia—signs, indications.

记号；表征

indict—formally, by a grand jury, accuse or charge (someone) with a crime.

控告；起诉

indictable—(of an offense) rendering the person who commits it liable to be charged with a crime that warrants a trial by jury.

可起诉的

indictment—formal accusation, "true bill", presented by a grand jury which charges a person with a crime.

有罪指控；起诉书

indigent—impoverished; needy; poor; without funds.

贫穷的；贫困的

indispensable—a person who must be made party to a legal action.

必不可少的；诉讼的一方

indispensable evidence—evidence that is necessary to prove a submitted fact.

不可或缺的证据

indispensable party—a party whose interest in a lawsuit is such that a final decree cannot be issued without either affecting that interest or leaving the controversy in such a condition that its final determination may be wholly inconsistent with equity and good conscience.

不可或缺的一方

indorsee—one to whom a negotiable instrument is assigned by indorsement.

被背书人

indorsement—signature placed upon the back of an instrument, with or without other words, whose effect is to transfer the instrument and create a new and substantive contract by which the indorser becomes a party to the instrument and liable, on certain conditions, for its payment.

背书

indorser—one who indorses negotiable paper. For instance, the payee or holder of a check may indorse the check by signing it on the back. An indorser is liable to pay the negotiable instrument in case it is dishonored.

背书人

inducement—a thing that persuades or influences someone to do something, especially enter into a contract.

引诱;劝诱(签约)

infamous—(of a person) deprived of all or some of a citizen's rights as a consequence of conviction for a serious crime.

(因犯罪)被褫夺(全部或部分)公权的;(罪行)可招致公权被褫夺的

infancy—the condition of being a minor; minority.

婴儿期;早期

infant—a person who has not attained legal majority.

婴儿;幼儿

infanticide—

1. the crime of killing one's newborn or a very young child.

杀婴罪

2. a person who kills an infant, esp. their own child.

杀婴者

inferior—(of a court or tribunal) subordinate to and able to have its decisions overturned by, a higher court.

低等的;下级的

inferior court—lower court. Any court subordinate to a higher appellate court in a particular judicial system.

下级法院

in flagrante delicto—in the very act of wrongdoing, esp. in an act of sexual misconduct.

在作案现场

influence—see *under the influence*.

影响;驱使

informal hearing—see *civil infraction*.
非正式听证

informant—a person who informs on another person to the police or other authority.
告发者;告密者

in forma pauperis—"in the manner of a pauper". Permission given to a person to sue without payment of court costs because of indigence or poverty.
诉讼救济

information—a formal accusation (criminal information) of a crime, differing from an indictment in that it is prepared and signed by the prosecuting attorney instead of the grand jury. This is the most common means employed in Michigan to bring an accused before the circuit court after a bind-over from the district court.
公诉书

informer—another term for *informant*.
告发者;告密者

infra—below.
以下;下文

infraction—a violation or infringement of a law, an agreement, the rights of others, or a set of rules. An infraction typically is a minor offense.
违背;违犯;犯规

infringe—actively break the terms of (a law, agreement, etc.)
违反(规章等)

inhere—(of rights, powers, etc.) be vested in a person or group or attached to the ownership of a property.
存在

inherent—vested in (someone) as a right or privilege.
固有的;内在的

inherit—receive (money, property, or a title) as an heir, by will or operation of law, at the death of the previous holder.
继承

inheritable—capable of being inherited.
可继承的

inheritance—property received from someone who dies, whether by will or by intestate succession. See also *intestate succession*.
继承物;遗产

inheritance tax—a state tax on property that an heir or beneficiary under a will receives from a deceased person's estate. The heir or beneficiary pays this tax.
遗产税;继承税

initlative—(*the initiative*)(*esp. in some US states and Switzerland*) the right of citizens outside the legislature to originate legislation.
立法提案权

initial appearance—in criminal law, the hearing at which a judge determines whether there is sufficient evidence against a person charged with a crime to hold him/her for trial. The Constitution bans secret accusations, so initial appearances are public unless the defendant asks otherwise; the accused must be present, though he/she usually does not offer evidence. Also called first appearance.
初审;首次出庭

injunction—a court order restraining a person from doing or continuing to do something that threatens or causes irreparable injury to another; or requiring the person to do a particular act. See *enjoin*, *temporary restraining order*.
命令;强制令;禁制令

1. *permanent injunction*—an injunction intended to remain in force unless and until modified by a later decree of a court.
永久禁令

2. *preliminary injunction*—an injunction granted during the pendency of a suit, to restrain a party from doing or continuing some act, the right to which is in dispute, and which may either be discharged or made permanent, according to the result of the controversy, as soon as the rights of the parties are determined.
暂时禁令

injurious—causing or likely to cause damage or harm.
伤害的;中伤的;不公正的

injury—an instance of being injured; the fact of being injured; harm or damage.
受伤;伤害

innocent—not guilty; acquitted of a crime.
清白的;无罪的;无辜的

inns of court—societies of barristers in England. American Inns of Court (AIC) are designed to improve the skills, professionalism and ethics of the bench and bar. An American Inn of Court is an amalgam of judges, lawyers, and in some cases, law professors and law students. Each Inn meets approximately once a month both to "break bread" and to hold programs and discussions on matters of ethics, skills and professionalism.
(英国的)律师学院;(美国的)法学会,法务工作者协会

innuendo—the defamatory meaning of a libel.
暗讽;含沙射影的诽谤中伤

in personam—made or availing against or affecting a specific person only; imposing a personal duty or liability.
对某人不利;将某人起诉

inquest—a legal inquiry generally before a court of law but in some instances before certain other officers legally empowered to hold inquiries, such as by a medical examiner investigating a death.
审讯;审理

inquisition—the verdict or finding of an official inquiry.
调查;审讯

inquisitorial—(of a trial or legal procedure) in which the judge has an examining or inquiring role.
审判官似的;调查官似的;爱打听的

in re—in the legal case of; with regard to.
关于

in rem—made or availing against or affecting a thing, and therefore other people generally; imposing a general duty or liability.

（指诉讼或判决）对物的

insanity—the state of being seriously mentally ill; madness.

精神错乱的；疯狂的

insider trading—the illegal practice of trading on the stock exchange to one's own advantage through having access, because of personal or business relationship, to confidential information.

内部交易

> 对于与证券发行、销售或者购买相关的任何欺诈性行为，《联邦证券法》均予完全禁止。此类禁止性规定是许多惩罚性行为，包括针对欺诈性内部交易所采取的惩罚措施的行使依据。任何人在其掌握某项尚未公开的实质性信息时，违反对该信息的保密义务，或者违反因其掌握该信息而不得进行相关交易的义务，从事相关的内部证券交易，均属非法。

insolvency—a financial condition in which one is unable to meet his obligations as they mature in the ordinary course of business or in which one's liabilities exceed his assets at any given time.

无力偿付债务；破产

inspectorial search—an entry into and examination of premises or vehicles by an inspector for the identification and correction of conditions dangerous to health or safety.

（为保护人身安全的）搜查

institute—

1. begin (legal proceedings) in a court.

对某人起诉

2. appoint (someone) to a position, esp. as a cleric.

使就职；授予圣职

instruct—give a person direction, information, or authorization, in particular.

命令；指导

instructions—judge's explanation to the jury before it begins deliberations of the questions it must answer and the applicable law governing the case. Also called charge to the jury.

（法官对陪审团审案的）指导

instrument—a formal document, esp. a legal one.

正式的法律文件

insurance policy—a document detailing the terms and conditions of a contract of insurance.

保险单

intangible assets—nonphysical items that have value, such as stock certificates, bonds, bank accounts, and pension benefits. Intangible assets must be taken into account in estate planning and divorce.

无形资产

intellectual property—a work or invention that is the result of creativity, such as a manuscript or a design, to which one has rights and for which one may apply for a patent, copyright or trademark.

知识产权

intent—intention or purpose.

意图；意向

interdict—an authoritative prohibition.

1. prohibit or forbid (something).

禁止；制止

2. intercept and prevent the movement of (a prohibited commodity or person).

封锁；阻断

interest—a legal concern, title, or right in property.

利益

interested party—one of the following: heir; devisee; beneficiary; a fiduciary of a legally incapacitated person who is an heir, devisee, or beneficiary; fiduciary or trustee named in an instrument involved; or, a special party.

有关当事人；有股权方

interested person—one of the following: interested party; creditor; surety; any person having a property right in a trust estate or estate of decedent or ward who may be affected by the proceedings, including a person nominated as personal representative; or, a fiduciary representing an interested person.

利害关系人

interim bond—refers to a bond that is set by a police officer when a person is arrested for a misdemeanor offense without a warrant. Any misdemeanor warrant may also have an interim bond endorsed on it by the issuing judge or magistrate. Allows one to be released pending an arraignment.

临时保释金

interim order—a temporary court decree, which is put into effect until something else is done.

暂时法令

interlocutory—temporary; not final, generally decides some point or matter between the beginning and end of a suit but is not a final decision of the case.

（判决等）在诉讼程序进行中（宣布）的；非最终的

interlocutory appeal—an appeal of a decision made by the court during the course of an action, but before the final order or outcome of the action.

中间（途）上诉

International Court of Justice—a judicial court of the United Nations, formed in 1945, that meets at The Hague.

国际法院；海牙国际法庭

> 国际法庭亦称为世界法院，是联合国的主要司法机关，其15名法官由大会和安全理事会分开并同时投票选举产生。国际法院负责在有关国家自愿参加诉讼的情况下裁决国家之间争端。一个国家如果同意参加诉讼，就有义务遵守法院的裁决。国际法院还应请求向联合国及其各专门机构提供咨询意见。

international law—a body of rules established by custom or treaty and recognized by nations as binding in their relations with one another.

国际法

interpleader—a legal action enabling a person to pay monies into court and force two or more persons having competing or conflicting claims against him or her for the same thing to dispute the matter among themselves.

交互诉讼;交互诉讼者

interrogatories—written questions posed prior to trial by one party to a civil case and served on another party to the case, who must answer them in writing under oath. See *discovery*.

讯问;质询(书)

interstate—involving two or more states.

州际的;跨州的

interstate income withholding order—an order entered to secure the enforcement of child support obligations by the withholding of income derived in this jurisdiction to enforce the child support order of another jurisdiction.

州际扣薪命令(不同州法院发出的定期扣交薪水用来抚养儿童的命令在各州皆有法律效力。)

intestate—dying without having made a valid will.

无遗嘱的(死者)

intestate succession—in cases where a decedent has left no valid will, a statutory determination of the right to inherit the decedent's property, made according to the heirs' relationship to the decedent.

无遗嘱继承

intervene—interpose in a lawsuit as a third party.

干涉;干预;调停

intervention—an action by which a third person that may be affected by a lawsuit is permitted to become a party to the suit.

(第三人)介入;干涉;干预

inter vivos—between living persons.

当事人活着时有效的

intoxication—state of drunkenness or inebriation or some similar condition caused by use of drugs other than alcohol.

中毒；喝醉

intrinsic evidence—part of the internal chain composing the process of adjudication. Where allegations of fraud in the complaint attacking a judgment in a former action were that false testimony was given, such allegations of fraud concerned "intrinsic fraud" and thus res judicata barred the complaint.

固有的证据；内部证据

inure—come into operation; take effect.

生效

invalid—(*esp. of an official document or procedure*) not valid; void because contravening a regulation or law.

无效的；无用的

invalidate—deprive (an official document or procedure) of legal efficacy because of contravention of a regulation or law.

使无效；使作废

inventory—a list of the assets of a decedent or ward required by law to be filed in probate court reflecting assets that are subject to management by the fiduciary.

财产清单

inventory fee—a statutory fee for services rendered to a decedent's estate by the probate court.

遗产检验费

investigatory powers—the powers given to governmental agencies and other entities to investigate violations of laws and to gather information regarding laws that are proposed to be enacted.

调查权

invitee—one who comes upon the land of another by the other's invitation, whether expressed or implied.

被邀请者；客人

invoke the rule—separation and exclusion of witnesses (other than parties) from the courtroom. The procedure known as "invoking the rule"— a rule of civil procedure that allows a party to request that a witness be prevented from hearing the testimony of other witnesses in the trial—can be distressing to witnesses. The intent is to prevent witnesses from refreshing their memory or shaping their testimony to fit other testimony. The rule is particularly frustrating to health care practitioners acting as expert witnesses. They will be asked to testify about the validity of other testimony that they are prevented from hearing. Since the attorneys are free to paraphrase the words of other witnesses, perhaps putting a different cast on them, the expert may be in the position of condemning another physician for something the physician did not say or do.

调用规则(在美国民事案件审理程序中,一方向法庭提出调用规则申请,法庭批准后就要指导特定证人离开法庭,避免听到其他证人的作证。)

involuntary—unwilling; forced; opposed; in criminal law, can act as a defense to a charge of committing a crime.

非自愿的;不随意的

ipso facto—by the fact itself; in and of itself.

根据事实本身

ipso jure—by the law itself; merely by the law.

根据法律本身

irrevocable trust—a trust that, once set up, the grantor may not revoke.

不可撤销的信托

issue—

1. of a person: all of the person's lineal descendants of all generations, except those who are descendants of a living descendant, with the relationship of parent and child at each generation being determined by the definitions of child and parent contained in the Probate Code.

子嗣;后代

2. in pleading: a single, certain, and material point, raised in the pleadings of the parties to a lawsuit, which is affirmed on the one side and denied on the other.

争议点

issue preclusion—the rendering of a decision that precludes the issue decided from being relitigated.

争点排除(美国民事诉讼法"既判力"理论及其中的"争点排除")

J

jail—a building used for the confinement of individuals awaiting trial, or who have been convicted of minor offenses.

看守所；拘留所

Jane Doe—an anonymous female party, typically the plaintiff, in a legal action.

女性原告

JD—doctor, the primary degree granted at most US law schools.

法学博士

jeopardy—danger (of conviction) arising from being on trial for a criminal offense.

（刑事被告所处的）危险处境

JIS—see *judicial information services*.

J.N.O.V.—an abbreviation for *judgment non obstante veredicto*, i.e., a judgment notwithstanding the verdict. See *judgment notwithstanding the verdict*.

但是裁决；反向裁决

John Doe

John Doe—an anonymous male party, typically the plaintiff, in a legal action.

男性原告

joinder—combining charges or defendants on the same complaint. Where a crime is committed by two people, both may be charged on one complaint. Joinder also applies in civil cases, where parties and claims may be joined in one complaint.

联合诉讼

joint—shared, held, or made by both houses of a bicameral legislature.

共同的;联合的

joint and several liability—a legal doctrine that makes each of the parties who are responsible for an injury liable for all the damages awarded in a lawsuit if the other responsible parties cannot pay.

连带责任;共同责任

joint custody—an order of the court in a domestic relations proceeding in which one or both of the followings are provided:

1) that the children live with one parent part of the time and with the other parent part of the time;

2) that the parents both share in making decisions on important issues dealing with the children.

共同监护权

joint enterprise—enterprise or undertaking founded on consensual agreement of parties. Its essential elements are agreement, common purpose, community of interest, and equal right of control.

合资企业

joint liability—shared liability which entitles any one party who is sued to insist that other be sued jointly with him.

连带责任

joint tenancy—a form of legal co-ownership of property (also known as survivorship). At the death of one co-owner, the surviving co-owner becomes sole owner of the property. Tenancy by the entirety is a special form of joint tenancy between a husband and wife.

共同保有;联合共有;共同财产权

> 共同保有指两人以上以同一名义共同保有某一地产,他们所享有的这种地产权是统一的一项权利,由同一地产转让契据创设,其权利同时开始,并不加分割地共同占有。其最大的特点是当共同保有人之一死亡时,该共同保有的地产并不予以分割,而是仍作为整体由生存者或遗属(survivor)继续共同保有,直至最后一个共同保有人死亡。共同财产权指二人以上共同对某一财产享有不可分割的权益,并彼此享有遗属权(right of survivorship);或是由某一契据或行为所创设的一项统一的财产权由二人以上共同享有;也指二人以上共同享有,但在整体中每人都有各自单独的权益并可平等享用该财产的情况。

joint tortfeasors—two or more persons who owe to another person the same duty and whose negligence results in injury to such other person, thus rendering the tortfeasors both jointly and severally individually liable for the injury.

共同侵权人

jointure—an estate in property secured to a prospective wife as a marriage settlement, to be enjoyed by her after her husband's decease.

寡妇所得的遗产;(丈夫生前指定的)由妻子继承的遗产

JP—justice of the peace.

治安法官

judge—a public official appointed or elected to decide cases in a court of law.

法官

judge advocate—attorneys who perform legal duties while serving in the U.S. Armed Forces. They provide legal services to their branch of the armed forces and legal representation to members of the armed services. In addition, judge advocates practice international, labor, contract, environmental, tort, and administrative law. They practice in military, state, and federal courts. A judge advocate attorney does not need to be licensed to practice law in the state in which he or she practices because they are part of a separate, military system of justice.

军事法官;军事检察官

judge advocate general—the officer in supreme control of the courts-martial of one of the armed forces.

军法署署长;军法局长

judge-made—created by judicial decisions rather than legislation.

法官制定的

judges' associations—associations formed by various groups of judges by court type to further understanding and cooperation between the judicial, legislative, and executive branches of government, to promote public awareness, to support activities designed for sound and efficient administration of justice, and to encourage high levels of judicial and legal competence.

法官协会

judgment—the decision of a court of law.

判决

judgment in default—(*chiefly Brit.*) another term for *default judgment*.

缺席判决

judgment notwithstanding the verdict—a judgment setting aside a jury's verdict.

但是裁决;反向裁决;不顾陪审团裁决之判决

> 这是美国法院中的一种判决实践。民事诉讼中的主审法官可以使陪审团的决定归于无效或推翻、修正陪审团的裁决。民事诉讼中提出这一请求后,这一救济方式允许法官行使自由裁量权去改变那种不能作为法律问题而成立的判决。法官很少同意败诉方律师提出的"不顾陪审团裁决之判决"申请;法官只在特定情形下,如陪审团裁定的民事损害赔偿金过于严重、过于不合理,或者完全没有法律依据,才有可能同意这一申请。在美国的刑事诉讼中,只有被告才可以提出"不顾陪审团裁决之判决"的申请。

judgment N.O.V.—an abbreviation for *judgment non obstante veredicto*, i.e., a judgment notwithstanding the verdict. See *judgment notwithstanding the*

verdict.
但是裁决;反向裁决;不顾陪审团裁决之判决

judicature—the administration of justice.
法官(总称)

judicial—of, by, or appropriate to a court of law or a judge.
司法的;法庭的

judicial activity report—monthly (district court) or quarterly (circuit court) report to the State Court Administrator on caseload and court activity.
司法活动报告

judicial immunity—the immunity of a judge from civil liability for any acts performed in the judge's official capacity. The immunity is absolute provided only that the judge is acting within his or her jurisdiction. The scope of the judge's jurisdiction must be construed broadly to protect the court's independence; therefore, the judge will not be deprived of immunity because the action taken was in error, was done maliciously, or was in excess of the judge's authority; rather, the judge will be subject to liability only when the action taken was in clear absence of all jurisdiction.
司法豁免权

Judicial Information Services /JIS—a data center providing systems analysis and data processing services to courts throughout the state.
司法信息中心

judicial review—the authority of a court to review the official actions of other branches of government. Also, the authority to declare unconstitutional the actions of other branches.
司法审查;复审

judicial separation—another term for *legal separation*.
合法分居;(并未解除婚姻关系夫妻的)法定分居

judicial tenure commission—the commission which reviews complaints against judges, investigates those complaints and reports to the Supreme Court recommending appropriate discipline or removal of the judge by the Supreme Court.

judiciary

司法督察委员会

<u>judiciary</u>—the judicial authorities of a country; judges collectively.
司法当局;法官、审判官(总称)

<u>jural</u>—formal of or relating to the law.
法律上的;有关权利义务的

<u>jurat</u>—certificate of officer or person whom writing was sworn before. Typically, "jurat" is used to mean the certificate of the competent administering officer that writing was sworn to by person who signed it.
宣誓证明(附于宣誓书后,证明宣誓时间、地点、监视人等)

<u>juridical</u>—of or relating to judicial proceedings and the administration of the law.
司法的;法院的

<u>jurisdiction</u>—the court's authority to decide cases. Two major aspects of a court's jurisdiction are:

1) *subject matter jurisdiction*: the authority to hear a particular type of case; for example, the circuit court has jurisdiction over divorce cases, and the district court has jurisdiction over small claims cases.

2) *personal jurisdiction*: the legal power of a court to render a judgment against a party to a proceeding.

See also *concurrent jurisdiction*, *waiver of jurisdiction*.
管辖权;司法权;审判权

> Jurisdiction 常常译为司法权、管辖权或审判权。在中文语境里,这几个术语含义是有区别的。比如司法权在我国是指包括法院、检察院,甚至公安部门和司法行政管理机关所行使的权力;管辖权是指法院与法院之间管辖第一审案件的分工;审判权是指审判具体案件的特定法庭所行使的审理和裁判权力。但 jurisdiction 在美国民事司法制度中的含义却是相同的,无论翻译为司法权、管辖权或审判权,都是指特定法院基于宪法和法律的授权所享有的对争议事项进行审判的权力,这一制度既要调整法院与其他国家机构和纠纷解决组织之间的职能范围,也要调整联邦法院与州法院以及州法院与州法院之间受理初审案件的权限范围。由于美国上诉法院与初审法院

之间的职能泾渭分明,因而不存在所谓"级别管辖"问题,所以当 jurisdiction 用于确定法院解决争议的权限范围时统译为"管辖权",在少数情况下当它作为与当事人诉权相对应的概念时则译为审判权或司法权。当 jurisdiction 在复合概念中时,要注意有关术语的翻译。如 jurisdiction district 译为"司法区";personal jurisdiction 译为"州域管辖权"或"区域管辖权";territorial jurisdiction 可译为"属地管辖权",体现了美国"实际控制"的管辖权原理;in rem jurisdiction 译为"对物管辖权";subject matter jurisdiction 译为"事项管辖权"。

juris doctor—the degree bestowed by law schools upon students who have earned sufficient academic credit to be eligible to practice law.

法学博士;JD

美国的法学学位有 JD,LLM 和 SJD(Doctor of Judicial Science)。在美国,本科是没有法学专业的,法学院的学位主要有 JD,LLM,JSD 之分。除了 JD 之外,美国法学院的学历教育还有一年制的硕士学位课程(Master of Laws,简称 LLM)和 2—4 年的博士学位(Doctor of Judicial Science,简称 JSD 或 SJD),但这两个学位通常是为国际学生而开设的。美国人一般选择读 JD 学位,这是一个注重法律实务的博士学位,而 SJD 侧重理论研究。JD 学位在美国被广泛认可。

jurisprudence—the study of law and the structure of the legal system.
法学;法理学

jurist—an expert in or writer on law.
法学家

juror—a member of a jury.
陪审员

juror disqualified—juror excused from a trial.
取消资格的陪审员

jury—a body of persons sworn to consider the evidence presented, to determine issues of fact, and to deliver a verdict in a judicial proceeding. There are 6 jurors for district court in civil and criminal matters. In circuit court, there are 6 jurors for civil matters and 12 for criminal matters. There are 6 jurors in probate court. See also *grand jury*, *petit jury*.

陪审团

jury array—the whole body of prospective jurors summoned to court from which the jury will be selected. Also called "jury panel".

陪审团成员审选;陪审团成员名册

jury box—a segregated area in which the jury sits in a court of law.

陪审团席

jury commissioner—the officers responsible for choosing the panel of persons to serve as potential jurors for a particular county.

陪审团审查官

jury instructions—directions given by the judge to the jury informing the jurors of the law applicable to the case.

陪审团指导

jury panel—the group of prospective jurors, from which the trial jury of 6 or 12 is chosen.

候选陪审员

jury polling—the procedure by which each individual juror is asked to affirm his or her verdict in open court at the conclusion of a trial.

陪审团员投票;陪审团员表决

jury trial—a trial in which the jury judges the facts and the judge rules on the law.

陪审团审判

jus cogens—the principles that form the norms of international law and that cannot be set aside by treaty, etc.

国际法准则

jus gentium—international law.

国际法

justice—

1. just behavior or treatment.

正义;公正;合理

2. judge or magistrate, in particular a judge of the supreme court of a country or state.

大法官

justice of the peace—a magistrate appointed to hear minor cases, perform marriages: grant licenses, etc., in a town, county, or other local district.

地方治安法官

justiciable—issues and claims capable of being properly examined in court.

可在法庭审判的;可在法庭裁决的

justifiable homicide—the killing of a person in circumstances (especially self-defense) that allow the act to be regarded in law as without criminal guilt.

正当杀人(指因执行死刑或正当防卫而导致的杀人)

justification—just cause or excuse; just, lawful excuse for an act; reasonable excuse showing of a sufficient reason in court why defendant did what he is called upon to answer for, so as to excuse liability.

理由;辩护;认为有理;认为正当

juvenile—a minor under the age of 17. See also *minor*.

未成年人

juvenile code—the group of statutes governing juvenile delinquency proceedings, designated proceedings, and child protective proceedings.

青少年法典

juvenile court—a court of law responsible for the trial or legal supervision of children under a specified age (18 in most countries).

少年法庭

juvenile delinquency—the committing of criminal acts or offenses by a young person, esp. one below the age at which ordinary criminal prosecution is possible.

少年犯罪

juvenile delinquency proceedings—proceedings in the family division of the circuit court regarding a minor under age 17 who has: committed an offense that would be a crime if committed by an adult, including a misdemeanor traffic offense; deserted his or her home; been absent from school; repeatedly violated school rules; or, disobeyed the reasonable and lawful commands of his or her parents.

少年犯诉讼程序

juvenile offender—a person below a specific age (18 in most countries) who has committed a crime.

少年犯

juvenile officer—see *county agent*.

主管少年犯罪的警官

K

kangaroo court—the term descriptive of a sham legal proceeding in which a person's rights are totally disregarded and in which the result is a foregone conclusion because of the bias of the court or other tribunal.

私设的法庭；非法法庭

KC—(*in the UK*) King's Counsel.

王室律师；皇家律师

keelage—the right of demanding money for the bottom of ships resting in a port or harbor. The money so paid is also called keelage.

停泊费；入港费

keyage—a toll paid for loading and unloading merchandise at a key or wharf.

码头费

kin—relationship by blood.

亲属；家族

King's Bench—(*in the UK*) in the reign of a king, the term for *queen's* bench.

英国高等法院

King's Counsel—(*in the UK*) in the reign of a king. The term for queen's counsel.

英国王室律师

King's Inns—the body responsible for the training of all barristers in Ireland.

爱尔兰律师培训中心

knock-for-knock—an arrangement between insurance companies whereby each company pays the claim of its own insured, on the basis that neither party will pursue a claim against the other.

自保原则(保险公司间达成协议,保险公司各自赔付自己的被保险人,并且双方不再起诉。)

knowingly and willfully—This phrase, in reference to violation of a statute, means consciously and intentionally.

故意违法

L

laches—unreasonable delay in making an assertion or claim, such as asserting a right, claiming a privilege, or making an application for redress, which may result in refusal.

懈怠;疏忽

land contract—a contract for the sale of land on a time payment plan.

土地契约

lapse—the termination of a right or privilege through disuse or failure to follow appropriate procedures;(of a right, privilege, or agreement) become invalid because it is not used, claimed, or renewed; expire.

丧失、失效(协议、法律权利等因未予应用、主张或放弃)

lapsed gift—a gift made in a will to a person who has died prior to the will-maker's death.

因失效而转归他人的赠与

larceny—the trespassory taking of property with the intent to permanently deprive the owner of its ownership rights.

盗窃(罪)

last antecedent doctrine—In statutory construction, under the last antecedent doctrine, relative or modifying phrases are to be applied only to words immediately preceding them, and are not to be construed as extending to more remote phrases, unless such is clearly required by the context of the statute or the reading of it as a whole. For example, in the phrase "the commercial vehicular license shall not apply to boats, tractors, and trucks under three tons", the qualifier "under three tons" applies only to trucks and not to boats or tractors.

紧邻先行词原理

last clear chance—the doctrine in some jurisdictions that a defendant may be liable for the injuries he caused, even though the plaintiff was guilty of contributory negligence, if the defendant could have avoided injury to the plaintiff by exercising ordinary care. The essential elements of the doctrine are: that the plaintiff by his own negligence placed himself in a position of danger; that the plaintiff could not extricate himself from the danger; that the defendant, seeing the plaintiff in a position of danger, or by the exercise of due care should have seen the plaintiff in such position, by exercising due care on his part had a clear chance to avoid injuring the plaintiff; that the defendant failed to exercise such due care; and that as a result of such failure on the defendant's part plaintiff was injured.

被告需承担损害责任原理(尽管原告也有疏忽)

latent ambiguity—language of legal effect that can be interpreted to have more than one meaning. Extrinsic evidence, when allowable, is often necessary to determine the correct interpretation of a latent ambiguity.

潜在的歧义

law clerks—persons trained in the law who assist judges in researching legal opinions.

(法官、检察官、律师)助理

Law Enforcement Information Network /LEIN—a computerized communications system for law enforcement agencies that contains information on such things as personal protection orders, pretrial release conditions in criminal cases, outstanding arrest warrants, driving records, and automobile registration.

法律实施信息网

lawful—conforming to, permitted by, or recognized by law or rules.
合法的;法定的;依法的

lawgiver—a person who draws up and enacts laws.
立法者

lawmaker—legislator.
立法者

lawman—a law-enforcement officer, esp. a sheriff.
执法者;警察

law office—a lawyer's office.
律师事务所

law of nations—international law.
国际法;万国公法

law of succession—the law regulating the inheritance of property.
财产继承法

lawsuit—a legal dispute brought before a court. A "lawsuit" is also referred to as an "action", "case", "cause of action", or "cause".
诉讼(尤指非刑事案件)

lawyer—see *attorney*.
律师

lay witness—any witness not testifying as an expert witness and who is thereby generally precluded from testifying in the form of an opinion.
普通证人;外行证人;非专家证人

leading case—a case continually cited for a proposition of law which controls in that particular area.
(作为先例援引的)案例

leading question—a question that suggests the answer desired of the witness. A party generally may not ask one's own witness leading questions. Leading questions may be asked only of adverse witnesses and on cross-examination.

（对答案）有诱导性的提问

lease—a contract or agreement for the renting of real or personal property for a specified or determined period of time and giving rise to the relationship of landlord (the lessor) and tenant (the lessee).

租约;租契

leaseback—the leasing of a property back to its seller.

反(回)租;售后回租

leasehold—the holding of property by lease.

(土地、房产等)根据地契而拥有的

LEC—Legal English Certificate

法律英语证书全国统一考试

legacy—a gift of personal property left by will. It is also called a "devise".

遗产;遗赠物

legal—

1. of, based on, or concerned with the law.

法律上的

2. permitted by law.

合法的;法定的

legal aid—payment from public funds allowed, in cases of need, to help pay for legal advice or proceedings.

法律援助

legal capacity—a person's authority under law to engage in a particular undertaking or maintain a particular status.

法定资格;法定身份

legal eagle—a lawyer, esp. one who is keen and astute.

精干律师

legalese—the formal and technical language of legal documents.

法律措词;法律术语

legal fiction—an assertion accepted as true, though probably fictitious, to achieve a useful purpose in legal matters.

法律虚拟(在法律事务上为权宜之计,在无真实情况依据下所做的假定。)

legality—the quality or state of being in accordance with the law.
合法性;法律性

legalize—make (something that was previously illegal) permissible by law.
使合法化;使得到法律认可

legally incapacitated person/LIP—an adult who is impaired by reason of mental illness, mental deficiency, physical illness or disability; chronic use of drugs, chronic intoxication, or other cause, to the extent that the person lacks sufficient understanding or capacity to make or communicate responsible decisions concerning his or her person.
无行为能力的人

legal permanent resident/LPR—an immigration term for an alien who has entered the United States and has legally established permission to remain. The person receives a document known as a green card and is entitled to live and work (unless the job is restricted to citizens) in the United States on a permanent basis, provided the person does not commit any actions that would make him or her removable under immigration law.
合法永久居民

legal person—an individual or incorporated entity that has legal rights and is subject to obligations.
法人

legal separation—
1. an arrangement by which a husband or wife remain married but live apart, following a court order. Also called *judicial separation*.
合法分居(法律判决过的夫妻分居)
2. an arrangement by which a child lives apart from a natural parent and with the other natural parent or a foster parent, following a court order.
父母和孩子分住(根据法庭命令)

legal tender—coins or banknotes that must be accepted if offered in payment of a debt.
法定货币

legatee—a person who receives property under a will. Under Michigan's

Revised Probate Code, this person is now called a "devisee".

遗产受赠人

legator—rare a testator, esp. one who leaves a legacy.

遗赠者;立遗嘱者

legislate—make or enact laws.

立法;制定法律

legislation—the action of making or enacting laws.

立法;法律的通过

legislative—having the power to make laws.

立法的

legislator—a person who makes laws; a member of a legislative body.

立法委员;立法者

legislature—the legislative body of a country or state.

立法机关;立法团体

legitimate—conforming to the law or to rules.

合法的;合情合理的

legitimize—make legitimate.

使合法;给予合法地位

leniency—recommendation for a sentence less than the maximum allowed.

宽恕;宽大处理

lessee—the tenant under a lease.

承租人;租户

lessor—the landlord under a lease.

出租人

letters of administration—legal document issued by a court that shows an administrator's legal right to take control of assets in the deceased person's name. Used when the deceased died without a will.

遗产管理证书(一般用于死者无遗嘱的情况下)

letters patent—a public document issued by a government or monarch conferring a patent or other right.

专利特许证

letters rogatory—a request by one court of another court in an independent jurisdiction that a witness be examined upon interrogatories sent with the request.

司法协助函(指一州法院委托他州法院对一诉讼案件所需证据就地进行调查的一种公函。)

letters testamentary—legal document issued by a court that shows an executor's legal right to take control of assets in the deceased person's name. Used when the deceased left a will.

遗嘱执行人授权书(一般用于死者留有遗嘱的情况下)

levy—a seizure; the obtaining or money by legal process through seizure and sale of property; the raising of the money for which an execution has been issued.

征收；征税

lex fori—the law of the state or country in which an action is brought.

所在地法(审理涉外民商事案件的法院所在地国家的法律。它常用来解决涉外民事诉讼程序方面的法律冲突。)

lex loci—the law of the state or country in which a contract is made, a transaction is performed, a tort is committed, or a property is situated.

地方法

lex talionis—the (supposed) law of retaliation, whereby a punishment resembles the offense committed in kind and degree.

同态复仇法

liable—legally responsible.

有法律责任的；有义务的

libel—injury to a person's character or reputation by print, writing, pictures, or signs.

(书面)诽谤

libelous—containing or constituting a libel.

损害名誉的；用言语中伤他人的

liber—Latin for "book". Sometimes used to refer to the large, bound book(s) of records in a court clerk's office, register of deeds, etc.

登记册

liberty—the state of being free within society from oppressive restrictions imposed by authority on one's way of life, behavior, or political views.

自由；自主

license—

1. a permit from an authority to own or use something, do a particular thing, or carry on a trade (esp. in alcoholic beverages).

批准；许可

2. grant a license to (someone or something) to permit the use of something or to allow an activity to take place.

颁发执照

licensed—having an official license

得到许可的；有执照的

licensee—the holder of a license.

执照持有者

lie—(of an action, charge, or claim) be admissible or sustainable.

可立案；可受理

lie detector—an instrument for determining whether a person is telling the truth by testing for physiological changes considered to be associated with lying. Compare with *polygraph*.

测谎仪

lien—a claim against property to secure a debt or other obligation.

留置权；扣押权

life estate—an estate whose duration is limited to or measured by the life of the person holding it or that of some other person pur autre vie. It is a freehold interest in land, whereas a right of homestead includes only right of occupancy and use of the surface of the land.

终身产权

life expectancy—the period of time a person is predicted to live, based on their present age and sex. This figure is most frequently used by actuaries to determine insurance premiums.

预期寿命;平均寿命

life interest—a right to property that a person holds for life but cannot dispose of further.

终身利益

life sentence—a criminal punishment of imprisonment for life.

无期徒刑

limitation—

1. the action of limiting something.

限制;局限

2. (*also limitation period*) a legally specified period beyond which an action may be defeated or a property right is not to continue. See also *statute of limitations*.

时效;时限

limited guardian—a guardian for a minor or legally incapacitated person whose powers over the person have been limited by a court's order.

有限监护人

limited jurisdiction—refers to courts that are only authorized to hear and decide certain or special types of cases. Examples include small claims courts and the court of claims. Also known as special jurisdiction.

有限管辖权

limited liability—the limitation placed on the amount an investor of a corporation can lose resulting from a lawsuit against the corporation or other loss suffered by the corporation; the liability for losses that is limited to the amount an investor or shareholder invests in the corporation, unless that amount is determined by a court to have been fraudulently insufficient. The corporation itself also enjoys limited liability inasmuch as the corporation's obligations are always limited to its assets unless, with regard to particular transactions, personal responsibility is assumed by an officer or shareholder of the corporation.

有限责任

lineage—race; family; kin; blood. A common ancestor with all ascending and descending persons.

血统;门第

lineal—refers to descent by a direct line of succession in ancestry. Parents, children, great-grandchildren, etc., form a *lineal line* as opposed to the line of a brother or sister which would be a *collateral line*.

直系的;嫡系的

lineup—a police procedure by which the suspect in a crime is exhibited, usually as one of a group of similar-appearing persons, before the victim or witness to determine if he or she can be identified as the person who committed the offense.

列队辨认(嫌犯)

liquidate—close the affairs of (a company or firm) by ascertaining liabilities and apportioning assets.

清算;结算

lis pendens—control that a court acquires over property that is the subject of litigation. Where real estate is the subject of litigation, a "notice of lis pendens" may be filed with the register of deeds in the county where the property is located. This notice warns persons who deal with the property that it is subject to litigation and that they may be bound by the court's judgment regarding the property.

未决诉讼

listed stock—stork of a company traded on an organized stock exchange. In addition to satisfying the registration requirements imposed by the Securities and Exchange Commission, a company must comply with the rules imposed by the exchange on which its stock is traded.

上市股票;交易所登记股票

literary executor—a person entrusted with a dead writer's papers and copyrighted and unpublished works.

遗稿保管人

litigant—party to a lawsuit.

诉讼当事人

litigate—go to law; be a party to or subject of a lawsuit.
提出诉讼

litigation—the process of resolving a dispute over legal rights in court.
诉讼

litigious—concerned with lawsuits or litigation.
好诉讼的；好争论的

living trust—a trust set up and in effect during the lifetime of the grantor. Also called *inter vivos trust*.
生存者信托；生前信托（信托合约规定信托人在世有效）

living will—a written statement detailing a person's desires regarding their medical treatment in circumstances in which they are no longer able to express informed consent, esp. an advance directive.
生前遗嘱

LLB—Bachelor of Laws, formerly the first degree in law.
法学学士

LLD—Doctor of Laws, typically an honorary degree.
法学博士（荣誉学位）

LLM—Master of Laws.
法学硕士

local court rules—rules adopted by a particular local trial court to govern procedural matters in that court.
地方法院规则

locus—the place where a particular event, especially a trespass, occurred.
所在地；场所

locus delicti—the place of the offense.
犯罪地点

lodge—present (a complaint, appeal, claim, etc.) formally to the proper authorities.
向……起诉

loiter—stand or wait around idly or without apparent purpose.

闲逛；游荡

long arm statutes—statutes that allow local courts to obtain jurisdiction over nonresident defendants when the cause of action is generated locally and affects local plaintiffs.

美国的长臂法

> 美国的长臂法指法院对外国（州）被告（非居民）所主张的特别管辖权的总称。根据普通法传统，美国的民事诉讼区分为对人诉讼与对物诉讼，相应地，美国法院的管辖权也有属人管辖权与属物管辖权之区分。长臂管辖权即是属人管辖权发展的结果。美国法院的"长臂管辖权"加大了法官的自由裁量权，一方面有利于保护弱方当事人的利益，另一方面也增加了当事人"挑选法院"的机会，使法院歧视得以大行其道。

loss of consortium—see *consortium*.

配偶权利的丧失

lower court—a court whose decisions may be overruled by another court on appeal.

下级法院

LSAT—Law School Admissions Test. A standardized examination administered by a private, nonprofit testing organization known as the Educational Testing Service and used by law schools as one factor in accepting applicants.

北美法学院入学考试

lump-sum payment—a single amount of money; a sum paid all at once rather than in part or in installments.

一次性付费；总付费

lynch—(of a mob) kill (someone), esp. by hanging, for an alleged offense without legal authority.

（暴民）以私刑处死

M

magistrate—Used generally, this title means a judge. In a district court magistrate is a quasi-judicial official of the district court given the power to set bail, accept bond, accept guilty pleas and sentence for traffic and other related violations, and to conduct informal hearings on civil infractions.

地方法官;治安官

Mail Box Rule—a common law doctrine providing that an acceptance made in response to an offer is valid and forms a binding contract at the time of its dispatch, as when it is placed in the mail box, if that method of accepting is a reasonable response to the offer.

投递生效原则;投邮主义

> 英美法系采取投递生效原则。英美法系认为,接受一旦投邮发出,立即生效,合同成立,所以,不存在撤回问题。

maim—at common law, to deprive a person of such a part of his body as to render him less able in fighting or defending himself than he would otherwise have been.

伤残的；有缺陷的

maintenance—providing for the support of a ward or the minor children or surviving spouse of a decedent.

赡养费

majority—the age when a person is legally considered an adult, in most contexts either 18 or 21.

法定年龄；成年

majority opinion—a written decision announcing the court's ruling in a case on appeal. The majority opinion explains the reasoning following by a majority of the judges who heard the case, and is binding on the lower courts in future cases. See also *concurring opinion*, *dissenting opinion*.

判决书

mala praxis—Latin expression, to signify bad or unskillful practice in a physician or other professional person, such as a midwife, lawyer, etc., whereby the health or welfare of the patient or client is injured. The failure of a professional to follow the accepted standards of practice of his or her profession.

医疗失误；医疗过失

> mala praxis 系拉丁语，Sir William Blackstone 在 1768 年编写其法律巨著 *Commentaries on the Laws of England* 时，将 mala praxis，即现代英文 malpractice 定义为"由于内科医师、外科医师或药师等人的疏忽与不当管理……所造成的伤害。如此的伤害破坏了患者对该医师的信任，并且也导致病患的毁灭。"据统计，英国每年有四万多人死于医疗失误；美国每年有近十万人死于医疗失误。

mala prohibita—those things which are prohibited by law, and therefore unlawful. A distinction was formerly made in respect of contracts, between mala prohibita and mala in se; but that distinction has been exploded, and, it is now established that when the provisions of an act of the legislature have for their object the protection of the public, it makes no difference with respect to contracts, whether the thing be prohibited absolutely or under a penalty.

法律所禁止的;非法的

> mala in se 意为"本身错误的",指实质上违反社会伦理道德的违法行为,这种行为因侵害了公共秩序、善良风俗而为一般社会正义所不容。mala prohibita 则是本质上并不违反伦理道德,而是因为维护行政管理秩序的需要而为法律所禁止的行为。在刑事犯罪中,mala in se 寓恶于已,不待法律之特别规定即可认为是犯罪;mala prohibita 则寓恶于禁,必须由法律之专门规定才能成立犯罪。显然,mala in se 寓居的范围早已超出了实定法的界限。

malfeasance—evil doing, ill conduct; the commission of some act which is positively prohibited by law.

不法行为;渎职

malice—evil intent, motive or purpose.

恶意;蓄意

malice aforethought—a special form of the intention to kill or harm, which is held to distinguish manslaughter from murder.

(谋杀罪中的)恶意预谋

malicious abuse of process—tort involving a litigant's malicious misuse of the power of the judiciary. The elements of this tort are: 1) initiation of judicial proceedings against the plaintiff by the defendant; 2) an act by the defendant in the use of process that would not be proper in the regular prosecution of the claim; 3) a primary motive by the defendant in misusing the process to achieve an illegitimate end; and 4) damages.

恶意诉讼;恶意滥用诉讼权

malicious prosecution—In New Mexico, the tort of "malicious prosecution" no longer exists. It has been combined with "abuse of process" to form a new tort, "malicious abuse of process."

恶意诉讼(其性质严重,带有明显无任何理由而提起刑事或民事指控之恶意。)

malpractice—a kind of lawsuit brought against a professional person, such as a doctor, lawyer or engineer, for injury or loss caused by the professional's failure to abide by accepted standards of practice.

玩忽职守；渎职；不法行为

mandamus—Latin expression means "we command". A writ of mandamus is a written order requiring the person to whom it is addressed to do some specified act, generally connected with his or her duty as a public official.

书面训令

mandate—the official decree by a court of appeal.

法院授权

mandatory—required by law or rules; compulsory.

强制的；义务的

manslaughter—the unlawful killing of another without intent to kill; either voluntary (upon a sudden impulse), or involuntary (during the commission of an unlawful act not ordinarily expected to result in great bodily harm.)

非预谋杀人罪

mare clausum—a sea or body of navigable water under the jurisdiction of a particular country.

领海

mare liberum—a sea open to all nations.

公海

marital deduction—an estate tax deduction allowed a surviving spouse of half of the value of the estate of the deceased spouse.

配偶扣除额；婚姻抵税

> 一般来说，美国的赠与税 Gift Tax 和财产税 Estate Tax 对于配偶间的财产转移，在赠与受益人是美国公民的情况下，允许无限金额赠与的免税。因为从经济的层面来说，夫妻被视为同一个经济体，可以享受婚姻抵税。只有在将财产转移给第三者时才会被课以赠与税或财产税。但是赠与的受益人如果不是美国公民的话，就不能享有这个婚姻抵税的优惠，即使配偶是美国永久居民也不可以。

marital estate (property)—property acquired by a husband and wife during the marriage. Division of the property upon dissolution of the marriage is decided by the court unless a marital agreement exists.

夫妻不动产(所有权)

maritime law—the traditional body of rules and practices particularly relating to commerce and navigation, to business transacted at sea or relating to navigation, ships, seamen, harbors, and general maritime affairs.

海商法;海洋法

marriage—the formal union of a man and a woman, typically recognized by law, by which they become husband and wife.

结婚;婚姻状况

marriage license—a document giving official permission, as from a county, to marry.

结婚证书

marry—join in marriage.

结婚;嫁娶

marshal—a federal or municipal law officer, typically with specified duties relating to court functions.

执法官

martial law—military government involving the suspension of ordinary law.

戒严法;戒严令

master—an officer of the court, usually an attorney, appointed for the purpose of taking testimony and making a report to the court, most frequently in divorce cases.

(常指离婚法庭上的)法庭官

master in chancery—an officer of a court of chancery who acts as an assistant to the judge.

衡平法院法官助理

material—(of evidence or a fact) significant or influential, esp. to the extent of determining a cause or affecting a judgment.

重要的;重大的

material evidence—such as is relevant and goes to the substantial issues in dispute.
实质上的证据；主要证据

materiality—the quality of being significant or influential.
重要性；实质性

maternal—of the mother; belong to or coming from the mother.
母性的；母亲的

matricide—the crime of killing one's mother.
弑母罪

matter—something that is to be tried or proved in court; a case.
案件；问题

maturity—the date at which legal rights in an obligation ripen; in the context of commercial paper negotiable instruments, it is the time when the paper becomes due and demandable, that is, the time when an action can be maintained thereon to enforce payment.
成熟期；到期日

maxims—statements espousing general principles of law; not usually used to justify a court decision based on law, but frequently used to determine the equities of a situation.
准则；普遍真理；行为准则

mayhem—chiefly historical the crime of maliciously injuring or maiming someone, originally so as to render the victim defenseless.
伤人致残罪；严重伤害罪

measure—a legislative bill.
措施；办法；议案

mediation—generally, a form of alternative dispute resolution in which a neutral third party assists the parties to a dispute in reaching an agreement to settle their differences. The parties are not required to reach agreement, but if they do, the agreement is binding.
调解；调停

medical jurisprudence—forensic medicine.

法医学

memorialized—in writing.
书面请愿

mens rea—the "guilty mind" necessary to establish criminal responsibility. In criminal law, it is viewed as one of the necessary elements of some crimes. The standard common law test of criminal liability is usually expressed in the Latin phrase, *actus reus non facit reum nisi mens sit rea*, which means "the act is not culpable unless the mind is guilty". Thus, in jurisdictions with due process, there must be an *actus reus*, or "guilty act", accompanied by some level of *mens rea* to constitute the crime with which the defendant is charged. As a general rule, criminal liability does not attach to a person who merely acted with the absence of mental fault. The exception is strict liability crimes. In civil law, it is usually not necessary to prove a subjective mental element to establish liability for breach of contract or tort, for example. However, if a tort is intentionally committed or a contract is intentionally breached, such intent may increase the scope of liability as well as the measure of damages payable to the plaintiff. Therefore, *mens rea* refers to the mental element of the offence that accompanies the *actus reus*. In some jurisdictions, the terms *mens rea* and *actus reus* have been replaced by alternative terminology. In Australia, for example, the elements of the federal offenses are now designated as "fault elements" or "mental elements" (*mens rea*) and "physical elements" or "external elements" (*actus reus*). This terminology was adopted to replace the obscurity of the Latin terms with simple and accurate phrasing.
犯罪意图

> mens rea 系拉丁语,意谓"犯罪的意图",即实施犯罪行为的目的。犯罪意图又称为犯罪心理,就是行为人在实施社会危害行为时应受社会谴责的心理状态,它是英美法系犯罪构成的主观要件。"没有犯罪意图的行为,不能构成犯罪"是英美刑法的一条原则,它充分体现了犯罪意图在构成犯罪中的重要意义。在美国刑法中,犯罪意图分为以下四种:1. 蓄意(mention),指行为人行动时自觉目的就是引起法律规定为犯罪的结果,或者自觉目的就是实施法律规定为犯罪的行为。2. 明知(knowingly),指行为人行动时明知道

mental cruelty

> 他的行为就是法律规定为犯罪的行为或者明知道存在着法律规定为犯罪的情节。3. 轻率(recklessly)，指行为人轻率地对待法律规定为犯罪的结果或情节，当行动时他认识到并有意漠视可能发生此种结果或者存在此种情节的实质性的无可辩解的危险。4. 疏忽(negligence)，指行为人疏忽地对待法律规定为犯罪的结果或情节，当行为时他没有察觉到可能发生此种结果或者存在此种情节的实质性的无可辩解的危险。从犯罪意图的内容来看，主要是行为人对于其犯罪行为的一种心理状态，它是构成犯罪的基本因素。

mental cruelty—the conduct that makes another person, especially one's spouse, suffer but does not involve physical assault.

精神虐待

mental health code—the statutes that govern, among other things, care and hospitalization of the mentally ill and guardianships for the developmentally disabled. See also *developmentally disabled person*.

心理健康法典

mental illness—

1. "mental illness" means a substantial disorder of thought or mood which significantly impairs judgment, behavior, capacity to recognize reality, or ability to cope with the ordinary demands of life.

精神病（多限于法律事务中，指刑法上导致反复的刑事犯罪或反社会行为的一种非正常精神病状。）

2. means mental disease to such an extent that a person so afflicted requires care and treatment for his or her own welfare, or for the welfare of others or of the community.

精神疾患（医学上所认知的精神上的疾病或病症）

mentally retarded—significantly below average intellectual abilities which originate during physical development (especially during pregnancy and early infancy). See also *developmentally disabled person*.

弱智，（尤指儿童）智力发育迟缓

merchant—a person who regularly deals in goods of the kind being sold or who otherwise holds himself out as having a special knowledge of the goods sold. For example, Bob owns a clock shop and sells clocks, so he would be considered a merchant of clocks. However, if Bob sold his car to someone, he would not be considered a merchant of cars.

商人;经销商

merger clause—merger clauses state that the written document contains the entire understanding of the parties. The purpose of merger clauses is to ensure that evidence outside the written document will not be admissible in court to contradict or supplement the express terms of the written agreement.

合并条款

meritorious—(of an action or claim) likely to succeed on the merits of the case.

值得称赞的;有功的

merits—the substantive claims and defenses raised by the parties to an action.

有理;法律依据

mesne—intermediate; intervening.

中间的

mesne profits—the profits of an estate received by a tenant in wrongful possession and recoverable by the landlord.

中间利益

messuage—a dwelling house with outbuildings and land assigned to its use.

家宅

military law—the law governing the armed forces.

军法

minimum wage—the lowest wage permitted by law or by a special agreement (such as one with a labor union).

最低工资

ministerial—of or relating to the duties of a government official.

行政性的

minor—In delinquency cases, a minor is someone under age 17. In most other proceedings, a minor is someone under age 18. Some court rules also

minor offense

provide that a "minor" may include a person age 18 or older if delinquency or child protective proceedings were commenced in juvenile court prior to the person's 18th birthday and the juvenile court continues to have jurisdiction over the person. See also *adult*, *juvenile delinquency proceedings*.

未成年人

minor offense—a misdemeanor or ordinance violation for which the maximum permissible imprisonment does not exceed 92 days and the maximum permissible fine does not exceed $500.00.

轻微犯罪（或违规）

Miranda—refers to a United States Supreme Court decision, *Miranda v. Arizona*, 348 US 436 (1966), from which the rules governing "the right to remain silent" were taken.

米兰达原则（有权保持沉默）

Miranda warning—also referred to as *Miranda rights* or *Miranda rule*, is a right to silence warning given by police in the United States to criminal suspects in police custody (or in a custodial interrogation) before they are interrogated to preserve the admissibility of their statements against them in criminal proceedings. The Miranda warning is part of a preventive criminal procedure rule that law enforcement are required to administer to protect an individual who is in custody and subject to direct questioning or its functional equivalent from a violation of his or her Fifth Amendment right against compelled self-incrimination. In *Miranda v. Arizona*, the Supreme Court held that the admission of an elicited incriminating statement by a suspect not informed of these rights violates the Fifth Amendment and the Sixth Amendment right to counsel, through the incorporation of these rights into state law. Thus, if law enforcement officials decline to offer a Miranda warning to an individual in their custody, they may interrogate that person and act upon the knowledge gained, but may not use that person's statements as evidence against him or her in a criminal trial. In *Berghuis v. Thompkins*, the Supreme Court held that unless a suspect expressly states that he or she is invoking this right, subsequent voluntary statements made to an officer can be used against him in court, and police can continue to interact with (or question) the suspect.

米兰达警告

> 米兰达警告是指美国警察,包括检察官,根据美国联邦最高法院在1966年"米兰达诉亚利桑那州案"(Miranda v. Arizona, 384 U.S. 436〈1966〉)一案的判例中,最终确立的米兰达规则。在讯问刑事案件嫌疑人之前,必须对其明白无误地告知其有权援引宪法第五修正案(刑事案件嫌疑人有不被强迫自证其罪的特权[Privilege Against Self-incrimination]),而行使沉默权和要求得到律师协助的权利。有关警告虽然源自美国,但由于证供的可信性在普通法系的法庭非常重要,这项警告对司法过程有重要影响,因为这项声明确保了犯人所提供的证供的可信性。即使犯人在侦讯时提供假口供,亦会因为提供假口供或发假誓而受到惩处。而另一方面,这项声明亦在某种程度上保障了犯人避免被屈打成招。因此,现时世界上采用普通法系的地区都吸纳了这项警告的精神,以保障犯人的权利及司法的公正。

misadventure—an accident. A homicide by misadventure results from a lawful act unaccompanied by criminal carelessness or recklessness. It differs from involuntary manslaughter in that the homicide by misadventure must be the result of a lawful act.
意外(致死);事故

misappropriation—the intentional, illegal use of the property or funds of another person for one's own use or other unauthorized purpose, particularly by a public official, a trustee of a trust, an executor or administrator of a dead person's estate or by any person with a responsibility to care for and protect another assets (a fiduciary duty). It is a felony (a crime punishable by a prison sentence).
挪用(未经物主同意,擅自取用他人的财产或金钱的行为,如果有证据显示挪用者有意永久占有该财产,则挪用者的行为属于侵占行为。)

miscarriage of justice—a failure of a court or judicial system to attain the ends of justice, esp. one that results in the conviction of an innocent person.
审判不公;误判

mischief—harm or trouble caused by someone or something.
损害;危害

misdemeanant—a person convicted of a misdemeanor.
行为不端的人

misdemeanor—a violation of a penal law of this State which is not a felony, or a violation of an order, rule or regulation of a state agency that is punishable by imprisonment or by a fine that is not a civil fine.
轻罪（与重罪相对）

misfeasance—the improper performance of some act or duty.
不法行为；不当行为

misjoinder—the joining together of distinct counts in a single indictment or complaint, which counts ought not to be tried together.
非法的共同诉讼；诉讼当事人的不当联合

mislaid property—property that owner has intentionally placed where he can resort to it, but which place is then forgotten.
遗忘物；错置财产

misnomer—a mistake in the word or combination of words constituting a person's name and distinguishing him from other individuals.
（在诉讼等中的）写错姓名（或地名）

misprision—(*chiefly historical*) the deliberate concealment of one's knowledge of a treasonable act or a felony.
包庇罪行

misrepresentation—a false or misleading statement.
不实陈述；误述

mistrial—a trial declared defective and void due to prejudicial error in the proceedings, or the failure of a jury to agree upon a verdict.
无效审判

mitigating circumstances—those facts which do not constitute a justification or excuse for an offense but which may be considered as reasons for reducing the degree of blame.
可使罪行减轻的情节行为

mitigation—reduction of penalty or punishment.
减轻处罚、惩罚

mittimus—Latin for "we send":

1. a written court order directed to the keeper of a jail or prison, directing that he or she receive and safely keep an offender awaiting trial or sentence.

收押令

2. a writ directing the transfer of records from one court to another. Contrast with *commitment*.

调卷令

moiety—each of two parts into which a thing is or can be divided, especially a joint tenancy.

一半；一部分

money judgment—a judgment ordering the payment of a sum of money. Such judgments may be executed under a writ of execution.

金钱支付判决

money order—a credit instrument, either negotiable or nonnegotiable, calling for payment of money to a named payee, and involving the payee, drawee, and remitter.

汇票

monogamy—polygamy.

一夫一妻制

monopoly—a description of a market condition where all or nearly all of an article of trade or commerce within a community or district is brought within the single control of one person or company, thereby excluding competition or free traffic in that article.

垄断；独占；专营

moot—usually in reference to a court's refusal to consider a case because the issue involved has been resolved prior to the court's decision, leaving nothing which would be affected by the court's decision. Moot court is a practice court for law students.

虚拟诉讼；模拟法庭

moot case—a case seeking to determine an abstract question which does not rest upon existing facts or rights, or which seeks a judgment in an alleged controversy when in reality there is none; a case which seeks a decision in advance about a right before it has actually been asserted or contested, or a judgment upon some matter which when rendered for any cause cannot have any practical effect upon the existing controversy.

未决案件

moot court—a mock court at which law students argue imaginary cases for practice.

模拟法庭

moral turpitude—conduct contrary to honesty, modesty or good morals.

道德败坏

moratorium—a legal authorization to debtors to postpone payment.

延缓;暂停

mortgage—a lien on real property to secure the performance of some obligation, and to be discharged upon payment or performance as stipulated. It is a pledge or security of particular property for the payment of a debt.

抵押借款;抵押借款利息

mortgagee—one who holds a mortgage; the creditor.

抵押贷款人

mortgagor—the maker of a mortgage; the debtor.

抵押借款人

motion—an application to the court for the purpose of obtaining a certain order or decision in favor of the applicant.

(向法庭)申请;请求

motions calendar—motions pertaining to the calendaring of court appearances in a case such as motions to continue, advance or reset.

庭审日历

motions in limine—a motion to exclude certain testimonial evidence from admission into evidence at trial.

证据排除申请

motion to expunge—a motion to delete material from official court records, such as a record of juvenile conviction.

消除法庭记录的申请

motion to mitigate sentence—a motion to reduce the sentence.
减刑申请

motion to seal—a motion to close records to public inspection.
封存记录申请

motion to quash—see *quash*.
宣布无效申请

motions to suppress—In common law legal systems, a motion to suppress is a formal, written request to a judge for an order that certain evidence be excluded from consideration by the judge or jury at trial. In the United States, the term "motion to suppress" typically encompasses motions in criminal cases where the proposed basis for exclusion arises from the United States Constitution, a state constitution, or a specific statute permitting the exclusion of certain types of evidence (for instance, a complaint that police procedures in a given case violated the defendant's Fourth Amendment right to be free from unreasonable searches and seizures). A motion to exclude evidence where the proposed basis for exclusion arises from the rules of evidence is more commonly termed a motion in limine.
排他证据申请(在美国,一般是在刑事案件中向法官提出的正式书面申请排除由于非法搜查得到的证据,或由于没有根据法律程序对被告宣读权利所获得的证据。)

mouthpiece—(*informal*) a lawyer.
辩护律师;代言人

movable—(of property) of the nature of a chattel, as distinct from land or buildings; personal.
活动的;可移动的

movant—a person who applies to or petitions a court or judge for a ruling in his or her favor.
请求胜诉的人

move—make a formal request or application to (a court or assembly) for something.

提议;行动

mulct—a fine or penalty imposed for an offense.

罚金

multifarious suit—suit wherein distinct and independent matters are improperly joined..., and thereby confounded—as for example, where several perfectly distinct and unconnected matters against one defendant are united in one bill.

混合诉讼

multiplicity of actions—numerous and unnecessary attempts to litigate the same right.

重复诉讼

municipal court—a trial court whose authority is confined to the city or community in which it is established. Municipal court civil jurisdiction is limited to $1,500.

市法院;(地方)自治法院

murder—the unlawful killing of a human being with deliberate intent to kill. Murder in the first degree is characterized by premeditation; murder in the second degree is characterized by a sudden and instantaneous intent to kill or to cause injury without caring whether the injury kills or not.

谋杀(按其情节分为一级和二级等多种等级。)

mutuality—a meeting of the minds of contracting parties regarding the material terms of the agreement.

相互性;相互关系

mutual wills—wills made by two people (usually spouses, but could be "partners") in which each gives his/her estate to the other, or with dispositions they both agree upon. A later change by either is not invalid unless it can be proved that there was a contract in which each makes the will in the consideration for the other person making the will.

共同遗嘱;联合遗嘱

mutual wills

共同遗嘱也称合立遗嘱、共立遗嘱,是指两个或两个以上的遗嘱人共同订立同一份遗嘱,对其死亡后各自或共同遗留的财产指定继承人继承的一种遗产继承方式。这是一种特殊的遗嘱方式,多数情况下发生在夫妻之间。共同遗嘱从遗嘱内容上可分为相关的共同遗嘱和单纯的共同遗嘱两种,同一份共同遗嘱也有单纯和相关之分。相关的共同遗嘱是相互依存的,即当一方的遗嘱内容发生变更或撤回时,对方的遗嘱内容也因而随之发生变化;在遗嘱生效前,即使有遗嘱人先死亡,其遗产也不得被擅自分割。而单纯的共同遗嘱人之间的关系,则是相互独立的,遗嘱人各自可自由变更、撤销其遗嘱而互不相干。可见,单纯的共同遗嘱实为数份独立遗嘱,只不过在形式上合而为一而已,而内容相关的共同遗嘱则要复杂得多,任何一位遗嘱人皆不得擅自变更或撤回遗嘱内容,通常要等到最后一位遗嘱人死亡后,继承才真正开始。

N

natural child—any child by birth as opposed to an adopted child.
亲生子;嫡血

naturalized citizen—one who, having been born in another country or otherwise reared as a foreigner, has been granted U. S. citizenship and the rights and privileges of that status. The process by which such a person attains citizenship is called naturalization.
已入籍公民;归划公民

natural law—law which so necessarily agrees with the nature and state of man, that without observing its maxims, the peace and happiness of society can never be preserved; knowledge of natural laws may be attained merely by the light of reason, from the facts of their essential agreeableness with the constitution of human nature.
自然法

natural law theory—in jurisprudence, the view that the nature and value of any legal order is best understood by studying how the positive law of that legal order agrees or contrasts with natural law.

自然法理论

natural person—a human being, as opposed to artificial or fictitious "person" such as corporations.

（区别于法人的）自然人

necessarily included offense—where an offense cannot be committed without necessarily committing another offense, the latter is a necessarily included offense; sometimes referred to as lesser included offense.

连锁冒犯；连锁违法（行为）

ne exeat—a court order forbidding the person to whom it is addressed to leave the country, the state or the jurisdiction of the court.

禁止出境令

negative averment—an averment in some of the pleadings in which a negative is asserted.

否定的申辩

negative pregnant—refers to a denial which implies an affirmation of a substantial fact and hence is beneficial to opponent. Thus, when only a qualification or modification is denied while the fact itself remains undenied, the denial is pregnant with the affirmation.

带有肯定意味的否定

neglect—

1. *n.* the omission of proper attention; avoidance or disregard of duty from heedlessness, indifference, or willfulness;

忽视；疏忽

2. *v.* failure to do, use, or heed anything.

疏忽

neglect hearing—hearing held in the family division of the circuit court; involves child abuse or those situations where the children are not being properly cared for.

虐待儿童听证

negligence—failure to exercise the degree of care that a reasonable person would exercise under the same circumstances.

过失

negligent—failing to take proper or reasonable care in doing something.
疏忽的;玩忽的

negotiable—open to discussion or modification.
可谈判的;可协商的

negotiable instrument—a writing which is signed by the maker or drawer, contains an unconditional promise or order to pay a sum certain in money, is payable on demand or at a definite time, and is payable to order or to bearer.
可流通票据(证券);可转让票据

nemo est supra legis—nobody is above the law.
任何人不得凌驾于法律之上

net estate—the portion of an estate subject to federal and state estate taxes; the estate remaining after all debts of decedent, funeral and administrative expenses, and/or other deductions prescribed by law, have been deducted from the gross estate total valuation of the estate's assets at decedent's death.
净资产;净遗产

net income—the gross total income less deductions and exemptions allowed by law.
纯收入;净收入

neutrality laws—laws governing a country's abstention from participating in a conflict or aiding a participant of such conflict, and the duty of participants to refrain from violating the territory, seizing the possession, or hampering the peaceful commerce of the neutral countries.
中立法

next friend—a person appointed by the court to appear on behalf of a minor or incompetent person who is a plaintiff in a civil action.
诉讼代理人(由法庭指定,代表在民事诉讼中未成年人或无民事行为能力的原告。)

next of kin—the term is used generally with two meanings: 1) nearest blood relations according to law of consanguinity and 2) those entitled to take under statutory distribution of intestates' estates. In the latter case, the term is not necessarily confined to relatives by blood, but may include a relationship existing by reason of marriage, and may well embrace persons, who in the natural sense of the word, bear no relation of kinship at all.

近亲

nisi—(of a decree, order, or rule) taking effect or having validity only after a specified period of time, as long as certain changes of condition have not occurred.

非最后的;非绝对的

nisi prius—courts for the initial trial of issues of fact as distinguished from appellate courts.

由一个法官和陪审团审理的民事诉讼初审

no bill—This phrase, endorsed by a grand jury on the indictment, is equivalent to "not found" or "not a true bill". It means that, in the opinion of the jury, evidence was insufficient to warrant the return of a formal charge.

指控不成立

no contact order—a provision in a court order (e.g., an order for the defendant's pretrial release in a criminal case) that the person subject to the order refrain from having contact with another named person.

禁止接触令

no-contest clause—language in a will providing that a person who makes a legal challenge to the will's validity will be disinherited.

无争议条款

no contest plea—see *nolo contendere*.

无罪申诉(刑事诉讼中,被告不认罪但又放弃申辩。)

no fault—a case which is decided without making a determination as to which party is at fault.

不追究责任

no-fault proceedings—a civil case in which parties may resolve their dispute without a formal finding of error or fault.

不追究过失责任的;无责任认定的

no-knock—denoting or relating to a search or raid by the police made without warning or identification.

(逮捕、搜查等)强行闯入;破门而入

nolle pros—abandon or dismiss (a suit) by issuing a nolle prosequi.
中止诉讼

nolle prosequi—the prosecutor declines to prosecute, but may still initiate prosecution within the time allowed by law.
原告撤诉

nolo contendere—no contest. A plea through which the defendant does not admit guilt, but which has the same legal effect as a plea of guilty in a criminal case. However, the no contest plea may not be used in a civil action related to the criminal charge to prove the defendant's civil liability. For example, a plea of nolo contendere for a traffic citation that resulted from an accident cannot be used to convince a judge in a civil case that the defendant is guilty of causing an accident.
无罪申诉（刑事诉讼中，被告不认罪但又放弃申辩。）

nominal party—one who is joined as a party or defendant merely because the technical rules of pleading require his presence in the record.
名义上的当事人

nonappearance—failure to appear or be present in a court of law, esp. as a witness, defendant, or plaintiff.
指当事人或证人在规定期限内未出庭

noncapital—(of an offense) not punishable by death.
罪不该死；不判死刑的谋杀罪

non compos mentis—"not of sound mind"; insane.
精神不正常的；心神丧失的

non-custodial parent—the parent who does not have custody of a child. See *child custody*.
无监护权父母

non est factum—It is not his or her deed. Non est factum is a defence to an action founded on a document where the defendant alleges that even though they may have signed the document they did not know what the document contained.
这不是我所签署的

> non est factum 系拉丁语,意为"这不是我的契约"it is not my deed。很多时候,此词是作为被告的辩词,声称被告没有签署文件,又或被告签署文件的时候并不知道文件的内容。

nonfeasance—failure to perform an act that one should perform.
不履行义务;懈怠

non jury trial—a case tried by a judge on the facts as well as the law.
非陪审团审判

non obstante veredicto—notwithstanding the verdict, i.e., an order of the judge entering a judgment for the defendant notwithstanding a jury verdict for the plaintiff.
但是裁决;反向裁决;不顾陪审团裁决之判决

non-recourse—without personal liability. An obligation that is non-recourse does not provide a basis for federal taxation purposes for individuals or partnerships except in certain limited cases such as when real estate is involved.
无追索权;不承担责任

non-service—in either a civil or criminal case, where a summons or warrant is issued but not served, or no arrest made.
没有送达

non sui juris—not by his own authority or legal right. This maxim refers to those who are not legally competent to manage their own affairs as regards contracts and other causes; this incompetency restricts their granting power of attorney or otherwise exercising self-judgment.
无法律行为能力

non-suit—a ruling by the judge in a lawsuit either when the plaintiff (the party who filed the suit) does not proceed to trial at the appointed time or has presented all his/her/its evidence and, in the judge's opinion, there is no evidence which could prove the plaintiff's case. A non-suit terminates the trial at that point and results in a dismissal of the plaintiff's case and judgment for the defendant.
驳回起诉

nonsuit

> non-suit 是指法官所作出的一项裁定,一般是起诉人没有在规定的时间内提起诉讼,或者是法官看来没有证据能够支持起诉人的案件。non-suit 不同于 ignore 驳回诉讼。两者的具体区别在于:1. 适用法律不同。驳回起诉适用程序法;而驳回诉讼请求既可适用程序法,又可适用实体法。2. 适用的诉讼主体不同。驳回起诉适用的诉讼主体是单一的,主要适用针对原告的起诉;而驳回诉讼请求适用的主体是多元的,既可以针对原告的诉讼请求,也可针对被告的反诉请求以及有独立请求权的第三人的诉讼主张。3. 采用的裁判形式不同。驳回起诉是对程序意义上诉权的确认,应当采用裁定形式;驳回诉讼请求则是实体意义上诉权的确认,必须采用书面判决。

nonsuit—(of a judge or court) subject (a plaintiff) to the stoppage of a suit on the grounds of failure to make a legal case or bring sufficient evidence.

诉讼驳回

nonsupport—the failure to provide support that one can provide and that one is legally obliged to provide to a spouse, child, or other dependent.

不履行抚养;不负担抚养费

non vult—abbreviation of non vult contendere ("he will not contest"). It refers to a plea by one charged with a crime that does not expressly admit guilt, but acknowledges that the defendant will not contest the charge and therefore agrees to be treated as though he had been found guilty.

不许争辩

no probable cause—insufficient grounds to hold the person who was arrested.

无合理依据

no progress—in a civil case, where a case is filed but not followed up; a case or cases which may be dismissed (disposed of) by the court because parties have done nothing to process the case from stage to stage.

无疾而终的民事诉讼

notarize—have (a document) legalized by a notary; (of a notary) legalize a document by certifying its authenticity.

公证

notary—a person who is authorized by the state or federal government to administer oaths and to certify the authenticity of signatures or documents.

公证人；公证员

notary public—see *notary*.

公证人；公证员

notice of appeal—a document filed with a clerk to inform the court of the appellant's intention to appeal a decision handed down by a lower court.

上诉通知书

notice of hearing—document notifying a person of the time, date, place, and subject matter of an upcoming court proceeding.

听证通知

notice of lis pendens—a notice filed on public records to warn all persons that the title to certain property is in litigation, and that if they purchase or lease that property they are in danger of being bound by an adverse judgment. The notice is for the purpose of preserving rights pending litigation.

未决诉讼公告

notice to produce—in practice, a notice in writing requiring the opposite party to produce a certain described paper or document at the trial.

要求制作、出示法庭指定的文件的通知

notice to quit—

1. a written notice by a landlord to his/her tenant demanding that the tenant surrender and vacate the property, terminating the tenancy.

中止租赁并腾空通知

2. a notice to pay back rent in seven days or vacate.

交房租或腾空租房通知

notification of parents, record of notice—Whenever a child is taken into custody by any peace officer, that officer is required to notify the parents of the child. A written record of the names of the persons notified, the manner and times of notification, or reasons for failure to notify must be made and preserved.

（警察签发给被拘留未成年人父母的）拘留通知书

novation—the substitution of a new contract (especially with a substitute debtor) in place of an old one.

更新

nuisance—an unreasonable, unwarranted, or unlawful use of one's property that annoys, disturbs, or inconveniences another in the use of his or her property; violation of an ordinance that forbids annoyance of the public in general.

妨害行为

null—having no legal or binding force; invalid.

无效的

nullity—an act or thing that is legally void.

法律上无效

nuncupative will—an oral (unwritten) will.

口头遗嘱

nunc pro tunc—Latin phrase meaning "now for then"; an order allowing acts done after they should have been done (now) to be effective retroactively to when they should have been done (then).

追溯既往令；弥补已生效的判决

nunc pro tunc amendment—an amendment or correction given retroactive effect by court order.

追溯既往令修正

nunc pro tunc filing—the filing of a pleading to take effect as of an earlier time.

追溯生效起诉

nunc pro tunc judgment—a method of amending the record of a judgment which is in accord with what was actually pronounced and done, so that the record will be accurate and true. It is a procedural device often employed in correcting defects in titles in real estate.

追溯性判决

nuncupative—(of a will or testament) declared orally as opposed to in writing, often by a mortally wounded person.

（遗嘱、证词等）口头的

O

oath—a declaration of a statement's truth, which renders one willfully asserting an untrue statement punishable for perjury.

宣誓；陈述真实性的声明

obiter dictum—an incidental comment, not necessary to the formulation of the decision, made by the judge in an opinion which is not binding as precedent.

法官在意见书中做出的不受先例约束的附带意见

objection—the process by which one party tries to prevent the introduction of evidence or the use of a procedure at a hearing. An objection is either sustained (allowed) or overruled by the judge.

拒绝、反对（引入新证据）

obligation—the condition of being morally or legally bound to do something.

义务

obligee—a person to whom another is bound by contract or other legal procedure. Compare with *obligor*.

债权人（与债务人相对）

obligor—a person who is bound to another by contract or other legal procedure. Compare with *obligee*.

债务人（与债权人相对）

obscene—(of the portrayal or description of sexual matters) offensive or disgusting by accepted standards of morality and decency.

淫秽的；猥亵的

obscenity—the state or quality of being obscene; obscene behavior, language, or images.

淫秽，猥亵；淫秽的词语或举动

obstruct—commit the offense of intentionally hindering (a legal process).

故意阻碍的违法行为

occupancy—the action or fact of occupying a place.

占有；占有的行为或事实

occupant—a person holding property, esp. land, in actual possession.

占有人（占有财产，尤其是占有土地）；事实上的占有

occupational disease /injury—a disease which is the natural incident or result of a particular employment, usually developing gradually from the effects of long continued work at the employment.

职业病

occupational hazard—a risk that is peculiar to a particular type of employment or workplace, and which arises as a natural incident of such employment or of employment in such a place.

职业风险

of counsel—a phrase commonly applied to counsel employed to assist in the preparation or management of the case, or its presentation on appeal, but who is not the principal attorney of record.

法律顾问；律师

offense—a crime or ordinance violation. The word "offense" generally implies an act infringing public as distinguished from private rights. In respect to minors, an offense is any act which violates provisions of the Juvenile Code and thus places the person committing the act in the jurisdiction of the juvenile court. It does not include civil infractions.

犯罪或违反法令（通常指行为侵犯公共利益，而非私人利益。）

> 如果是未成年人犯罪，则指其行为违反未成年人法令中的任意条款，从而将该行为实施人送交具有管辖权的青少年法庭。

offense against child—any act or acts by a person other than the child asserted as grounds for bringing such child within the provisions of the Juvenile Code.

针对未成年人的犯罪

offense by child—any act or acts by a child asserted as grounds for bringing the child within the provisions of the Juvenile Code.

未成年人犯罪

offer—an expression of willingness to enter into a bargain that is definite and certain in its terms and that is communicated to the offeree. Once accepted, the offer is transformed into a contractual obligation.

要约

offeree—the person to whom an offer is made.

受要约人

offeror—the person who makes an offer.

要约人

officer—a bailiff.

法庭官员；法警（其职责通常为维持法庭秩序）

old bailey—the central criminal court in London, England.

位于英国伦敦的中央刑事法院

omission—a failure to do something, esp. something that one has a moral or legal obligation to do.

疏忽；懈怠；失败做某事（尤其是负有道德或法律义务的事）

one day, one trial—a method of summoning and utilizing jurors whereby an individual serves as juror for either one day or for the length of one trial. The purpose of this method is to reduce the term of service and expand the

opening

number of individual jurors called.

一天一审

> 为了解决陪审团职责中某些令人厌烦的问题,美国一些法院采取"一天一审"的制度。这种新的制度规定,陪审员或任职一天或在案件的某个审期期间任职。陪审员、法官、法院行政管理人员认为"一天一审"制度节约了成本,是陪审团制度极大的改进。

opening—an attorney's preliminary statement of a case in a court of law.
(在法庭上律师对案件的)预备陈述

opening statement—the initial statement made by attorneys for each side, outlining the facts each intends to establish during the trial.
律师开场辩论

opinion—a formal statement of reasons for a judgment given.
判决理由

opinion evidence—evidence of what the witness thinks, believes or infers in regard to fact in dispute, as distinguished from his personal knowledge of the facts; not admissible except (under certain limitations) in the case of experts.
意见证据(根据英美法意见证据规则,普通证人意见不可采,专家证人意见具有可采性,但在适用上都有例外。)

oral argument—an opportunity for lawyers to summarize their positions before the court and also to answer the judges' questions.
口头辩论

ordeal—an ancient test of guilt or innocence by subjection of the accused to severe pain, survival of which was taken as divine proof of innocence.
无罪测试;清白测试(使被告遭受痛苦的一种测试有罪或清白的古老的方法,能够幸存的被神灵证明是清白的。)

order—a direction of a court made or entered in writing. One which terminates the action itself, or decides some matter litigated by the parties.
命令;法庭作出的书面命令

order assigning residue—a probate court order which names the persons entitled to receive parts of an estate and that share allotted to each.

遗嘱法庭遗产分配令

ordinance—a local law or regulation enacted by a municipal government. It has no effect outside that city or village.

地方性法规或规章

organic law—the fundamental law of a country, state, or society; the law upon which its legal system is based, whether that law is written, such as a constitution, or unwritten.

组织法;基本法;建制法

organized crime—a syndicate of professional criminals who rely on unlawful activities as a way of life. Often called the family, the mafia, or the mob.

帮会犯罪;集团犯罪

original jurisdiction—the authority of a court to hear and decide a matter; prior to any other court's review of the matter.

(法院的)最初审理权

oust—deprive (someone) of or exclude (someone) from possession of something.

剥夺;排除(某人占有某物)

ouster—ejection from a freehold or other possession; deprivation of an inheritance.

(从不动产或其他占有中)排除;剥夺遗产

out—

1. no longer detained in custody or in jail.

不再被羁押或监禁

2. (of a jury) considering its verdict in secrecy.

裁审团秘密考虑其判决、裁定

outlaw—a person who has broken the law, esp. one who remains at large or is a fugitive.

歹徒;逃犯

out-of-court—(of a settlement) made or done without a court decision.

不经法院;被驳回

overreaching—in commercial law, taking an unfair advantage over another through fraudulent practices or abuse of superior bargaining power.

(商法中)滥用议价权;欺骗

overrule—a judge's decision not to allow an objection. Also, a decision by a higher court finding that a lower court decision was in error.

推翻;驳回;否决

例如:In 1991, the Court of Appeal overruled this decision. 1991 年,上诉法院驳回了这一判决。

overt act—open act; in criminal law, an outward act done in pursuance of a crime and in manifestation of an intent or design, looking toward the accomplishment of a crime.

公开的行为

owner—the person who has legal title to property; the person in whom ownership, dominion, or title of property is vested.

物主;所有人

ownership—one's exclusive right of possessing, enjoying, and disposing of a thing.

所有权

oyer—hearing. At common law, the reading to a defendant upon his demand the writ upon which the action is brought.

听诉;听审

P

pack—fill (a jury, committee, etc.) with people likely to support a particular decision or tendency.

挑选(陪审团员、委员会成员等)可能支持某个特殊决定或倾向的人

pain and suffering—a species of damages that one may recover for physical or mental "pain and suffering" that result from a wrong done or suffered. The loss of ability or capacity to work because of physical pain or emotional or mental suffering is a type of pain and suffering and a proper element of damages.

疼痛和痛苦;折磨

palimony—a court-ordered allowance for support paid by one person to his or her former lover or live in partner (living together out of wedlock) after they have separated.

分居扶养费;分手赡养费

> 这是一个新词汇,单词的前一部分 pal 的意思是伙伴,后一部分 alimony 的意思是扶养费,放在一起就是伙伴扶养费。夫妻按法庭判决离婚或合法

pander

> 分居后,原配偶中收入较多的一方应该付给另一方一定的赡养费。英语中管这种赡养费叫 alimony。由于婚姻的自由化,不少人同居多年都不愿意结婚,但是一旦他们分手,法律却无法在经济上保护同居者的利益。直到 20 世纪 70 年代,"分居扶养费"palimony 才首次登上美国法庭的"大雅之堂",从此未婚同居者分居后也可以理直气壮地向对方索取生活费了。alimony 一词的起源可以追溯到拉丁语 alere,其表示"滋养、喂养、使健壮、使生存",传到英语中自然就表示"赡养费"了。另外,除了 alimony 和 palimony,还有 flirt-imony 调情损失费,date-imony 约会补助费等名目。

pander—to pimp, to cater to the lust of another; a panderer is thus a pimp, procurer, male bawd, one who caters to the lust of others.

怂恿者;迎合(不良需求)

panel—

1. the jurors serving a specific court. See also *jury panel*.

全体陪审员

2. the three judges who sit together to decide cases brought before the Court of Appeals.

三位上诉法庭法官

paralegal—a person trained in subsidiary legal matters but not fully qualified as a lawyer, who typically works as an assistant to a lawyer.

律师助理(不完全具有律师资格,协助律师工作的人)

paramount title—a title that will prevail over another title asserted against it.

最优先的所有权

paramour—a lover; one who stands in the place of a husband or wife, but ordinarily without the legal rights attached to the marital relationship.

情人;情夫(妇)

parcener—at common law, one who jointly holds an estate by virtue of descent(i.e., inheritance).

共同继承人

pardon—a remission of the legal consequences of an offense or conviction, and often implicitly from blame.

宽恕；赦免

parens patriae—the government, or any other authority, regarded as the legal protector of citizens unable to protect themselves.

政府监护

parens patriae doctrine—the inherent power and authority of state to protect the person and property of a person who is legally unable to manage his/her own affairs.

政府监护原则

parental liability—responsibility of parents for tortious acts committed by their minor children. While at common law, parents did not have such liabilities, the fact that juvenile misbehavior resulted in uncompensated victims led many states to enact statutes imposing liability on parents for the tort of their minor child. These statutes vary widely, but usually limit the parents' liabilily to a small dollar amount.

父母对未成年子女的侵权行为应承担的责任

parenting time—the time a child spends with a non-custodial parent. Parenting time was formerly referred to as "visitation".

和父母团聚的时间；探望父母

parol—given or expressed orally.

口头的

parol evidence rule—when parties put an agreement in writing, all previous oral agreements merge with the writing and subsequent oral evidence cannot modify the agreement.

口头证据规则

> 作为合同解释规则，美国合同法中的"口头证据规则"是指："如果合同主体同意书面文件是他们之间协议条款的最终和完整的表达，那么协议前或同时的证据就不能被采纳用以否定或改变书面文件或给书面文件增加新的条款。"

parole—conditional release from prison before the end of sentence; if the parolee observes the conditions, he or she need not serve the rest of his or her term.

假释(刑满前有条件地被释放;如果被假释者遵守条件,将不必执行剩下的刑期。)

parricide—the killing of a parent or other near relative.

谋杀父母或其他近亲属

partial guardian—in cases under the Mental Health Code, a guardian with some—but not all—legal rights and powers over the person and/or estate of a developmentally disabled person. A partial guardian's rights, powers, and duties are specifically enumerated by court order.

有限监护人(有限的权利义务在法庭命令中载明)

partition—a judicial separation of the respective interests in land of joint owners or tenants in common thereof, so that each may take possession of, enjoy, and control his separate estate at his own pleasure.

财产分割

partnership—a contract of two or more competent persons to place their money, effects, labor and skill, or some or all of them, in lawful commerce or business, and to divide the profit and bear the loss in certain proportions; an association of two or more persons to carry on as co-owners a business for profit.

合作(伙伴)关系

party—

1. a person concerned with or taking part in a matter or transaction, such as a party to a contract.

一方

2. a person by or against whom a lawsuit is brought, i.e., the plaintiff or defendant.

一方;当事人(提起或应诉的人,原告或被告)

pass—

1. be transferred from one person or place to another, esp. by inheritance.

从某人或某处被转移,特别是通过遗产

2. (of a legislative or other official body) approve or put into effect (a proposal or law) by voting on it.

（立法机关或其他官方主体）通过投票表决，批准通过或使（提议或法律）生效

3. pronounce (a judgment or judicial sentence).

判决；宣判

pat—patent.

专利权

patent—

1. a government authority to an individual or organization conferring a right or title, esp. the sole right to make, use, or sell some invention.

政府授予个人或组织权利，特别是制作、使用，或销售一些发明的专有权。

2. obtain a patent for (an invention).

获得（发明）专利

patentee—a person or organization that obtains or holds a patent for something.

专利权所有人

patent infringement—the act of trespassing upon the incorporeal rights secured by a patent; any person who, without legal permission, makes, uses, or sells to another to be used, the thing which is the subject matter of any existing patent, is guilty of an infringement, for which damages may be recovered at law or which may be remedied by a bill in equity for an injunction.

专利侵权

patent office—an office from which patents are issued.

专利授予办公室

paternity—fatherhood.

父子关系

paternity suit—a suit to establish the identity of a child's father and to determine the father's obligation to support the child.

亲子鉴定并确定父亲抚养义务的诉讼

patricide—the killing of one's father.

杀父

patronage—giving either protection or support.
赞助；资助

pauper—indigent; one who is unable to provide his own support and is otherwise without financial resources. Under the Equal Protection Clause to the United States Constitution, indigents and paupers may be excused from paying certain court costs and other legal fees so that they may have equal access to the courts.
贫民；被救济者

pawn—to give personalty to another as security for a loan; property deposited with another as security for the payment of a debt.
典当物；抵押物

payee—any person to whom a debt should be paid.
受款人；收款人

peaceable possession—possession that is continuous and not interrupted by adverse suits or other hostile action intended to oust the possessor from the land.
和平拥有；不间断的占有

peace officer—any public officer or official having authority to arrest to enforce the law and preserve the peace, and generally includes any sheriff or deputy sheriff, any state or municipal police officer, and any state conservation officer. It may also include judges of courts of criminal jurisdiction. Some other public officials (i.e., Mayor) may be designated by law as a peace officer for specific limited purposes.
太平警官（有逮捕权，执行法律以及维护和平的公共事务官员，通常包括治安官、市政警察和保安员。）

penal—of, relating to, or prescribing the punishment of offenders under the legal system.
刑事的；刑罚的

penalize—(*often be penalized*) make or declare (an act or offense) legally punishable.
作出或宣布（行为或犯罪）在法律上的可罚性

penalty assessment—procedure in which traffic offender is allowed to mail in a fine (plead guilty by mail). Points may be assessed against the person's driving record for penalty assessment offenses.

（交通违章）处罚认定

pendente lite—during litigation.

在诉讼过程中

per capita—a method by which an estate is divided equally among a given number of persons.

人均；均等分割不动产的方式

per curiam—by decision of a court in unanimous agreement.

法庭一致通过

peremptory—not open to appeal or challenge.

强制的；不得上诉和挑战的

peremptory challenge—the right of the prosecution or defendant to challenge (remove) a certain number of jurors without giving any cause or reason. The right of the parties at a hearing to challenge a certain number of jurors without giving cause.

无因回避（不陈述理由而要求陪审团回避的权利）

peremptory writ—a species of original writ commencing certain lawsuits at common law and directing the sheriff to have the defendant appear in court, provided that the plaintiff has given the sheriff security for the prosecution of the claim.

拘传票

perfect—satisfy the necessary conditions or requirements for the transfer of (a gift, title, etc.).

转移（礼物、权利等）满足必要条件或要求

perfect obligation—one which gives a right to another to require us to give him something or not to do something. These obligations are either natural or moral, or they are civil.

合法的债务；具有完备手续的债务

performance—the fulfillment of an obligation; a promise kept; refers especially to completion of one's obligation under a contract.

执行；履约

performance bond—a bond which guarantees against breach of contract.

履约保证书

peril—risk, such as the risk that is insured in an insurance policy.

冒险；危险

例如：The embankment is in great peril. 河堤岌岌可危。

perjure—(*perjure oneself*) willfully tell an untruth when giving evidence to a court; commit perjury.

（作证时）发伪誓；伪证罪

perjured—(of evidence) involving willfully told untruths.

伪证

perjury—the offense of willfully telling an untruth, especially in a court, after having taken an oath or made an affirmation.

伪证罪；在法庭上发誓或声明后作虚假证词

permanent injunction—one intended to remain in force unless modified by a later decree of a court.

永久禁止令（故意使其有效，除非被其后的法庭判决更改。）

permanent ward—a child who is permanently placed under the care of the court or other guardian because the parents' rights to the child have been permanently terminated by the family division of the circuit court.

永久被监护儿童；儿童因父母权利被法庭终止，而由法庭或其他人监护

permissive—allowed or optional, but not obligatory.

许可的；可选择的；非必须的

perpetuity—a thing that lasts forever or for an indefinite period, in particular.

永久的或无限期的事物

per procuration—from Latin *procurare*, meaning "to take care of", is the action of taking care of, hence management, stewardship, agency. The word is applied to the authority or power delegated to a procurator, or agent, as well as to the exercise of such authority expressed frequently by procuration (*per* *procurationem*), or shortly *per pro.*, or simply *p.p.*

由……代理；代签

per se law—In the Motor Vehicle Code, the per se crime is driving with a blood alcohol level of .08 or greater, as established through a valid testing procedure. No proof is required to show that the defendant was under the influence since the law concludes that driving with a blood alcohol content (BAC) of .08 or greater is driving while intoxicated. (DWI can be proved by other evidence even if a defendant's BAC is less than .08.)

醉驾自证法（驾驶机动车时，当然的犯罪是指驾驶员体内每 100 毫升血液酒精含量超过 80 毫克，这个事实本身自动被认定为醉驾，不需要其他证据。）

personal injury—injury inflicted on a person's body or mind, as opposed to damage to property or reputation.

人身伤害；对身体或精神造成伤害，与财产或名誉损害相对

personal jurisdiction—is a court's jurisdiction over the parties to a lawsuit, as opposed to subject-matter jurisdiction, which is jurisdiction over the law and facts involved in the suit. If a court does not have personal jurisdiction over a party, its rulings or decrees cannot be enforced upon that party, except by comity; i.e., to the extent that the sovereign having jurisdiction over the party allows the court to enforce them upon that party. A court that has personal jurisdiction has both the authority to rule on the law and facts of a suit and the power to enforce its decision upon a party to the suit. In some cases, territorial jurisdiction may also constrain a court's reach, such as preventing hearing of a case concerning events occurring on foreign territory between two citizens of the home jurisdiction.

州域管辖权；区域管辖权

personal property—all of someone's property except land and those interests in land that pass to their heirs.

个人财产（不包括地产以及转移给继承人的有关地产的权益）

personal protection order—one of two types of orders issued by a circuit court protecting an individual from stalking or domestic abuse.

个人保护令；人身保护令

personal recognizance—the release that is gained in a criminal case without the necessity of having to post money or have any surety sign a bond with the court. The court takes the defendant's word that he or she will appear for a scheduled matter or when advised to appear.

自我担保获释（被告在刑事案件中，无需缴纳保证金或由保证人签署保证协议而获得释放。法庭要求被告承诺在被传唤时到庭。）

personalty—a person's personal property. The opposite of *realty*.

动产（与不动产相对）

per stirpes—by right of representation; it is the method of dividing an estate where a group of distributees take the share to which their deceased ancestor would have been entitled, such as where children take the share to which their parents would have been entitled.

代位继承（遗产继承的一种方式）

> "代位继承"是一种继承制度，和"本位继承"相对应，是法定继承的一种特殊情况。它是指被继承人的子女先于被继承人死亡时，由被继承人子女的晚辈直系血亲代替先死亡的长辈直系血亲继承被继承人遗产的一项法定继承制度，又称间接继承、承租继承。先于被继承人死亡的继承人，称被代位继承人，简称被代位人。代替被代位人继承遗产的人称代位继承人，简称代位人。代位人代替被代位人继承遗产的权利，叫代位继承权。

pertain—belong to something as a part, appendage, or accessory.

附属物；配件

petit—(of a crime) petty.

（犯罪）轻微的；次要的

petition—

1. an application made in writing to a court.

上诉状

2. In juvenile delinquency or child protective proceedings before the family division of the circuit court, a petition is the instrument used to set forth the allegations (complaint) against the party before the court. Petitions in such proceedings must be verified. Jurisdiction of the court can only be invoked by petition. See *child protective proceedings*, *juvenile delinquency proceedings*, *verification*.

起诉状;起诉书(在巡回法庭审理的少年犯罪或儿童保护程序中,起诉书是提起控诉的正式文书,是法院行使管辖权的依据。)

petit jury—the ordinary jury (of 6—12 persons) selected to hear the trial of a civil or criminal case and to determine issues of fact; so called to distinguish it from the grand jury.

小陪审团(陪审民事或刑事案件并决定事实问题的6—12人的小陪审团,区别于大陪审团。)

petty larceny—theft of personal property having a value less than a legally specified amount.

轻微盗窃罪

petty misdemeanor—a crime that allows less than six months of jail time upon conviction.

轻微犯罪(一般不超过6个月刑期)

physical evidence—The evidence that is presented during a trial usually plays a major role in the outcome. There are several types of evidence that can be used. One type, physical evidence, refers to items that can be brought into a courtroom for observation. Examples of this type of evidence include a bloody shirt, the mold of a foot print, and a bullet casing. In many instances, law officials are the first to discover and handle physical evidence. This is because such items are often obtained from crime scenes, meaning that suspects have not been named, and therefore no lawyers are involved at that point. The manner in which this type of evidence is collected and maintained is important because such items can be crucial in winning a case. If it is not obtained according to procedure or it is damaged, it may be deemed inadmissible or useless.

物证

physician-patient privilege—privilege protecting communications (including oral statements by the patient and visual observations by the physician) between a physician and a patient in the course of their professional relationship from disclosure unless consent is given by the patient. This privilege is statutory and did not exist under common law. Its purpose is to allow persons to secure medical service without the fear of betrayal, or humiliation. Treatment need not be rendered.

医患保护隐私特权

pierce the corporate veil—to prove that a corporation exists merely as a completely controlled front (alter ego) for an individual or management group, so that in a lawsuit the individual defendants can be held responsible (liable) for damages for actions of the corporation.

揭开公司面纱;揭下法人面纱

> 通常情况下,公司人格理论承认公司是独立的主体,享有与自然人一样的人格,从而使得公司可以承担独立的责任,使股东承担有限责任。但在特定情况下,公司的独立人格可能遭到否认,使股东直接对公司债务承担责任。这就是通常所谓的"揭开公司面纱"原则。"揭开公司面纱"是普通法系国家法律在处理公司人格否认时所运用的重要方法。著名的1905年美国诉密尔沃冷藏运输公司一案中,法官认为:"公司形式不得被用来破坏公共便利,或使不法正当化,或用来维护欺诈、保护犯罪,否则法律将视公司为数人之组合。"目前,该原则已为一些大陆法系国家所继受。揭开公司面纱原则是指,在一定条件下,法院可能会拒绝承认公司人格的独立存在,即使它符合法律上设立公司的全部要件。该原则的核心是否定公司人格,使股东对公司的债务承担责任。这一原则是对公司独立人格和股东有限责任的一种修正,其主要功能是对股东滥用有限责任的情形予以矫正和补救。

piracy—the practice of attacking and robbing ships at sea.

海盗行为

plagiarism—appropriation of the literary composition of another and passing off as one's own the product of the mind and language of another.

抄袭;剽窃

plain error (rule)—rule requiring an appellate court to reverse a conviction and award a new trial when an obvious error in the trial proceedings, which was not objected to during the trial and went uncorrected by the trial court, affected the defendant's fundamental right to a fair trial.

上诉法院对一审法院的明显程序错误进行重审(原则)

plaintiff—In civil cases, the person who initiates the lawsuit is the plaintiff. In criminal matters, the prosecuting attorney is the plaintiff.

原告（民事诉讼中，提起诉讼的一方是原告；刑事诉讼中检察官是原告。）

plain view doctrine—the doctrine that permits a law enforcement officer to lawfully seize incriminating evidence not specifically sought but readily visible in the course of a valid search.

紧急侦查原则（该刑事程序规则是指如果警方有理由相信某物品是犯罪证据，警方有权在没有搜查证的情况下查封或使用在法律调查中从法律角度认定是犯罪证据的物品。）

plea—the defendant's response to a criminal charge (e.g., guilty, not guilty, nolo contendere).

抗辩；被告对刑事指控的答复（例如有罪、无罪以及无罪申诉。）

plea agreement—an agreement between the prosecutor and the defendant, presented for the court's approval, regarding the sentence the defendant should serve upon a plea of guilty, an Alford plea, or a no contest plea. Typically, the defendant pleads guilty in exchange for some form of leniency. For example, the defendant may plead to lesser charges so that the penalties are diminished. Or, the defendant may plead to some, but not all of the charges so that others are dropped. The agreement may include sentencing recommendations. Such bargains are not binding on the court.

认罪协议

plea-bargaining—in criminal cases, a process of negotiation between the prosecutor and defense counsel that typically involves the prosecutor's agreement to dismiss pending criminal charges against the defendant in exchange for the defendant's plea of guilty to another (usually lesser) offense.

认罪协商（一种在刑事案件中公诉人与辩护人的谈判过程，特别是指公诉人和辩护人依据由公诉人提出的协议，撤销对被告的原刑事指控来交换被告对另一个〈通常是较轻的〉罪名的请求。）

plead—in a criminal case, to respond to the charge (e.g., by pleading guilty, not guilty, nolo contendere, etc.).

答辩（刑事案件中，对指控的答复，例如认罪、不认罪以及无罪申诉。）

pleadings—in a civil lawsuit, the papers that set forth the parties' claims and defenses. The plaintiff's pleadings state his or her claims against the defendant. The defendant's pleadings state his or her defenses to the plaintiff's claims.

民事诉讼答辩状；诉状

pledge—

1. a thing that is given as security for the fulfillment of a contract or the payment of a debt and is liable to forfeiture in the event of failure.

（用于确保履行合同或偿还债务的）抵押物

2. give as security on a loan.

抵押

plenary guardian—under the Mental Health Code, a guardian with full power over the person and/or estate of a developmentally disabled person.

全权监护人（依据精神健康条例，监护人对被监护人及其财产有充分的权利。）

pocket veto—a means by which the president of the United States may effectively veto an act of Congress without exercising the presidential veto right. Under the U. S. Constitution, the president must veto legislation within 10 days after it has been passed by both the Senate and the House of Representatives, or else the legislation will become law. However, if Congress adjourns before the end of the 10-day period the legislation will only become law if the president has signed it. Accordingly, the president may effectively veto legislation that was passed within the last 10 days of the congressional session merely by not signing it into law.

搁置否决权

> 美国总统可以否决国会通过的法案，退还国会复议，如该法案经国会两院以2/3的多数通过，则即行生效；在法案送交总统签署的10天内（不包括星期天）未被退回国会，就被认为总统已经批准；如国会在规定期限届满之前休会，总统就可以把法案搁置不理，装进自己的口袋，使法案自行无效，这就是所谓的搁置否决权。

points or point information—penalty points imposed by the Motor Vehicles Division after conviction of a traffic offense.

（交通违章）扣分

police power—power of a government to exercise reasonable control over people and property within its jurisdiction in the interest of general security, health, safety, morals, and welfare. It is generally regarded as one of the powers reserved to the states under the U.S. Constitution. In considering cases involving the exercise of police power, the courts have applied a doctrine called balance of interests to determine when the public's right to health and well-being outweighs private or individual concerns. Of equal concern is that due process of law be observed.

社会治安综合治理权(包括政府的安全、健康、道德、教育等权力。)

> 根据宪法,州拥有非列举权力。联邦政府拥有列举性的权力,而没有在宪法中明确列举的权力留给各州行使。社会治安综合治理权是美国宪法性法律中用以指政府为全体公民的利益管理安全、卫生、福利和伦理等方面事务的权力的名称,由于宪法中体现了州处理内部事务的原则,所以大部分的社会治安综合治理权属于州。

policy—a contract of insurance.
保险单

polling the jury—a practice whereby the jurors are asked individually whether they assented, and still assent, to the verdict.
陪审团投票表决

poll tax—a capitation tax; a tax of a fixed amount upon all the persons, or upon all the persons of a certain class, resident within a specified territory, without regard to their property or the occupation in which they may be engaged.
人头税

polygamy—in criminal law, the offense of having more than one spouse at one time.
多配偶罪;重婚罪

polygraph—a machine designed to detect and record changes in physiological characteristics, such as a person's pulse and breathing rates and used esp. as a lie detector.

测谎仪（一种用来检测和记录生理特征，例如脉搏和呼吸频率的设备，尤其用来作为测谎仪使用。）

posse—(*historical*) a body of men, typically armed, summoned by a sheriff to enforce the law.

地方武装团队（历史原因形成的，由县司法长官召集执行法律的武装团队。）

posse comitatus act—a federal statute prohibiting use of the military in civilian law enforcement.

禁止使用武装力量强制执行民事判决的联邦条例

possess—have possession of as distinct from ownership.

占有（区别于所有权）

possession—

1. visible power or control over something, as distinct from lawful ownership; holding or occupancy.

占有；实际控制；持有；居住（区别于合法所有）

2. an item of property; something belonging to one.

财产，财物

possessor—a person who takes, occupies, or holds something without necessarily having ownership, or as distinguished from the owner.

占有人或持有人（无所有权，区别于所有权人）

possessory action—a lawsuit brought for the purpose of obtaining or maintaining possession of real property and not for a determination of rightful title.

确认所有权的诉讼

possessory interest—a right to exert control over certain land to the exclusion of others, coupled with an intent to exercise that right.

（排他性）占有权益

postnuptial agreement—an agreement entered into by a husband and wife to determine the rights of each in the other's property in the event of death or divorce.

婚后协议

pourover—a provision in a will, or a whole will, declaring that money or other valuables are to be distributed to a previously established trust; in rare instances, a provision in a trust placing the trust assets in a will.

"倾倒"条款;财产"倾倒"(遗嘱的一条或整个遗嘱声明金钱和其他有价值的财务全部归入以前所设立的信托。)

power of appointment—power to decide the disposal of property, in exercise of a right conferred by the owner.

财产处理决定权,(决定遗产归属的)提名权

power of attorney—a written instrument appointing and authorizing a person to act in the place of another as agent or substitute. One holding a power of attorney is called an attorney in fact, and may or may not be a lawyer.

授权委托书(指定或授权代理人的书面文书,持有该文书的人被视为事实代理人,事实代理人可以不是律师。)

practice—

1. the carrying out or exercise of a profession, especially that of a lawyer or doctor.

执业,尤其指律师或医生

2. actively pursue or be engaged in (a particular profession, especially law or medicine).

从业(尤其指法律或医学)

praecipe—a form used in some jurisdictions to ask a court clerk to do something (such as issue a summons after a complaint is filed, etc.).

法院书记员工作任务一览表

preamble—the introductory part of a statute, deed, or other similar document, stating its purpose, aims, and justification.

序言(法规、契约或其他类似文书中的介绍部分,描述其目的、目标及正当性。)

precatory—(in a will) expressing a wish or intention of the testator that is advisory but not binding.

遗嘱中委托的;嘱托的(遗嘱人表达的,供参考但不具有法律约束力的愿望或意图。)

precedent—a previous case or legal decision that may be or must be followed in subsequent similar cases.
判例,先例

precept—a writ or warrant.
命令书;令状

preempt—
1. (of a superior authority) take action to prevent an inferior authority from acting.
先发制人
2. take (something, esp. public land) for oneself so as to have the right of preemption.
先占(尤其指土地)

preemption—
1. action by a superior authority that prevents an inferior authority from acting.
优先行使权
2. the purchase of goods or shares by one person or party before the opportunity is offered to others.
优先购买权

prefer—submit (a charge or a piece of information) for consideration.
提交(指控或信息)供审理

preference—a prior right or precedence, esp. in connection with the payment of debts.
优先权(尤其指债权人优先得到偿还的权利)

prejudice—harm or injury that results or may result from some action or judgment.
1. give rise to prejudice in (someone); make biased.
引起偏见
2. cause harm to (a state of affairs).
造成损害

prejudicial—harmful to someone or something; detrimental.

侵害行为

prejudicial error—"reversible error"; an error in the course of a trial serious enough to require an appellate court to reverse the judgment.

"可逆转的错误";可更改的错误(初审法院审理过程中的严重错误,须上诉法院撤销原判决。)

preliminary examination—a hearing in a felony case before a district judge at which the prosecution presents evidence (the defendant and his or her counsel being present) from which the district judge decides whether there is probable cause to believe that a crime has been committed, that the defendant committed the crime and to "bind over" or refer the defendant to the circuit court for trial. Testimony of some witnesses and presentation of some exhibits are offered at such examination.

预先审查;初步审查

> 审理重罪前,原告向地方法院法官和原告及其辩护人提交证据,地方法院法官决定是否有理由相信案件的发生和被告实施了犯罪行为,以及"发誓"或将被告送交法庭审理。该审查程序中包括询问证人及展示证物。

preliminary hearing—the first stage of processing a juvenile delinquency or child protective proceeding when the juvenile is in custody, or custody/placement is requested.

预审(在少年犯被拘留、羁押的情况下,审理少年犯罪或儿童保护程序的第一步。)

preliminary inquiry—the first stage in the processing of a child protective or juvenile delinquency case when the juvenile is not in custody. An informal procedure in the family division of the circuit court.

初步调查(当少年犯未被羁押时,这是审理儿童保护或少年犯罪程序的第一步,是巡回法庭家庭法部门的非正式程序。)

premeditate—think out or plan (an action, esp. a crime) beforehand.

预谋(犯罪行为)

premises—a house or building, together with its land and outbuildings, occupied by a business or considered in an official context.

房产;房屋(及其附属建筑、地基等)

prenuptial agreement—an agreement made by a couple before they marry concerning the ownership of their respective assets should the marriage fail.
婚前协议(如果离婚各自的财产所有权归属)

preponderance of evidence—greater weight of evidence, or evidence which is more creditable and convincing to the mind, not necessarily the greater number of witnesses.
优势证据

> 优势证据制度就是指在民事诉讼中实行优势证据证明标准,即如果全案证据显示某一待证事实存在的可能性明显大于其不存在的可能性,使法官有理由相信它很可能存在,尽管还不能完全排除存在相反的可能性,也应当允许法官根据优势证据认定这一事实。

prerogative—
1. a right or privilege exclusive to a particular individual, institution, or class.
特权
2. arising from the prerogative of the Crown (usually delegated to the government or the judiciary) and based in common law rather than statutory law.
特权(基于普通法而非成文法,由王权特权产生,通常代表政府或法官。)

prerogative writ—an order in exercise of a court's discretionary power.
特权令状

prescription—the establishment of a claim founded on the basis a long or indefinite period of uninterrupted use or of long-standing custom.
习惯;惯例

prescriptive—(of a right, title, or institution) having become legally established or accepted by long usage or the passage of time.
约定俗成的;惯例的

presentence investigation—investigation of the relevant background of a convicted offender. Usually conducted by a probation officer and designed to act as a sentencing guide for the judge. See *presentence report*.

判决前调查;量刑调查(对罪犯相关背景的调查,通常由缓刑监督官实施,作为法官的判决指导。)

presentence report—written report prepared by the Probation Department containing the family and personal history of the accused, evaluation of the crime and its ramifications, and recommendations as to sentencing. Required in all felony cases. Presented to the judge as a guide in determining sentence.

判决前调查报告;量刑前报告

> 判决前调查报告内容包括对犯罪嫌疑人的个人情况和在社区中的有关情况的详细说明,以及这些情况与犯罪关系的分析,同时提出对犯罪嫌疑人的判决建议等。

presentment—a written finding by a grand jury of an offense, from their own knowledge or observation.

大陪审团观察报告(陪审团根据自身知识观察了解情况所提出的报告)

presiding judge—

1. the judge conducting a hearing or trial; the judge in charge of a case.

审判长;庭长

2. formerly, the chief judge of a court composed of two or more judges. The presiding judge in this sense is now called the Chief Judge.

首席法官

presumption—attitude adopted in law or as a matter of policy toward an action or proposal in the absence of acceptable reasons or proof to the contrary.

推定;假设

presumption of fact—an inference as to the truth or falsity of any proposition of fact, drawn by a process of reasoning in the absence of actual certainty of its truth or falsity, or until such certainty can be ascertained.

事实推定

presumption of innocence—in American law, one of the most sacred principles presumes a defendant innocent until proven guilty. What that means is the prosecution must prove beyond a reasonable doubt, each element of the

presumption of law

crime charged.

无罪推定；疑罪从无

> presumption 来自拉丁文 praesumprio，也称"假定"。它是现代刑事诉讼法中的一项原则，其含义是：任何人在法院作出有罪判决之前，不得认为其犯罪，并处以刑罚。所谓"推定"presumption，是指依照法律规定或者由法院按照经验法则，从已知的基础事实推断未知的推定事实的存在，并允许当事人提出反证予以推翻的一种证据法则。英美法理论上一般把推定分为：1. 不可反驳的法律推定 irrebuttable presumptions of law；2. 可反驳的法律推定 rebuttable presumptions of law；3. 可反驳的事实推定 rebuttable presumptions of fact。

presumption of law—a rule of law that courts and judges shall draw a particular inference from a particular fact, or from particular evidence.

法律推定

presumptive—giving grounds for the inference of a fact or of the appropriate interpretation of the law.

推定的；假定的

presumptive evidence—prima facie evidence or evidence that is not conclusive and that may be contradicted; evidence that must be received and treated as true and sufficient until and unless rebutted by other evidence, i. e., evidence that a statute deems to be presumptive of another fact unless rebutted.

推定证据

pretermitted child—a child born after a will is executed, who is not provided for by the will. New Mexico law provides for a share of estate property to go to such children.

遗腹子；被遗漏的继承人（因为孩子是遗嘱被执行后才出生的。）

pretrial conference—hearing in a criminal or civil case between the judge and the attorneys to discuss any questions or matters that can be resolved prior to the trial to assist in expediting or simplifying the trial. Such hearing is usually informal and without client participation.

预审会议；审前会议（刑事或民事案件审理前，法官和律师讨论可以在审判前解决的问题或事项,以加快或简化法庭审理,该审理通常是非正式的,没有委托人参加。)

pretrial intervention—programs to aid certain qualifying criminal defendants by diverting them from prosecution and enrolling them in rehabilitative programs. Upon successful completion of the required program(s), the criminal case is dismissed. Pretrial intervention is most often used in substance abuse and domestic violence where the crime charged is the defendant's first offense.

审前干预

pretrial hearing—see *pretrial conference*.

预审

pretrial release—release by sheriff's personnel after arrest and before any court appearance, but with a court appearance date.

保释;保外候审;取保候审

preventive detention—the imprisonment of a person prior to conviction, with the aim of preventing them from committing further offenses or of maintaining public order.

防范性拘留;预防性拘留(定罪前将被告关押,目的在于防止其继续犯罪,维持社会治安。)

prima facie—

1. The term "prima facie case" refers to those facts that will establish a party's right to legal relief if no evidence to the contrary is offered by the party's opponent.

表面上证据确凿的案件

2. The term "prima facie evidence" refers to evidence that is sufficient to prove a fact unless overcome by other evidence.

表面真实的证据(证据能充分证明事实,除非有其他更有力的证据)

principal—

1. one who has permitted or directed another (an agent) to act for his or her benefit. See also *agent*.

被代理人;委托人

2. the person having primary liability to pay a debt. See also *guarantor*, *surety*.

保证人;对债务负主要责任的人

3. property, as opposed to the income from the property. The term is often used to designate the property put into a trust. See also *trust*.

财产(区别于财产收入,经常被用来指定信托财产。)

priority of liens—the precedence in which liens on property are honored and paid. The general rule is "first in time, first in priority", although certain liens, such as those for unpaid taxes, may have priority regardless of when they attached to the property.

留置权优先受偿

prison—a building or place to which people are legally committed, typically as a punishment for crimes they have committed.

监狱;牢狱

prisoner—a person legally committed to prison as a punishment for crimes they have committed.

囚徒;囚犯

private law—a branch of the law (such as contract, tort, or property law) that deals with the relations between individuals or institutions, rather than relations between these and the government.

私法(合同、侵权、财产法等处理个人及单位之间关系的法律)

private practice—the work of a professional practitioner, such as a lawyer or doctor, who is self-employed or employed by a firm or group rather than by the government.

(律师)私人开业;(医生)私人诊所

privilege—

1. (in a parliamentary context) the right to say or write something without the risk of incurring punishment or legal action for defamation.

特权

2. grant a privilege or privileges to.

授予特权

privileged—(of information) legally protected from being revealed in the legal process or made public.

保密的(在法律程序中信息不被公开,不被公众知晓的)

privity—a relation between two parties that is recognized by law. Particularly by contract or property interest.

(同一权利或财产)当事人间的相互关系

probable cause—in criminal cases, reasonable grounds for believing that the facts justify issuance of an arrest or search warrant, or further legal action.

合理依据;合理根据

> 为了取得逮捕或搜查许可令,警方必须至少有足够理由显示某人可能已涉足刑事犯罪行为。要满足这一标准,应当提供诸如警方对犯罪行为的直接观察、告发者的直接观察和物证,或目击者对犯罪行为的描述等证据。当然,警方即使没有逮捕状也可以行动,但是在行动时必须已存在合理依据。合理依据所要求的证据标准不同于要证明有罪所要求的证据标准那样,后者必须是实质性的。合理依据与合理推论有关,它不是一个基于严格要求的技术判断。美国在判例实践中确立的标准坚持认为,当权力机构知晓的真实情况足以使人合理地注意到可以相信某种犯罪已经发生或正在发生时,便意味着存在合理依据。其证据强度约为50%以上。

probate—the process by which a decedent's estate is transferred to its rightful owners.

遗嘱检验程序,通过该程序死者的遗产转移给合法继承人

probate court—the court that handles the process by which a decedent's estate is transferred to its rightful owners. This court also handles matters relating to the commitment of mentally ill persons, guardianship matters, conservatorship matters, and trusts; however, if one of these matters arises from a child protective proceeding, a juvenile delinquency proceeding, or a domestic relations custody case, it is properly heard in the family division of the circuit court.

遗嘱检验法院;遗产认证法院

> 此法院受理涉及死亡事务的案件,包括遗嘱的合法性和遗产的管理。这些法院同时也有权处理收养事务。遗嘱检验法院法官经选举产生。

probate estate—estate property that may be disposed of by a will.
遗嘱处理遗产（根据遗嘱处理分配的财产）

probate register—a person who serves both as clerk of probate court and in a quasi-judicial manner in estates.
遗嘱检验登记员

probation—allowing a person convicted of an offense to remain in the community instead of going to jail or prison as long as the offender fulfills the conditions of the probation. One's probation is usually supervised by a probation officer. If a person violates probation, probation can be revoked and the defendant resentenced.
缓刑（由缓刑监督官监管）

probationer—a person who is serving a probationary or trial period in a job or position to which they are newly appointed.
缓刑犯

probation officer—a person appointed to supervise offenders who are on probation.
缓刑监督官；监护官

probative—having the quality or function of proving or demonstrating something; affording proof or evidence.
检验的；提供证明或证据

probative value—evidence has "probative value" if it tends to prove an issue. It is evidence that furnishes, establishes, or contributes toward proof.
证据的证明价值；证据力

pro bono—a term used to describe legal services provided to a client free of charge.
（法律等专业性）无偿服务

pro bono publico—for the public good or for the welfare of the whole, usually referring to voluntary service rendered by attorneys. Commonly abbreviated as "pro bono".
为公众利益

procedure—legal method; the machinery for carrying on the suit,

including pleading, process, evidence and practice.
诉讼程序

proceed—start a lawsuit against someone.
起诉

proceeding—any hearing or court appearance related to the adjudication of a case.
提起诉讼;诉讼程序

process—a court order to appear in court or enforce a judgment. Subpoenas and summonses are examples of process.
诉讼程序;法律手续

process server—a person employed to deliver a summons or complaint to a person being sued or to deliver a subpoena to a witness.
传票送达员

proclamation—a public announcement giving notice of an act done by the government or to be done by the people.
声明;公告书

pro con divorce—an uncontested divorce. The proceeding consists of a short hearing at which only plaintiff appears, the defendant not contesting anything, after which the divorce is granted.
无争议离婚;协议离婚(只有原告出庭,被告无争议,经简单审理后准予离婚。)

proctor—an attorney in an admiralty court.
海事法庭律师

procurator—an agent representing others in a court of law in countries retaining Roman civil law.
代理人;检察官

prohibition—
1. the action of forbidding something, esp. by law.
禁令
2. the prevention by law of the manufacture and sale of alcoholic beverages, esp. in the US between 1920 and 1933.

禁酒令(生产销售酒精饮料的禁令)

promisee—a person to whom a promise is made.

受约人；接受承诺者

promisor—a person who makes a promise.

立约人；契约者；做出承诺者

promissory—conveying or implying a promise.

承诺的；有约束力的

promissory estoppel—equitable doctrine allowing the court to enforce a promise even though a valid contract was not formed when a person reasonably acted in reliance on that promise. Promissory estoppel allows the court to compensate the person for their expenditures and/or to avoid the unjust enrichment of the other party.

允诺禁止反言原则；允诺后不得否认原则

> 允诺禁止反言原则产生于英美法系国家，它的构成须符合允诺、信赖和公平等要件，并具有暂时性、抗辩性等法律特征。允诺禁止反言原则克服了英美法传统的"约因理论"适用范围狭窄、缺乏灵活性等不足，因而被誉为是法院的一种尝试，以使救济与在整个商业交易中已提高的要诚信表述的良知齐头并进。

promissory note—a signed document containing a written promise to pay a stated sum to a specified person or the bearer at a specified date or on demand.

本票；期票

pronounce—declare or announce, typically formally or solemnly.

(庄重、严肃地)宣布；声明

proof—the evidence in a trial.

证明；证据

pro per litigant—a person who represents himself or herself in court without the aid of a lawyer.

自行辩护

property—anything that may be the subject of ownership. See *personal*

property, real property.
财产

property bond—a signature bond secured by mortgage or real property.
财产债券

propria persona—see *pro per litigant*.
自行辩护;自我辩护

prosecute—institute legal, especially criminal, proceedings against (a person or organization).
检举

prosecuting attorney—a public officer whose duty is the prosecution of criminal proceedings on behalf of the people of the State of Michigan.
检察官

prosecution—the institution and conducting of legal proceedings against someone in respect of a criminal charge.
提起刑事诉讼

prosecutor—a prosecuting attorney. An elected official in each county; the chief law enforcement officer of each county.
检察官;公诉人;原告

prosecutorial waiver—see *waiver of jurisdiction*.
起诉转移;管辖权转移

pro se litigant—a person who represents himself or herself in court without the aid of a lawyer.
自行辩护

protected person—a minor or legally incapacitated person whose estate is under the care of a conservator.
被保护人

protest—
1. a written declaration that a bill has been presented and payment or acceptance refused.
拒付声明

2. write or obtain a protest in regard to (a bill).
出具或收到拒付声明

prothonotary—(*chiefly historical*) a chief clerk in some courts of law.
首席书记官

protocol—

1. the official procedure or system of rules governing affairs of state or diplomatic occasions.
外交礼仪；规约程序

2. the original draft of a diplomatic document, esp. of the terms of a treaty agreed to in conference and signed by the parties.
外交条约的草案；议定书（尤指在会议中达成的条约）

prove—demonstrate the truth or existence of (something) by evidence or argument.
证明；检验

provocation—action or speech held to be likely to prompt physical retaliation.
挑衅；激怒

proximate cause—one of the four requirements for a tort; that which produces an event without which the injury would not have occurred.
近因

public act—an act of legislation affecting the public as a whole; public law.
有关国家、社会公众的法案；公法

public defender—a lawyer paid by the county to defend one who is indigent (without funds).
公共辩护律师

public domain—the state of belonging or being available to the public as a whole.
公有土地

public law—

1. the law of relationships between individuals and the government, such as constitutional, criminal, and administrative law.

公法（调整个人和政府间关系的法律，例如宪法、刑法和行政法。）

2. another term for *public act*.

有关公众的法案

public nuisance—an act, condition, or thing that is illegal because it interferes with the rights of the public generally.

公害；妨害公共利益

public prosecutor—a law officer who conducts criminal proceedings on behalf of the government or in the public interest.

公诉人；检察官

public trust doctrine—The public trust doctrine obligates government to protect and preserve waterways for public uses. As opposed to one single law or policy, the public trust doctrine is a guiding principle of government, composed of a body of laws and legal precedents. The public trust doctrine asserts that the state holds water ways "in trust" for use by the public. These public uses typically include navigation, recreation, fishing, but in California, have been expanded to include ecological values. As the trustee for the citizens, the state is obligated by the doctrine to protect rivers and wetlands for use by the public. To better understand what the doctrine obligates the state to do and what implementation of the doctrine looks like, we must understand the doctrine's history and examine the role the public trust doctrine played in its most prominent case, the Mono Lake decision.

公共信托原则

> 公共信托原则的内涵可以概括为：政府对一些特殊的财产应承担起受托人的义务，即依财产本身的性质最大限度地保障社会公众能实现对这些财产所应当享有的权益。公共信托原则的这一概念包含了三个重要因素：公共信托财产、政府义务和社会公众的权益。这三个要素在逻辑上具有紧密的内在关系。
>
> 公共信托原则的相应内容在罗马法与在英国法上的体现尚处于简单而较为原始的状态。公共信托原则被引入美国后取得了迅猛的发展，主要体现在公共信托原则从对王权的限制转而成为对政府权力的限制。同时由于时代变迁等原因公共信托原则在这一阶段的发展中引发了诸多的分歧与争议。

> 美国不存在国王,公共信托原则也就不存在限制国王行使其所有权的问题,人们转而运用公共信托原则限制政府。美国早期最著名的公共信托原则案例——伊利诺伊中央铁路公司诉伊利诺伊州案就是一个典型的限制政府权力的例子。该案强调:"州政府不得放弃其对大片土地的管理权。"而且这里显而易见的是,受到限制的不仅仅是所有权,更多获得关注的是政府处置公共资源的行政权力。随之而来产生的问题是在多大的范围内限制政府的这一权力?如果公共信托原则要求政府维持公共资源的现状而绝对不得将其转让或不得更改其用途,则很难想象社会经济能得以正常发展。相反,如果公共信托完全默许政府遵循一般法则行使权力而无额外限制,则无法保证被异议的政府行为是出于公共目的而不仅仅是为了私人目的而把公共财产当作馈赠的礼物。那么公共信托原则的课题之一是能否找到这样一个定位:在涉及海洋、公共用地等利益交易的政府行为领域,既要适用严格于一般政府事务的标准,同时为政府能合理有效利用资源留有一定余地。由此,在市场经济深入发展之后私人主体则有更多机会以所有权等方式控制和占有自然资源。仅将政府权力作为公共信托原则的限制对象已远远不能满足公众对自然资源正当需求,也与公共信托原则思想的初衷不能完全相符。公共信托原则究竟应延伸至何处呢?

publish—communicate (a defamatory statement) to a third party or to the public.

向第三方或公众传播(诽谤言论)

punitive damages—damages exceeding simple compensation and awarded to punish the defendant; exemplary damages.

惩罚性损害赔偿

pur autre vie—In property law of the United States and some Canadian provinces, *pur autre vie* (Old French for "for another['s] life") is a duration of a property interest. While it is similar to a life estate, it differs in that a person's life interest will last for the life of *another person* instead of their own. For example, if Bob is given use of the family house for as long as his mother lives, he has possession of the house pur autre vie. Pur autre vie can occur when a contingent remainder is destroyed, in a Doctrine of Merger situation, where one person acquires the life estate of another and thereby destroys a remainder not already vested.

为他人的终生利益

purchase—

1. acquire (something) by paying for it; buy.

购买

2. the acquisition of property by means other than inheritance.

通过非遗产继承方式获得财产

purchase-money mortgage—a mortgage given, concurrently with a conveyance of land, on the same land, by the vendee to the vendor, to secure the unpaid balance of the purchase price.

置产抵押;购买财产担保(在转让地产的同时,买卖双方在交易的地产上办理抵押贷款,以确保余款的支付。)

purge—atone for or wipe out (contempt of court).

偿还;消除

purposely—deliberately or intentionally. As used in criminal statutes to define murder, "purposely" means intentionally, and as an act of the will, not accidentally.

故意地;蓄意地

purview—the enacting part or body of a statute as distinguished from other parts of it, such as the preamble.

主体条款;主体部分;范围

putative—alleged; supposed; commonly used in family law, e.g., a "putative" marriage is one which is actually void but which has been contracted in good faith by the two parties, or by one of the parties.

公认的;推定的;假定存在的;普遍认可的

Q

QC—Queen's Counsel. An archaic designation of a barrister, phased out in most jurisdiction, indicating of its title holder faithfulness to the Crown, but more recently, contribution to the profession of lawyers.

英国王室法律顾问

quaere—query; question; doubt.

询问

qualification—a condition that must be fulfilled before a right can be acquired; an official requirement.

资格;条件

quantum meruit—"as much as he deserves"; absent a contract/agreement, the law implies a promise to pay a reasonable amount for services or materials received from another.

合理价格;合理给付(应得的数额;在没有合同或协议的情况下,按劳动力价值及合理价格支付。)

quash—to nullify a conviction or order. For example, a motion to quash may be initiated for the purpose of setting aside a bind over after a preliminary examination.

撤销；废止（判决或命令）

quasi contract—an obligation of one party to another imposed by law independently of a formal agreement between the parties.

准合同

quasi judicial—authority or discretion vested in an officer, wherein his acts partake of a judicial character.

准司法的

Queen's Bench—(*in the UK*) a division of the High Court of Justice.

英国高等法院

Queen's Counsel—a senior banister appointed on the recommendation of the Lord Chancellor.

英国王室法律顾问

question of fact—an issue of factual circumstances, decided at trial, usually by a jury, and not appealable.

事实问题（通常由陪审团决定，不可上诉。）

question of law—an issue of the law's application, decided by a judge and appealable.

法律问题（法官决定，可以上诉。）

quid pro quo—("something for something" or "this for that" in Latin) means an exchange of goods or services, where one transfer is contingent upon the other. English speakers often use the term to mean "a favour for a favour". Phrases with similar meaning include: "give and take", "tit for tat", and "you scratch my back, and I'll scratch yours". In common law, *quid pro quo* indicates that an item or a service has been traded in return for something of value, usually when the propriety or equity of the transaction is in question. A contract must involve consideration that is, the exchange of something of value for something else of value.

In the United States, if the exchange appears excessively one sided, courts in some jurisdictions may question whether a *quid pro quo* did actually exist and the contract may be held void. In the U.S., lobbyists are legally entitled to support candidates that hold positions with which the donors agree, or which will benefit the donors. Such conduct becomes bribery only when there is an identifiable exchange between the contribution and official acts, previous or subsequent, and the term *quid pro quo* denotes such an exchange.

公平交易;交换条件;(租赁合同中)的让步条件

quiet—not interfered with, as by an adverse claim.

无打扰的;相安无事的

quitclaim—a formal renunciation or relinquishing of a claim.

放弃合法权利或放弃索赔

quitclaim deed—a deed which releases only the grantor's interest in the property, but nothing more.

产权转让契约

quorum—the number of members of any body who must necessarily be present in order for the body to transact business.

法定人数

quotation—the allegation of some authority or case, or passage of some law, in support of a position which it is desired to establish. Quotations when properly made, assist the reader, but when misplaced, they are inconvenient.

引用;引证

quotient verdict—a money verdict determined by the following process: each juror writes down the sum he wishes to award by the verdict. These amounts are added together and the total is divided by 12 (the number of jurors). The quotient stands as the verdict of the jury by their agreement.

以金额平均数作裁决

quo warranto—the name of a writ which brings a person into court so that it may be determined by what right he or she exercises his or her authority, usually brought by the Attorney General to test a person's claim of right to hold public office.

权利开示令状;追究权利依据令状

R

racketeering—originally, an organized conspiracy to commit extortion. Today, punishable offenses created by congress to seek the eradication of organized crime by establishing new penal prohibitions and by providing enhanced sanctions and new remedies to deal with the unlawful activities of those engaged in organized crime.

(有组织)敲诈勒索罪;诈骗罪

raised check—a check whose face amount has been increased from the amount for which the check was originally issued.

变造面额的支票

ransom—the money or other consideration paid for the release of a kidnapped person; to redeem from captivity by the payment of money or other consideration.

赎金;赎回

rape—the crime, committed by a man, of forcing another person to have sexual intercourse with him without their consent and against their will, esp. by the threat or use of violence against them.

rapist

强奸罪

rapist—a man who commits rape.
强奸犯

ratable—taxable; proportional, capable of estimation.
应纳税的

ratification—to sanction or affirm.
批准；追认；认可

ratiocination—the process of reasoned, rational, exact thought.
推理；推论

ratio decidendi—Latin phrase meaning "the reason" or "the rationale for the decision". The rule of law on which a judicial decision is based.
判决理由，司法判决的一个原则

> 判决理由是对法官提供的法律要点的裁定，因为在法官看来，法律要点对于证明他的特定判决的公正是必要的。这样的裁定是判案所依据的理由。它可以是在以前的案例中制定的法律规则，或被其他人视为具有约束力的法律规则。它也可以是物证事实。相比之下，附带意见是由法庭作出的与判决没有必然关系的有关法律的陈述。如何确认一个案件中的判决理由是一个根本性的问题。对于什么是理由以及如何发现它，人们存在很大的争议。不同法庭的法官可能会持有不同的观点，以致一个原判法庭中的判决理由可能被上诉法院视为附带意见，反之亦然。

rational basis test—a method of constitutional analysis under the equal protection clause used to determine whether a challenged law bears a reasonable relationship to the attainment of some legitimate governmental objective; the principle that the constitutionality of a statute will be upheld, if any rational basis can he conceived to support it.
合理依据标准

real estate—another term for *real property*.
不动产

real evidence—an object relevant to facts in issue at a trial, and produced for inspection at trial rather than described by a witness.

物证

reasonable belief—land, and generally whatever is erected or growing upon or affixed to the land.

不动产（土地及上面的附着物）

realty—a brief term for real property; also for anything which partakes of the nature of real property.

不动产

reasonable belief—probable cause. The facts and circumstances within an arresting officer's knowledge, and of which s/he had reasonably trustworthy information, sufficient in themselves to justify a person of average caution in believing that a crime has been or is being committed. Facts sufficient to justify a warrantless arrest.

合理推测

reasonable doubt—such a doubt as would cause a careful person to hesitate before acting in matters of importance to himself/herself.

合理怀疑

> 合理怀疑是在刑事诉讼中陪审团认定被告人有罪时适用的证明标准。即只有控诉方提出的证据对被告人有罪的事实的证明达到无合理怀疑的确定性程度时，陪审团方可裁判被告人有罪，其证据强度必须超过90%。

reasonable person—a phrase used to denote a hypothetical person who exercises the qualities of attention, knowledge, intelligence, and judgment that society requires of its members for the protection of their own interest and the interests of others. This term is commonly used in torts, where the test of negligence is based on either a failure to do something that a reasonable person, guided by considerations that ordinarily regulate conduct, would do, or on the doing of something that a reasonable and prudent (wise) person would not do.

普通正常人

reasonable suspicion

> 这是法律上的假想人,被理想化和标准化了,具有法律所期望的一般人所应有的谨慎和理性。当判断被告行为是否谨慎时,我们要看一个"普通正常人"处在被告所处的情况下,会怎样行为。如果"普通正常人"处在被告的情况不会像被告那样行动,那么,被告的行为就有问题,就不符合"普通正常人"的标准,就可能是不谨慎的。这是一个客观的标准,它并不照顾被告的特殊弱点。不管是性急、害羞、愚蠢、健忘、反应慢、智商低,还是长期粗心大意的人,都适用同样的标准。因为,不管被告人是聪明还是愚蠢,他们的行为所带来的危险是一样的,并不因为被告的能力弱而有所减轻。

reasonable suspicion—level of suspicion required to justify law enforcement investigation, but not arrest or search. A lower level of suspicion or evidence than probable cause. An officer has reasonable suspicion when the officer is aware of specific, articulable facts, together with rational inferences from those facts, which, when judged objectively, would lead a reasonable person to believe that criminal activity occurred or was occurring.

合理怀疑

> 合理怀疑是最典型的警察作为,是盘查犯罪嫌疑人时的一个前提条件,其证据强度约30%以上,比 probable cause 弱。美国判例一直尊重必须要把警察本身"专业知识与多年经验"列入考量。

rebut—to introduce evidence disproving other evidence previously given or reestablishing the credibility of challenged evidence.

反驳

rebuttal—a refutation or contradiction.

辩驳;举反正

rebuttal witnesses—witnesses introduced to explain, repel, counteract, or disprove facts given in evidence by the adverse party

(对方)反驳证人;提出反证的证人

recall—a method of removing a public official from office by submitting to popular vote the issue of whether the official should continue in office.

罢免权;召回

recall a judgment—reversing or vacating a decision based on a matter of fact, as opposed to a matter of law.

撤销判决

recall order—court order recalling a warrant or capias (writ requiring an officer to take a named defendant into custody).

召回令

receivership—the state of being dealt with by a court-appointed receiver.

破产案产业管理人的职务或任期

recess—a brief time set by the judge when those in court including the jury may be excused from the courtroom.

休庭

recital—the part of a legal document, such as a deed, that explains its purpose and gives factual information.

叙述(法律文书中解释目的、描述事实的部分)

reckless—careless, heedless, inattentive to duty.

轻率的;不顾后果的

reckless disregard—refers to an act or conduct destitute of heed or concern for consequences; especially foolishly heedless of danger; headlong, rash; wanton disregard or conscious indifference to consequences. This implies a consciousness of danger and a willingness to assume the risk.

漠视

reckless driving—the criminal offense of operating a motor vehicle in a manner that shows conscious indifference to the safety of others. It is the operation of an automobile under such circumstances and in such a manner as to show a willful or reckless disregard of consequences. In such cases the driver displays a wanton disregard for the rules of the road; often misjudges common driving procedures and causes accidents and other damages. It is usually a more serious offense than careless driving, improper driving, or driving without due care and attention and is often punishable by fines, imprisonment, and/or driver's license suspension or revocation. As a general rule something more than mere negligence in the operation of an automobile is necessary to constitute the offense.

鲁莽驾驶罪

recognition—subjecting to tax, under the federal income tax system; the inclusion of gain in income so that it may be subject to federal income taxes.

承认；认可缴税义务

recognizance—

1. an obligation entered into before a court of record or duly authorized magistrate, containing a condition to do some particular act, usually to appear and answer a criminal accusation.

保证书

2. a term used interchangeably with "bail bond" in many statutes and court opinions.

保释金

recommit—commit again.

再犯

reconciliation—when the parties in a divorce action are attempting to work out their differences and wish to have enforcement of their court-orders suspended.

（离婚诉讼中的）和解

record—the word for word (verbatim) account by the official court reporter/recorder of all proceedings at the trial. See *docket*.

庭审记录

record on appeal—the pleadings, exhibits, orders or decrees filed in a case in the trial court, a copy of the docket entries, and a transcript of the testimony taken in the case, forwarded to the appellate court.

上诉复审案卷（移交上诉法庭的案卷，包括一审中的答辩状、证据、裁定、判决、摘要和鉴定结论等。）

recorder—in some jurisdictions, a public officer who has charge of the records of deeds, and instruments relating to real property, and other legal instruments required by law to be recorded. Also, a court recorder. See *court recorder*.

书记员(负责记录契约、不动产证明以及其他法律文书的公职人员)

records retention and disposal schedules—a system or plan covering all records kept by a court which states what must be kept permanently and what may be disposed of and when.

案卷存废期限表(法庭保留记录的制度或方案,载有哪些记录应当长期保留,哪些记录可以销毁以及何时销毁。)

recover—find or regain possession of (something stolen or lost).

重新获得;找回(遗失或被盗的财物)

recovery—the action or process of regaining possession or control of something stolen or lost.

(重新占有或控制遗失或被盗财物的)诉讼或程序

recusal—the voluntary action by a judge to remove himself or herself from presiding in a given case because of self-interest, bias, conflict, or prejudice. Also, the process by which a judge is disqualified from a case because a party objects.

宣布不合格;取消资格;回避

recuse—(of a judge) excuse oneself from a case because of a possible conflict of interest or lack of impartiality

回避;要求撤换(法官因利益冲突,影响公正的理由回避案件的审理)

redemption—to purchase back; to regain possession by payment of a stipulated price; repurchase.

回赎;回购

red herring—an issue, whether legal or factual, raised in a case or law school exam which may be important generally but which has no relevant importance to the question at hand.

与本题不相干的法律问题或事实问题

redirect examination—opportunity to present rebuttal evidence after one's evidence has been subjected to cross-examination.

再主询问(最初询问证人的当事人或律师对证人进行再询问。)

redress—remedy or set right (an undesirable or unfair situation); remedy or compensation for a wrong or grievance.

（对令人厌烦的或不公正的情形的）矫正；（对错误及不满的）补偿

reenact—bring (a law) into effect again when the original statute has been repealed.

再制定（法律）

reentry—the action of retaking or repossession of property that had been let or granted.

所有权的再获得

reexamine—examine again or further.

再检查；再审问

referee—a person who takes testimony, prepares reports, and makes recommendations to the court in domestic relations, juvenile delinquency, designated proceedings involving juveniles, and child protective proceedings.

仲裁人；调解人

referral—(*referral to a protective service*) If it appears that the best interest of the child and of society will be served, the court may refer the matter at hand to a public or private agency providing such service.

托付；提供（保护）

refunding—the process of selling a new issue of securities to obtain funds needed to retire existing securities.

借款偿债；退款

refusal—the rejection of something to which a person is entitled, such as the rejection of goods under a contract.

拒绝；优先权

regina—(*in the UK*) the reigning queen (used following a name or in the titles of lawsuits, e.g., Regina v. Jones: the Crown versus Jones).

女王（英国案件名称中的公诉人）

registrar—an official responsible for keeping a register or official records.

注册主管

rehear—hear (a case or plaintiff) in a court again.

复审；再审

rehearing—another hearing of a civil or criminal case or motion by the same court in which the matter was originally decided in order to bring to the court's attention an error, omission, or oversight in the first consideration.

复审;再审

reinstate—restore to a former state, authority, station, or status from which one has been removed; as applied to insurance, to restore all benefits accruing under a policy.

恢复

rejoinder—at common law, a pleading made by the defendant in response to the plaintiff's replication.

被告的答辩

relation back—the principle that an act done at a later time is deemed by law to have occurred at a prior time. In practice, an amended complaint will relate back to the time of the filing of the initial complaint for the purpose of the statute of limitations.

回溯

relator—a person who brings a public lawsuit, typically in the name of the attorney general, regarding the abuse of an office or franchise.

公诉方;原告(尤其指以首席检察官的名义提起有关滥用政府及选举权的诉讼。)

release—

1. allow or enable to escape from confinement; set free

释放

2. remit or discharge (a debt).

免除债务

release-on-recognizance/ROR—the pretrial release of an arrested person on his or her written promise to appear for trial at a later date, without deposit of cash or any surety. Used primarily with defendants as an alternative to monetary bail. See *ror*, *recognizance*.

具结释放(不交纳保证金、不提供保证人,而根据书面保证,审前释放被逮捕的人。)

relevant—(of evidence or a fact) pertinent; closely connected or appropriate to the matter at hand, especially to the extent of proving or disproving the matter.

相关的;相应的

relief—the redress of a hardship or grievance.

缓解;救济

remainder—an interest in an estate that becomes effective in possession only when a prior interest (devised at the same time) ends.

剩余权利;残留权(在同时产生的以前地产的终止之后才能转让的地产)

remand—to send a case back to the court from which it came for further proceedings, e.g., defendant waives a preliminary examination, thus the case goes from district court to circuit court, usually because the defendant intends to plead guilty to a charge. The defendant then decides not to plead guilty and requests a preliminary examination; if the request is granted, the case is "remanded" to district court. To send back to the lower or trial court from which it was appealed, with instructions as to what further proceedings should be had there.

送还,还押;发回重审

remedy—a means of legal reparation.

救济;弥补

remission—the cancellation of a debt, charge, or penalty.

豁免;赦免

remit—

1. cancel or refrain from exacting or inflicting (a debt or punishment)

取消债务;免除惩罚

2. send back (a case) to a lower court

(将案件)发回下级法院

remittitur—an order reducing an excessive jury damages award. An order in cases when a jury has made an award of damages which is excessive in which the amount of damages is reduced.

因陪审团裁决的赔偿金额过高,而作出的减少损害赔偿金的法令

removal—the transfer of a state case to federal court for trial.

移送

rendition—the transfer of a fugitive from the asylum state to the demanding state.

引渡

renounce—formally declare one's abandonment of (a claim, right, or possession).

声明放弃(权利、财产等)

renunciation—the formal rejection of something, typically a belief, claim, or course of action.

声明放弃(信仰、权利等);宣布断绝关系

reorganization—in corporate income tax law, a group of transactions including mergers, consolidations, recapitalizations, acquisitions of the stock or assets of another corporation, and changes in form or place of organization. The common element in each of these transactions is that if various technical requirements are met, the corporations or shareholders involved may not recognize any gain for income tax purposes, and the transaction will occur tax free.

重组;改组

repeal—

1. *v.* revoke or annul (a law or congressional act).

撤销、废除(法律或国会法案)

2. *n.* the action of revoking or annulling a law or congressional act.

撤销、废除法律或国会法案的行为

replevin—a civil action to recover: 1) property unlawfully taken or held by another; and, 2) damages sustained by the unlawful taking or retention. An action for replevin is also known as an action for claim and delivery.

临时归还令,要求获取:1)被非法扣押或占有的财产;以及2)因非法扣押或占有产生的损害赔偿金的民事诉讼

replevy—recover (goods taken or detained) by replevin.

凭令状追回、取回(被扣押或被占有财物)

reply—a plaintiff's response to the defendant's plea.

答辩

reporter—

1. a court official responsible for the verbatim record of most court proceedings, including the questions addressed to, and answers made by, witnesses, usually for the purpose of preparing a verbatim transcript.

法院书记官

2. a court official responsible for compiling, indexing and publishing the opinions of an appellate court.

法庭编辑

reports—

1. court reports: published judicial cases arranged according to some grouping, such as court jurisdiction, period of time, subject matter or case significance.

法院报告

2. administrative reports or decisions: published decisions of an administrative agency.

行政报告或决议

represent—

1. be entitled or appointed to act or speak for (someone), esp. in an official capacity, as a lawyer for a client

代表

2. (*with clause*) allege; claim.

主张

repudiate—refuse to fulfill or discharge (an agreement, obligation, or debt).

拒绝履行或解除(协议、义务或债务)

request for production—a formal court process by which one party requests that another produce certain documents or other tangible items.

请求出示规则(指一方当事人要求对方当事人及其他任何人提供他们所拥有的或控制的文件、信息及其他有形物的程序和方法。)

rescission—cancellation of a contract.

废除(合同)

reservation—a right or interest retained in an estate being conveyed.
保留；预定

res gestae—
1. a matter incidental to the main or principal fact which helps explain that fact.
与主要事实相关，能够解释主要事实的事件
2. acts and words which are so related to an occurrence as to appear to be evoked and prompted by it.
有关行为和语言

res gestae witness—person taking part and/or witnessing or at the scene of a crime who may have personal knowledge concerning the crime or the defendant's possible involvement.
目击证人

residence—the place where one presently lives, does not require that it be a permanent home as is the case with "domicile".
居所；住处（目前正居住的地点，不必是永久性住所。）

residuary—of or relating to the residue of an estate.
有关剩余财产的

residue—the part of an estate that is left after the payment of charges, debts, and bequests.
（支付费用、债务及履行遗赠后的）剩余财产

res ipsa loquitur—the principle that the occurrence of an accident implies negligence if circumstances were such that it would not ordinarily otherwise have happened.
事实自证原则（指在缺乏充分证明的情况下由事实决定，这时举证责任转移至被告，被告必须证明，如果没有过失，事故也会发生。）

res judicata—a rule that a matter once judicially decided is finally and conclusively decided and cannot be relitigated.
一事不再理；既判力理论（对已判决的案件不能再提起诉讼。）

respondeat superior—"a superior must answer". The doctrine which holds that an employer or principal is responsible for the acts and omissions of employees or agents, when those acts are within the scope of their duties as employees or agents.

雇主责任原则(即雇主应对他们雇员的侵权行为负责。为了促进雇主的工作,即使他在雇佣、训练、监督或不解雇等方面都没有过失,雇主仍对雇员负有责任。)

respondent—a party against whom a motion is filed in the course of a lawsuit; analogous to a defendant or an appellee.

被告

rest—conclude the case for the prosecution or the defense in a law case.

结案

restitution—

1. in criminal cases, the amount of money that the convicted defendant is required to pay the crime victim to compensate for damages suffered as a result of the crime.

赔偿金(刑事案件中,赔偿金额应弥补因犯罪行为遭受的损害。)

2. in civil cases, the amount of money necessary to restore a party who was wronged to the position he or she was in prior to suffering the wrong.

赔偿金;补偿金(民事案件中,赔偿应弥补或恢复无过错方因对方的过错而造成的损失。)

restraining order—see *injunction*, *temporary restraining order*.

法院制止令

restraint of trade—action that interferes with free competition in a market.

贸易管制(干扰市场自由竞争的行为)

restricted delivery mail—a new postal classification which takes place of certified mail. County clerks frequently use this type of mail in conducting the court's business.

限制快件(一种用来处理法院事务的邮件)

restrictive covenant—a covenant imposing a restriction on the occupancy or use of land, typically so that the value and enjoyment of adjoining land will be preserved.

(对土地占有或使用的)限制性条款

retain—secure the services of (a person, esp. an attorney) with a preliminary payment.

（通过支付预付款的方式）聘用律师

retainer—a fee paid in advance to an attorney in order to secure or keep their services when required.

律师费；顾问费

retrial—a second or further trial.

复审；再审

retroactive—(*esp. of legislation*) taking effect from a date in the past.

有溯及力的

retrospective—(of a statute or legal decision) taking effect from a date in the past; retroactive.

有追溯力的

retry—try (a defendant or case) again

再审

return—an endorsement or report by an officer, recording the manner in which he or she served, the process or order of the court.

（传票等向法院的）交还；（执令官对执行结果的）汇报书、报告

return date—the day on which process is due or an order is to be answered. Also called *return day*.

期限届满

return of service—a certificate of affidavit by the person who has served process upon a party to an action, reflecting the date and place of service.

送达回执

reversal—an annulment of a judgment, sentence, or decree made by a lower court or authority.

驳回下级法院的判决

reverse—to set aside a judgment on appeal or proceedings in error; to annul; to vacate.

驳回；宣告无效；撤销

reversible error—an error during a trial or hearing sufficiently harmful to justify reversing the judgment of a lower court.

可撤销的错误判决；可逆性瑕疵（初审法院层级所犯的错误由于情节严重,上诉法院必须推翻初审法院的判决。）

reversion—the right, esp. of the original owner or their heirs, to possess or succeed to property on the death of the present possessor or at the end of a lease.

复归（原主或其继承人）的权利

reversioner—a person who possesses the reversion to a property or privilege.

回复享有未来所有权权的人

revert—(of property) return or pass to (the original owner) by reversion.

（财产）复归所有

review—a reconsideration of a judgment, sentence, etc., by a higher court or authority.

（上级法院或有权机构对判决）再审

revocable trust—a trust that the grantor may change or revoke.

可撤销信托

revocation (of driver's license)—judicial termination of a driver's license and privilege to drive after conviction of DWI. The license shall not be renewed or restored for the duration of the revocation, except that an application for a new license may be presented and acted upon by the division after the expiration of at least one year after date of revocation. This kind of revocation is distinguished from an administrative revocation, in which the Motor Vehicle Division may terminate a driver's license for up to one year.

吊销（驾驶执照）

revocation of will—the annulling, or rendering inoperative an existing will, by some subsequent act of the testator.

撤销遗嘱

Rex—(in the UK) the reigning king (used following a name or in the titles of lawsuits, e.g., Rex v. Jones: the Crown versus Jones).

（英国）案例标题中的公诉人；英国国王

RICO—(in the US) Racketeer Influenced and Corrupt Organizations Act.

RICO is a United States federal law that provides for extended criminal penalties and a civil cause of action for acts performed as part of an ongoing criminal organization.

反敲诈勒索和腐败组织法

> 简单地说,这是美国一个针对黑社会团伙犯罪法例。不需要证明某人直接参与犯罪,只要证明这个人属于某黑社会团伙,就可以将之起诉甚至定罪。

rider—an addition or amendment to a document, esp. a piece of legislation or a contract.

(法律或合同的)附加条款

right—a moral or legal entitlement to have or obtain something or to act in a certain way.

权利

right of representation—see *per stirpes*.

代理权

right of way—

1. the legal right, established by usage or grant, to pass along a specific route through grounds or property belonging to another.

通行权

2. the legal right of a pedestrian, rider, or driver to proceed with precedence over other road users at a particular point.

优先通行权

3. the right to build and operate a railroad line, road, or utility on land belonging to another.

用地权

Riot Act—a law passed by the British government in 1715 and repealed in 1967, designed to prevent civil disorder. The act made it a felony for an assembly of more than twelve people to refuse to disperse after being ordered to do so and having been read a specified portion of the act by lawful authority.

反骚乱法(英国政府于1715年通过,1967年废除,旨在预防民事骚乱。)

ripe for judgment—the point in a case when everything seems to have been done that ought to be done before entry of a final adjudication upon the rights of the parties.

可做判决的

ripeness（doctrine）—doctrine in constitutional law under which the Supreme Court, in accordance with its policy of self-restraint, will not decide cases in advance of the necessity of deciding them.

司法审查成熟原则

rise—(*chiefly Brit.*)(of a meeting or a session of a court) adjourn.

（英国）休会；休庭

rob—take property unlawfully from (a person or place) by force or threat of force.

抢劫

robber—a person who commits robbery.

抢劫者

robbery—the action of robbing a person or place.

抢劫案

Roman law—the law code of the ancient Romans, which forms the basis of civil law in many countries today.

罗马法

> 　　从狭义上说，罗马法是罗马共和国及罗马帝国所制定的法律规范的总称。罗马法的系统推广历史开始于东罗马帝国时期，于东罗马帝国皇帝查士丁尼一世时期达到鼎盛。之后东罗马帝国自我封闭，西罗马帝国灭亡，欧洲大陆进入文化文明相对黑暗的中世纪，罗马法的主体一度失传超过 600 年之久。但是随着罗马法完整文献的出土和文艺复兴的思想，罗马法成为整个欧洲大陆各个势力争相研究和推广的对象。文艺复兴后的以古罗马法研究为基础而建立起的欧洲法律体系，也被称之为"公共法"ius commune 或者"民法"Civil Law，被视为整个欧洲文明共有的财富，以示与公元 6 世纪前的古典罗马法的区别。广义的罗马法可以包括民法的这一层含义。

rule against perpetuities

ror—see *release on recognizance*.

具结释放

royalty—a share of the product or of the proceeds therefrom reserved by an owner for permitting another to exploit and use his or her property; the rental that is paid to the original owner of property based on a percentage of profit or production.

（发明、创意、财产等的）使用费

rubric—the title of a statute; a statute regarded as authoritative.

红头文件；规则；成规

rule—

1. a regulation or principle of law.

规则；法条

2. an order made by a judge or court with reference to a particular case only.

案件适用规则

rule against perpetuities—the rule that no contingent interest is good unless it must vest, if at all, not later than twenty-one years after some life in being at the creation of the interest.

禁止永久权规则

> 禁止永久权规则指一个可期待利益最晚必须在其设立时活着的有关当事人死后21年内得以实现，否则它将失效。所以，该规则也被称为21年规则，用来限制土地所有者设立的未来利益，其目的在于反对土地的所有者试图将地产无休止地保存在自己家族中，而妨碍财产的可转让性。这一规则只限制被授予人的未来利益，不确定的剩余权、成员开放的确定剩余权、期待利益和优先购买权（rights of first refusal）。它不限制确定的剩余权，也不限制授予人的未来利益。在适用禁止永久性规则时，第一步要考虑这一规则是否适用；第二步应确定实现未来利益的先决条件；第三步确定有关当事人，即其在权益设立之时是活着的，其生死与先决条件实现相关；第四步确定未来利益是否可在有关当事人死后21年内成为即得的，如果可以成为即得，则该未来利益有效，如果不可成为即得，则未来利益无效。禁止永久性规则不适用于慈善团体之间的赠与。

rule in Shelley's case—when in the same conveyance an estate for life is given to the ancestor with remainder to the ancestor's heirs, then the ancestor takes the fee simple (or fee tail) remainder estate and his heirs take nothing.

谢利案规则

> 如果授与者将终身财产给予A并将剩余遗产给予A的继承人，A就有了不限制继承者身份的土地权（fee simple，即 full title，完整权利），而A的继承人却被除外。如果给予A的继承人的剩余遗产得到确认，那么A就很难将财产进行转让，因为在他死亡之前，其继承人是无法确定的。

rule in Wild's case—in property law, a rule of construction by which a devise to "B and his children", where B has no children at the time the gift vests in B, was read to mean a gift to B in fee tail, the words "and his children" thus being construed as words of limitation and not words of purchase.

怀尔德案规则

rule nisi, or rule to show cause—a court order obtained on motion by either party to show cause why the particular relief sought should not be granted.

提审裁决；否定裁决缘由

rule of court—an order made by a court having competent jurisdiction. Rules of court are either general or special: the former are the regulations by which the practice of the court is governed; the latter are special orders made in particular cases.

法院规程（则）

rule of the road—a custom or law regulating the direction in which two vehicles (or riders or ships) should move to pass one another on meeting, or which should yield to the other, so as to avoid collision.

行路规则

S

safe conduct—immunity from arrest or harm when passing through an area.

安全通行权

salvage—payment made or due to a person who has saved a ship or its cargo.

（对船只、货物的）救援费

sanction—

1. a penalty for disobeying a law or rule.

制裁

2. official confirmation or ratification of a law.

正式确认或正式批准法律

sanctuary—immunity from arrest.

庇护

satisfaction—a written acknowledgment of receipt of payment or performance of a judgment which, when filed with the court, discharges the obligation.

偿还；(债务等的)清偿

satisfaction of judgment—payment of all monies determined to be owed pursuant to a court judgment.

履行判决；确定债务清偿的判决

saving—a reservation; an exception.

保留意见；例外

saving clause—an exception in a statute preserving prior law from repeal.

保留条款

seal—

1. *n*. a piece of wax, lead, or other material with an individual design stamped into it, attached to a document to show that it has come from the person who claims to have issued it.

密封文档

2. *v*. fix a piece of wax or lead stamped with a design to (a document) to authenticate it.

密封(证明真实有效)

search—examination of a person's house or other building or premises, or of his person, or vehicle, with a view to discovery of contraband, illicit or stolen property, or some evidence of guilt to be used in the prosecution of a criminal action.

搜查

search and seizure, reasonable—in general, an examination without authority of law of one's premises or person with a view to discovering stolen contraband or illicit property or some evidence of guilt to be used in prosecuting a crime.

合理的搜查和扣押

search warrant—a written order from a judge or magistrate directing an officer to search a specific place for a specific object, issued upon a showing of probable cause.

搜查证

second-degree—denoting a category of a crime, esp. murder, that is less serious than a first-degree crime.

二等的;二级的

secured debt—In collection or bankruptcy proceedings, a debt is secured if the debtor gave the creditor a right to repossess the property or goods used as collateral.

有抵押或担保的债务

sedition—conduct or speech inciting people to rebel against the authority of a state or monarch.

煽动叛乱;反政府的煽动行为或言论

seditious—inciting or causing people to rebel against the authority of a state or monarch.

煽动叛乱的

seditious libel—a published statement that is seditious.

发布煽动言论

seisin—possession of land by freehold.

依法占有不动产

seize—

1. (of the police or another authority) take possession of (something) by warrant or legal right; confiscate; impound.

依授权或职权占有;没收;扣押

2. (*also seise, be seized of*) (*English Law*) be in legal possession of.

(英国法)法定占有

self-defense—the defense of one's person or interests, esp. through the use of physical force, which is permitted in certain cases as an answer to a charge of violent crime or a tort.

正当防卫

self-incrimination (privilege against)—the constitutional right of people to refuse to give testimony against themselves that could subject them to criminal prosecution. The right is guaranteed in the Fifth Amendment to the U. S. Constitution. Asserting the right is often referred to as "Taking the Fifth".

自证其罪(美国宪法第五修正案及许多州的宪法和法律都规定"任何人都

不得被强迫在任何刑事案件中自证有罪"。)

self-proving—(of a will) accompanied by a witnesses' affidavit for which no oral testimony is needed to be admitted to probate.

自证(遗嘱)

self-proving will—a will whose validity does not have to be testified to in court by the witnesses to it, since the witnesses executed an affidavit reflecting proper execution of the will prior to the maker's death.

自证遗嘱

senator—a member of a senate.

参议员

sentence—the punishment imposed upon the defendant following a conviction in a criminal proceeding. sentence

宣判;判决

sentence report—a document containing background material on a convicted person. It is prepared to guide the judge in the imposition of a sentence. Sometimes called a pre-sentence investigation.

判决前调查报告

separate maintenance—allowance granted for support to a married party, and any children, while the party is living apart from the spouse but not divorced.

(夫给予妻)分居赡养费

separation—the state in which a husband and wife remain married but live apart.

分居

separation of powers—phrase the vesting of the legislative, executive, and judicial powers of government in separate bodies.

政权(立法、司法、行政权)分离

separation of witnesses—an order of the court requiring all witnesses to remain outside the courtroom until each is called to testify, except the plaintiff or defendant.

隔离证人

sequester—

1. isolate (a jury) from outside influences during a trial.

隔离(隔离陪审团免受外界影响)

2. take legal possession of (assets) until a debt has been paid or other claims have been met.

扣押

sequestrate—another term for *sequester*.

没收；扣押

sequestration—

1. the action of taking legal possession of assets until a debt has been paid or other claims have been met.

没收；扣押

2. the action of isolating a jury during a trial.

隔离(陪审团)

sequestration of witnesses—a court order directing witnesses to stay outside the courtroom and not discuss testimony with other witnesses until they are called to testify to prevent witnesses from being influenced by the testimony of other witnesses.

分开隔离证人(防止受其他证人的影响)

sergeant-at-arms—an official of a legislative or other assembly whose duty includes maintaining order and security.

(会议、法庭等处的)警卫官

servant—an employee or one who acts for another.

雇员

serve—

1. spend (a period) in jail or prison.

服刑

2. deliver (a document such as a summons or writ) in a formal manner to the person to whom it is addressed.

送达文书

service—the formal delivery of a document such as a writ or summons.

service of process

递送法律文书

service of process—the service of writs, summonses, etc.; signifies the delivering to or leaving of such documents with the party to whom or with whom they ought to be delivered or left; and, when they are so delivered, they are then said to have been served.

送达法院令状

servitude—the subjection of property to an easement or other restriction.

地役权

set aside—overrule or annul (a legal decision or process).

驳回

set-off—a counterbalancing debt pleaded by the defendant in an action to recover money due the set-off may diminish or entirely cancel the claim of the plaintiff.

债的抵消

settle—end (a legal dispute) by mutual agreement.

解决

settlement—

1. a formal arrangement made between the parties to a lawsuit in order to resolve it, esp. out of court.

（和解）协议

2. an arrangement whereby property passes to a person or succession of people as dictated by the settlor.

转让财产协议

settlor—a person who makes a settlement, esp. of property.

托管财产者

several—applied or regarded separately. Often contrasted with *joint*.

各自的；分别的

severalty—the tenure of land held by an individual, not jointly or in common with another.

单独占有

severance—the action of ending a connection or relationship, especially a property interest among co-owners.

分割(财产)

sex crime—(*informal*) a crime involving sexual assault or having a sexual motive.

性犯罪

sex discrimination—discrimination in employment and opportunity against a person (typically a woman) on grounds of sex.

性别歧视

sexual harassment—harassment (typically of a woman) in a workplace, or other professional situation, usually involving the making of unwanted sexual advances or obscene remarks.

性骚扰

sg—solicitor general.

(美国)副司法部长;(美国一些州的)首席司法官

sheriff—(*in the US*) an elected officer in a county who is responsible for law enforcement and judicial administration.

(美国)县的司法长官

shoplifting—the criminal action of stealing goods from a store while pretending to be a customer.

入店行窃

show cause order—an order to appear in court and present reasons why certain circumstances/actions should be continued, permitted, or prohibited.

陈述理由令;示因命令

show up—see *lineup*.

到场;出席

sidebar—(*in a court of law*) a discussion between the lawyers and the judge held out of earshot of the jury.

(陪审团听力所及范围之外的)律师和法官之间的讨论

signature—a writing or other mark that is placed upon an instrument for the purpose of authenticating it or giving it legal effect.

签名;签字;签署

silent partner—an investor in a business enterprise who either does not take an active role in the management of the business, or whose identity is not revealed to third parties; a principal whose identity is not disclosed by his or her agent. While the identity of a silent partner may or may not be disclosed, the silent partner, nonetheless, participates in the profits or losses of the enterprise.

隐名合伙人

silk—(*Brit.*, *informal*) a Queen's (or King's) Counsel.

(英国)女王(国王)的法律顾问

sine die—(with reference to business or proceedings that have been adjourned) with no appointed date for resumption.

无期限的、无确定日期的审理中止

sine qua non—an indispensable requisite.

必要条件;要素

situs—the place to which, for purposes of legal jurisdiction or taxation, an act occurred or a property belongs.

(管辖、税收、行为发生、财产所在)地

slander—injury to a person's character or reputation by the spoken word.

诽谤

small claims court—a division of the district court. The jurisdiction of the small claims division is limited to civil cases where the amount claimed does not exceed \$1,750. Claims are handled without lawyers or juries, and the parties generally have no right to appeal.

小额赔偿法庭(限于民事案件,金额不超过1750美元,审理无须律师及陪审团,通常不得上诉。)

sole custody—an order of the court which states that the children live with one parent and that parent is responsible for making decisions on important issues dealing with the children.

单独监护权(孩子与父母一方生活,该方有权决定有关孩子的重要事项。)

solicit—incite or persuade (a person) to commit an illegal or insubordinate act.

教唆

solicitor—the chief law officer of a city, town, or government department.

(事务)律师

solicitor general—in the US Department of Justice, the law officer responsible for arguing cases before the US Supreme Court.

(美国)副司法部长;(美国一些州的)首席司法官

sovereign immunity—the doctrine that the government, state or federal, is immune to lawsuit unless it gives its consent, generally through legislation.

主权豁免

special damages—damages that are the actual, but not necessary, consequence of a breach of contract or injury. In contract law, special damages must have been reasonably foreseeable and must flow directly and immediately from the breach, or they are not enforceable.

特别损害赔偿

special verdict—a verdict that states facts as proved but leaves the court to draw conclusions from them in order to render judgment.

特别裁决(指陪审团将找到已证实的事实提交给法庭去推出法律上的结论。)

specie—in the real, precise, or actual form specified.

详述

specific performance—a court order directing a party to a contract who has breached its terms to do what he or she contracted to do; generally involved when the thing or service contracted for is unique so that money damages for breach of contract would be inadequate, i.e., breach of contract to sell water rights to one who has no alternative access to water.

依约履行;具体履行(合同义务)

speed limit—the maximum speed at which a vehicle may legally travel on a particular stretch of road.

速度限制

speedy trial—a criminal trial held after minimal delay, as a citizen's constitutional right.

spendthrift

快速审理

> 这是公民的宪法权利。美国宪法第六修正案规定:在所有刑事起诉中的被告,皆享有迅速暨公开审判之权利,此乃避免因审判程序久延,严重影响被告权益。然而何谓"迅速"并非明确。联邦最高法院虽曾于 1972 年指出较为明确之速审定方式,但仍有诸多疑义,国会遂于 1974 年制定"速审法"(Federal Speedy Trial Act),期能兼顾公众与被告之利益,将案件迅速审结。

spendthrift—a person who by excessive drinking, gaming, idleness, or debauchery of any kind shall so spend, waste, or lessen his estate as to expose himself or his family to want or suffering, or expose the State to charge or expense for the support of himself or family.
挥霍者;浪费者

spendthrift trust—a trust set up for the benefit of someone whom the grantor believes would be incapable of managing his/her own financial affairs.
规定受益人不得自由处理的信托资产

split decision—a decision based on a majority verdict rather than on a unanimous one.
基于大多数决定;非一致性决定

spoliation—the action of destroying, mutilating, or altering a document (e.g., a will) or evidence unfavorable to oneself.
篡改

spousal—of or relating to marriage or to a husband or wife.
结婚的;婚姻的;夫妻间的

spousal support—a sum of money that a court orders a spouse to pay to his or her separated or divorced spouse for support, aid, or maintenance. An award of spousal support does not include child support. See also *child support*.
离婚扶养费(不包括对子女的抚养)

stale—(of a check or legal claim) invalid because not acted on within a reasonable time.
(支票或诉求)已过时效的

stalking—a willful course of conduct involving repeated or continuing harassment of another person that would cause a reasonable person to feel terrorized, frightened, intimidated, threatened, harassed, or molested, and that actually causes the victim to feel this way.

跟踪骚扰；不断纠缠

stand—

1. *n*. a witness stand.

证人席

2. *v*. undergo or submit to, as in *stand trial*.

在证人席上

standard jury instructions—a collection of jury instructions approved by a Supreme Court Committee for use by trial court judges.

最高法院委员会认可的法官对陪审团的指示，对此陪审团应当遵守

standard of review—In law, the standard of review is the amount of deference given by one court (or some other appellate tribunal) in reviewing a decision of a lower court or tribunal. A low standard of review means that the decision under review will be varied or overturned if the reviewing court considers there is any error at all in the lower court's decision. A high standard of review means that deference is accorded to the decision under review, so that it will not be disturbed just because the reviewing court might have decided the matter differently; it will be varied only if the higher court considers the decision to have obvious error. The standard of review may be set by statute, rule or precedent. In the United States, "standard of review" also has a separate meaning concerning the level of deference the judiciary gives to Congress when ruling on the constitutionality of legislation.

审查标准

standing—the legal right to bring a lawsuit. Only a person with some legally recognized interest at stake has standing to bring a lawsuit.

起诉权

Star Chamber—an English court of civil and criminal jurisdiction that developed in the late 15th century, trying esp. those cases affecting the interests of the Crown. It was noted for its arbitrary and oppressive judgments and was

stare decisis

abolished in 1641.

星法院

> 星法院成立于1487年，由于位于西敏寺一个屋顶有星形装饰的大厅而得名。它同枢密院、高等法院等构成英国封建王朝最重要的专制机器，特别是在惩治出版商上一直充当急先锋的角色，成为英国报纸出现前一长段历史中禁止自由发表意见的又一障碍。英国许多报业先驱都受过这个机构的传讯、折磨或监禁。星法院也成为英国专制制度的象征，于1641年关闭。

stare decisis—the doctrine that the decisions of the court should serve as precedents for future cases.

遵循先例原则

> 这是判例法的一个基本原则，它是判例法得以形成的基础。遵循先例原则的基本含义就是，包含在以前判决中的法律原则对以后同类案件有约束力，具体说就是高级法院的判决对下级法院处理同类案件有约束力；同一法院的判决对其以后的同类案件的判决具有约束力。即指以前判决中的法律原则对以后同类案件具有约束力。具体表现为：高级法院的判决对下级法院处理同类案件有约束力；同一法院的判决对以后同类案件具有约束力，确切地说，是指一个判决中所含有的法律原则或规则，对其他法院或者甚至对本法院以后的审判，具有约束力（binding effect）或者说服力（persuasive effect）。

state—

1. *n*. the particular condition that someone or something is in at a specific time.

状态

2. *n*. the civil government of a country.

州

　　adj. of, provided by, or concerned with the civil government of a country.

州的

3. *v*. specify the facts of (a case) for consideration.

陈述；叙述

state case—refers to a violation of state law. The term is most often used in district courts and the remaining municipal courts to distinguish between the local ordinance violations they usually deal with and violations of state statutes. Violating a state law makes the case a "state case" in these jurisdictions.

违反州法律(区别于违反地方性法规)

statement—a formal account of events given by a witness, defendant, or other party to the police or in a court of law.

声明;陈述

state's attorney—a lawyer representing a state in court.

政府律师;政府法律顾问

state's evidence—evidence for the prosecution given by a participant in or accomplice to the crime being tried.

告发同犯的证据

statute—a written law passed by a legislative body.

法令;法规

statute book—a book in which laws are written.

法令全书

statute law—the body of principles and rules of law laid down in statutes. Compare with *common law*, *case law*.

成文法;制定法(区别于普通法、判例法)

statute of frauds—a legal doctrine or rule that certain types of agreements must be in writing or they will not be enforced by the courts. Real estate sales agreements are examples of agreements that must be in writing.

防止欺诈法(法律规定采用书面形式的合同,应当用书面形式,否则不具有强制力,例如,不动产买卖合同。)

statute of limitations—a statute prescribing a period of time limitation for the bringing of certain kinds of legal action.

限制法令;时效法

statutes at large—a country's statutes in their original version, regardless of later modifications or codification.

(未经修改或编纂的)法律汇编

status offense—a violation of the juvenile code by a minor that would not be considered a violation of the law if committed by an adult. Examples: runaway, school truancy, incorrigibility, etc.
身份犯罪

> 身份犯罪是指只有少年才能构成的犯罪。如果不具有"少年"这种身份，即使进行了这样的行为，也不构成犯罪。这类少年犯罪包括逃学，小偷小摸，恶意破坏，离家出走，不正当的性行为，结交少年犯罪人朋友，使用亵渎语言，饮酒，吸烟，违反宵禁令，不服从父母、老师和监护人的管教，不服从管理人员的管理以及懒惰、放荡、猥亵等不道德行为。

statutory—required, permitted, or enacted by statute.
依照法令的；法定的

statutory construction—process by which a court seeks to interpret the meaning and scope of legislation.
立法解释

statutory law—the body of law enacted by the legislative branch of government, as distinguished from case law or common law
成文法；制定法

statutory rape—sexual intercourse with a person under the age of consent.
法定强奸罪；强奸幼女罪（指与未满法定结婚年龄的人发生性行为。）

stay—the suspension of a judicial proceeding by court order.
延期审理

stipulation—an agreement between opposing attorneys on any matter relating to the proceedings or trial, i.e., to extend the time to answer, to adjourn the trial date, to admit certain facts at the trial, etc. It often requires court approval to be effective.
契约；约定；协定（双方辩护律师的协议书，须法庭确认生效。）

strict construction—a literal interpretation of a statute or document (e.g., a constitution) by a court.
狭义解释；严格解释

strict liability—liability that arises from certain actions without a showing of actual negligence or intent to harm.

无过失(过错)责任；严格赔偿责任

strike—cancel, remove, or cross out with or as if with a pen, particularly testimony or remarks in court.

排除；勾(划)掉

sua sponte—a court acts "sua sponte" when it takes action voluntarily ("on its own motion"), without first being requested to act by a party to a case.

自发的；依职权的

subject matter jurisdiction—power of a court to hear the type of case that is before it. Example: a municipal court has subject matter jurisdiction for cases involving violation of that municipality's ordinances, but does not have subject matter jurisdiction over felonies.

事项管辖权；诉讼事务管辖权

> 这是法院审理和裁决某一类案件的权限范围。在美国对不同州籍公民间民事争议的管辖权、联邦问题管辖权、对海事和破产案件的管辖权等都属于联邦法院的事物管辖权。该管辖权通常由制定法予以规定。

sub judice—under judicial consideration and therefore prohibited from public discussion elsewhere.

审理中的案件；未决案件

sublease—a lease of a property by a tenant to a subtenant. Another term for *sublet*.

转租

sublessee—a person who holds a sublease.

转租入人

sublessor—a person who grants a sublease.

转租出人

sublet—lease (a property) to a subtenant. Another term for *sublease*.

转租

submission—a proposition or argument presented by a lawyer to a judge or jury.

（律师向法官或陪审团提出的）建议；论点

submit—present (a proposal, application, or other document) to a person or body for consideration or judgment.

提交

subordination—to give one claim or debt a lower priority in relation to another claim or debt. A subordination agreement is one whereby a creditor agrees that claims of other creditors must be fully paid before there is any payment to himself or herself, the subordinated creditor.

放在次要位置；从属的

suborn—bribe or otherwise induce (someone) to commit an unlawful act such as perjury.

行贿；教唆；作伪证

subornation of perjury—the crime of procuring another to make a false oath.

唆使作伪证罪

subpoena—

1. (*in full subpoena ad testificandum*) a writ ordering a person to attend a court.

传票

2. summon (someone) with a subpoena.

用传票传唤

subpoena duces tecum—a writ ordering a person to attend a court and bring relevant documents.

随带证件到庭作证的传票

subrogation—the substitution of one party to the rights of another. Most commonly used in civil cases in which an insurance company (subrogee) which pays its policyholder is entitled to the policyholder's right to recover damages.

代位；代位偿清

> 代位是一种法律拟制,即债权人在他从第三人处收到所述债务款项的偿付时,应将他对债务人的权利和求偿转让给该第三人。在大陆法系中,存在法定代位和约定代位。在普通法中,代位可以是法定的,也可是约定的,还可以是法院同意的。

subsidiary—an inferior portion or capacity; usually used in describing the relationship between corporations.

子公司

substantive—defining rights and duties as opposed to giving the rules by which such things are established.

实体的;规定权利义务的

substantive law—the law dealing with rights, duties and liabilities, as distinguished from adjective law, which is the law regulating procedure.

实体法

substitute—

1. *n.* (in litigation) a party who acts or serves in place of another.

替代方

2. *v.* (in litigation) replace one party with another.

替代

succession—the action or process of inheriting a title, office, property, etc.

继承

successor—a person who succeeds to the office, rights, responsibilities, or place of another; one who replaces or follows another.

继承人;继任者

successor personal representative—A successor personal representative is appointed by the court to complete the administration of a decedent's estate in cases where the administration of the estate is left unfinished due to the death, removal, or resignation of the original personal representative. In some jurisdictions, a successor personal representative is called the "administrator de bonis non".

（执行遗产事宜的）私人代表继承人

sue—institute legal proceedings against (a person or institution), typically for redress.

起诉；控告

sufferance—the condition of the holder of an estate who continues to hold it after the title has ceased, without the express permission of the owner.

强制性租占；默许租占（当一个原合法占据某房地产的租客在租约期满后，在未取得房东的同意下，仍继续强制性地占据该房地产。）

suicide—the voluntary and intentional killing of one's self; suicide was a felony at common law, but modem statutory law is not unanimous in classifying it as a crime.

自杀

sui juris—of full age and capacity; independent.

完全行为能力人（指已到法定年龄并精神健全者）

suit—short for *lawsuit*.

诉讼

summary—(of a judicial process) conducted without the customary legal formalities.

即决的；简易的

summary disposition—in a civil lawsuit, a dismissal of or judgment on all or part of a claim, made by a judge prior to trial upon motion by one of the parties. A motion for summary disposition may be based on one or more of several grounds listed in MCR 2.116(C). Some of the grounds listed in the court rule are: the trial court lacks jurisdiction over the case or the parties; process or service of process was insufficient; the party asserting the claim has no legal capacity to sue; another action has been initiated between the same parties involving the same claim; the claim is barred by the statute of limitations; a party has failed to state a valid defense to the claim against him or her; the facts alleged in a party's complaint do not entitle the party to judicial relief.

简易判决；即决判决

> 这是英美民事诉讼的一项重要制度，尤其在美国，简易判决已成为近些年联邦和地方法院为过滤案件而大量适用的手段，甚至可以说民事案件的联邦判例大部分是简易判决的产物。这种判决方式及其程序指对于要件事实(material fact)不存在实质争点，且申请人有权将其主张或者抗辩作为法律问题(a matter of law)由法官进行裁判而获得的判决。法庭根据答辩状、申请以及当事人所举出的其他证据，来判断要件事实是存在实质争议还是仅仅存在法律问题争议。这一制度允许快速处理争议而无需经过庭审。

summary judgment—see *summary disposition*.
简易判决；即决判决

summary proceedings—proceedings where the court decides an issue in a prompt and simple manner, often without the aid of a jury.
简易程序

summation—an attorney's closing speech at the conclusion of the giving of evidence.
（律师的）法庭辩论总结

summons—a notice given to a party stating that proceedings have been instituted against him or her and directing that the person appear in court at a given date and time to answer the complaint; and further, should he or she fail to answer a judgment will be entered against him or her.
传票

sum up—(*summed up, summing up*) (of a judge) review the evidence at the end of a case, and direct the jury regarding points of law.
向陪审团概述案情

sunset law—a law that automatically terminates a regulatory agency, board, or function of government on a certain date, unless renewed.
（公共开支）日落法；日暮法（国会在批准成立一个新的行政机构或批准一个联邦计划项目时，明确规定该机构或该项目的终止日期。）

sunshine law—a law requiring certain proceedings of government agencies to be open or available to the public.
阳光法（规定管理机构某些会议必须公开。）

superintending control—the constitutional doctrine that the Michigan Supreme Court has general administrative supervision over all the courts of the state. The circuit courts of each county have similar administrative supervisory power over the various lower courts within their jurisdiction.

监管控制

superior court—

1. (*in many states of the US*) a court of appeals or a court of general (original) jurisdiction.

上诉法院;高等法院

2. a court with general jurisdiction over other courts; a higher court.

上级法院

supersedeas—a writ containing a command to stay proceedings at law, such as the enforcement of a judgment pending an appeal.

停止控告的令状

support order—in a domestic relations proceeding, an order for payment of money to meet the ongoing financial needs of a child, spouse, or former spouse. Support may include health care and educational expenses. See also *child support*, *spousal support*.

供养令(家庭关系诉讼中,支付儿童、配偶、前配偶的生活费,包括医疗教育支出。)

support trust—a trust that instructs the trustee to spend only as much income and principal (the assets held in the trust) as needed for the beneficiary's support.

必需的生活费用信托

suppress—to suppress a court record is to prevent its release; to suppress evidence is to forbid it from being introduced at a trial or other court proceeding.

禁止;使止住

suppression hearing—a hearing caused by a defense motion to prohibit the use of evidence alleged to have violated, when obtained, the defendant's rights. This hearing is held outside the presence of the jury, either prior to or at trial and the state has the burden of going forward with the evidence and establishing that the defendant's rights were not violated in the process of obtaining the evidence. Suppression hearings are held only in criminal cases.

证据禁止之听证

> 这是开庭前对于审查证据是否合法,是否该禁止的一种听证会。辩护方对于排除某一控方证据的申请,一般要在"审前动议"阶段提出,并由法官主持专门的证据禁止之听证。

supra—Latin for above.
在上;在前面

surety—a person who agrees to fulfil another person's financial obligation in the event the other person fails to fulfill it. The other person is known as the "principal." A surety's obligation typically arises from the same contract that binds the principal. See also *guarantor*, *principal*.
担保人;保证人

surety bond—a bond purchased at the expense of the estate to insure the executor's proper performance.
履约保证券

surrender—cease resistance to an enemy or opponent and submit to their authority.
投降;放弃

surrogate—a substitute, esp. a person deputizing for another in a specific role or office.
代理

surrogate mother—one who bears a child for a person or a couple unable to have children, usually for monetary compensation.
代孕母亲

surveillance—oversight or supervision. In criminal law, an investigative process by which police gather evidence about crimes or suspected crime through continued observation of persons or places.
监视

survivor—a joint tenant who has the right to the whole estate on the other's death.

（在共有财产产权人中的）生存者；幸存者

survivorship—a right depending on survival, esp. the right of a survivor of holders of a joint interest to take the whole on the death of the others.

生存者取得权（在共有财产中生存者对死者名下享有权利的取得权）

suspend—prevent from continuing or being in force or effect, in particular.

暂停；终止

suspended sentence—postponed execution of sentence; sentence is imposed, and execution of sentence is suspended, postponed, or stayed for a period and on conditions set by the judge.

缓刑

suspension (of driver's license)—the driver's license and privilege to drive are temporarily withdrawn, but only during the period of such suspension. No reapplication is necessary to obtain license.

暂时中止；暂扣（驾驶执照）

sustain—uphold, affirm, or confirm the justice or validity of (especially an objection to the introduction of evidence in court).

支持；认可；保持（合法有效）

swear—take a solemn oath as to the truth of (a statement).

宣誓

sworn complaint affidavit—a sworn, witnessed complaint filed with the clerk of the court.

（经过宣誓、见证的）起诉书

syllabus—a summary of the opinion of a court.

判决摘要

T

tacit—implied or indicated, but not actually expressed; arising without expressing contract or agreement.

默示的；推定的

tack—to add or join together.

附加；追加；合并

take—as used in probate, to acquire title or to be entitled to an estate, such as the person is entitled to "take" under the will.

根据遗嘱占有

talesman—a person summoned to act as a juror from among the bystanders in a court.

候补陪审员

tariff—a tax or duty to be paid on a particular class of imports or exports.

关税

例如：fix the price of (something) according to a tariff. 根据关税定价

tax—

1. *n.* a compulsory contribution to federal, state, or municipal revenue, levied by the government on income and business profits or added to the cost of some goods, services, and transactions.

税

2. *v.* impose a tax on (someone or something).

征税

3. *v.* examine and assess (the costs of a case).

检验评估

tax avoidance—the arrangement of one's financial affairs to minimize tax liability within the law. Compare with *tax avoidance*.

避税

tax evasion—the illegal nonpayment or underpayment of tax. Compare with *tax avoidance*.

逃税；漏税

technical—according to a strict application or interpretation of the law or rules.

专业的（根据法律法规严格适用或解释的）

technicality—a precise, usually procedural point of law or a small detail of a set of rules.

术语

temporary relief—any form of action by a court granting one of the parties an order designed to protect its interest pending further action by the court.

临时救济

temporary restraining order—an order of the court that is intended to restrain a person's actions and preserve the status quo until a hearing can be held to determine if a preliminary injunction should be issued.

暂时禁令

temporary ward—a minor who is under the supervision of the family division but whose parents' parental rights have not been terminated.

临时监护

tenancy—possession of land or property as a tenant.

租赁

tenancy in common—a shared tenancy in which each holder has a distinct, separately transferable interest.

分别共有财产权（指由两个或者两个以上的人共享所有权，可能是等额或者不等额。在其中一个共有人死后，他/她在财产中的份额转移给他/她的继承人，而不是转给其他生存的共有人。）

tenant—a person who rents property from the owner (called a landlord); one who occupies the property of another for a temporary period, with the landlord's consent.

承租人

tenant at will—a tenant who has no stated lease term and can be evicted, or can vacate, at any time, provided statutory notice requirements are met.

不定期租赁；没有订契约的房客（根据法律规定可随时被赶走。）

ten percent bond—a procedure that allows persons to pay to the court ten percent (10%) of the bond otherwise required of them to obtain their release. This procedure reduces the actual monetary amount paid so that most persons can arrange bond without the services of a bondsman or other surety.

10%保证金程序

tenure—

1. *n.* the conditions under which land or buildings are held or occupied.

保有

2. *n.* the holding of an office.

在职

3. *n.* guaranteed permanent employment, esp. as a teacher or professor, after a probationary period.

固定职业

4. *v.* give (someone) a permanent post, esp. as a teacher or professor.

提供固定职业

term—

1. (also *term for years* or *Brit. term of years*) a tenancy of a fixed period.

租期

2. (*terms*) conditions under which an action may be undertaken or agreement reached; stipulated or agreed-upon requirements.

期限

term of court—the designated period of time a court is allowed by law to sit and hear cases.

审理期限

termination hearing—a hearing held in the family division of the circuit court to determine if the parental rights are to be taken away from the parties involved, and therefore the child will become a ward of the court. The prosecutor is required to attend. This is the final scheduled hearing of a neglect/abuse case.

家事庭决定撤销侵权的听证

territorial—

1. of or relating to the ownership of an area of land or sea.

属地的;领地的;领海的

2. of or relating to a particular territory, district, or locality.

地方性的;区域性的

territorial waters—the waters under the jurisdiction of a state, esp. the part of the sea within a stated distance of the shore (traditionally three miles from low-water mark, but extended in the 20th century by most countries).

领海

territory—an area of land under the jurisdiction of a ruler or state.

领土

testament—a person's will. esp. the part relating to personal property.

遗嘱

testamentary—of, relating to, or bequeathed or appointed through a will.

遗嘱的

testamentary capacity—the legal ability to make a will.

遗嘱行为能力

testamentary trust—a trust set up by a will. This trust becomes effective only upon the death of the testator.

遗嘱信托

testate—dying having made a valid will.

留有遗嘱的

testate succession—inheritance of a decedent's property under the direction of the decedent's will.

遗嘱继承

testation—the disposal of property by will.

立遗嘱

testator—one who has made a will. (A female testator is known as a "testatrix".)

留有遗嘱的人

test case—a case initiated to set a precedent for other cases involving similar questions of law.

判例案件

testify—give evidence as a witness in a law court.

作证；证明

testimony—the statement of a witness under oath which is given as evidence.

证词

theft—the action or crime of stealing.

盗窃

thief—a person who steals another person's property, esp. by stealth and without using force or violence.

小偷；盗贼

thieve—be a thief; steal something.

偷

thievery—the action of stealing another person's property.

偷窃

third-degree—long and harsh questioning, esp. by police, to obtain information or a confession.

third party

刑讯逼供

third party—a person, business, organization or government agency not actively involved in a legal proceeding, agreement, or transaction, but affected by it.

第三方

third-party claim—an action by the defendant that brings a third party into a lawsuit.

第三方请求

third-party complaint—in a civil lawsuit, a complaint that the defendant files against a "third-party", i. e., someone who is not already named in the lawsuit. This "third-party complaint" alleges that the third-party is or may be liable to the defendant for some or all of the plaintiff's claim.

索赔涉及第三方的诉讼

third person—a third party.

第三方

threat—

1. a statement of an intention to inflict pain, injury, damage, or other hostile action on someone in retribution for something done or not done.

威胁;恐吓

2. a person or thing likely to cause damage or danger.

威胁;恐吓

three strikes—legislation providing that an offender's third felony is punishable by life imprisonment or another severe sentence.

事不过三

> 这个词源于美国的棒球运动。棒球用语有一句名言"Three strikes, and you are out",意思是在棒球比赛中,击球手若三次都未击中投球手所投的球,必须出局。引申至法律,"three strikes law"规定,因暴力或严重罪行"进宫"两次者,以后每再犯一次,无论新罪严重与否,都要受到重判甚至是终身监禁。该法旨在严惩累犯。

time served—actual number of days already served in jail on a charge or offense before conviction.

审前羁押日期

tipstaff—a bailiff.

法警

title—a right or claim to the ownership of property or to a rank or throne.

权益；权利

title deed—a legal deed or document constituting evidence of a right，esp. to ownership of property.

所有权证书（尤指地契）

torrens system—a system of land title registration adopted originally in Australia and later in some states of the US，under which a judicial decree and registration obviate the need for title insurance.

托伦斯登记制

> 这种登记制度由托伦斯爵士于 1858 年在澳大利亚首创，其基本内容包括：由国家主持进行一次全面的不动产资源调查，根据调查的情况进行一次总登记，并由政府根据登记簿的情况制作权利书状交付权利人，未确定各权利人的权利，该权利证书具有证明权利存在的效果。

tort—an injury or wrong committed against the person or property of another，arising out of violation of a duty established by law rather than by contract.

侵权

tortfeasor—a person who commits a tort.

侵权行为人

tortuous—constituting or pertaining to a tort.

构成侵权

trademark—

1. *n.* a symbol，device，or words legally registered or established by use as representing a company or product.

（注册）商标

2. *v*. provide with a trademark.
提供（注册）商标

traditional waiver—see *waiver of jurisdiction*.
放弃管辖

transcript—the verbatim record of proceedings in a trial or hearing.
审理、听证记录

transfer—

1. *v*. make over the possession of (property, a right, or a responsibility) to someone else.
转让；转移

2. *n*. a conveyance of property, esp. stocks, from one person to another.
转让；转移

transitory—Actions are "transitory" when they might have taken place anywhere, and are "local" when they could occur only in some particular place.
短期的；短暂的

traverse—deny (an allegation) in pleading.
否认；反驳

treason—the crime of betraying one's country, esp. by attempting to kill the sovereign or overthrow the government.
叛国罪

treasure trove—valuables of unknown ownership that are found hidden, in some cases declared the property of the finder.
埋藏物；无主财宝

treaty—a formally concluded and ratified agreement between countries.
条约

trespass—

1. *v*. enter the owner's land or property without permission
非法侵入

2. *n*. entry to a person's land or property without their permission
侵占；侵犯

triable—able to be tried in court; liable to trial.
应受审讯的;可审讯的

trial—a formal examination of evidence by a judge or tribunal, especially a jury in order to determine the facts in criminal or civil proceedings.
审理;审判

trial by jury—trial by a body of persons selected from the citizens of a particular district and brought before the court where they are sworn to try one or more questions of fact and determine them by their verdict.
陪审团审理

trial court—the court where trial takes place. Examples of Michigan trial courts are district, circuit, and probate courts.
一审法庭;初审法院

trial de novo—a retrial in district court that is conducted as if no trial had occurred in the lower court.
重新审理

trial lawyer—a lawyer who practices in a trial court.
出庭辩护律师

tribunal—a court of justice.
审理委员会;特别法庭;法官席

trier—a person or body responsible for investigating and deciding a case judicially.
实验者

-trix—forming feminine agent nouns corresponding to masculine nouns ending in -tor (such as *executrix* corresponding to *executor*).
女性;阴性名词后缀

true bill—a bill of indictment found by a grand jury to be supported by sufficient evidence to justify the hearing of a case.
正式起诉状;(大陪审团认为证据充分而准予受理的)起诉书

true copy—an exact copy of a written instrument.
真实的副本;经核准无误的复印件

trust—a right of property, real or personal, held by one party for the benefit of another.

信托；托管

trust agreement or declaration—the legal document that sets up a living trust. Testamentary trusts are set up in a will.

信托协议；信托声明

trust company—a company formed to act as a trustee or to deal with trusts.

信托公司

trust deed—a deed of conveyance creating and setting out the conditions of a trust.

信托书；信托契据

trustee—a person in whom property is vested in trust for others.

受托人

trustee in bankruptcy—a person taking administrative responsibility for the financial affairs of a bankrupt and the distribution of assets to creditors.

破产管理人；破产财产分配受托人

try—subject (someone) to trial.

审理；审讯

try title—to submit to judicial scrutiny the legitimacy of title to property.

产权确认之诉

turner hearing—a proceeding to determine if the defendant was entrapped by law enforcement officials into committing the offense.

特纳听证（决定被告是否因执行人员的误导而犯罪的程序）

U

UCC—Uniform Commercial Code. The UCC applies to the sale of movable goods to or by a merchant.

《美国统一商法典》

> 该《法典》于1952年公布后,又作了多次修改,现行的是1977年公布的文本。该《法典》不同于大陆法国家的商法典,它不是美国国会通过的法律,而只是由一些法律团体起草,供各州自由采用的一部样板法。这是因为美国是联邦制国家,联邦和各州都在宪法规定的范围内享有立法权。根据美国宪法的规定,有关贸易方面的立法权原则上属于各州,联邦只对涉及州际之间的贸易和国际贸易的事项享有立法权。所以,各州对于是否采用上述统一法典,有完全的自主权。但该《法典》详尽完备,灵活适用。它既考虑到过去和现在,又兼顾了未来;既保持了英美法的特点,又兼采了大陆法的长处,能够比较适应当代美国经济发展的要求,因此,现在美国50个州中,除保持大陆法传统的路易斯安那州外,其他各州均已通过本州的立法采用这部《法典》。

ultimate facts—facts said to lie in the area between evidence and a conclusion of law. They are the essential and determining facts on which the final conclusion of law is predicated.

基本事实；主要事实

ultrahazardous activity—an activity which gives rise to strict liability, because it necessarily involves a risk of serious harm to the person, land or chattels of others, which cannot be eliminated by the exercise of utmost care and it is not a matter of common usage.

高危行动；高危行业

ultra vires—(Latin: "beyond the powers") an action which is invalid because it exceeds the authority of the person or organization which performs it. A company cannot normally be bound by an act which it is not empowered to do by its memorandum of association.

超越权限

unalienable—another term for *inalienable*.

（指权利等）不能让与、不能剥夺的

unappealable—(of a case or ruling) not able to be referred to a higher court for review.

不可上诉的

uncharged—not accused of an offense under the law.

未被指控的

unclean hands—one of the maxims of equity embodying the principle that a party seeking redress in a court of equity (equitable relief) must not have done any dishonest or unethical act in the transaction upon which he or she maintains the action in equity, since a court of conscience will not grant relief to one guilty of unconscionable conduct, i. e., to one with unclean hands.

不洁之手原则

> 不当行为是美国法院在专利审判实践中针对专利侵权行为设立的一项衡平抗辩制度，其理论依据在于衡平法中的"不洁之手"原则，美国最高法院在 Keystone Driller Co. v. General Excavator Co. 案、Hazel-Atlas Glass Co.

v. Hartford-Empire Co. 案、Standard Oil Co. v. United States 案以及 Precision Instruments Manufacturing Co. v. Automotive Maintenance Machinery Co. 等案件中对其进行了阐述。如果专利权人实施了不当行为，即使该专利权是有效的并且侵权行为成立，法庭也可以根据衡平规则确定该专利权不可实施（unenforceable）。

unconscionable—so unreasonably detrimental to the interest of a contracting party as to render the contract unenforceable.
显失公平的；极不公平的

unconstitutional—conflicting with some provision of constitution, most commonly the United States Constitution.
违宪的

uncorroborated—not confirmed or supported by other evidence or information.
未经证实的

undefended—not defended.
无辩护人的

undersheriff—a deputy sheriff.
代理郡长

undertaking—enforceable promise given to court.
承诺；保证

under the influence—(*informal*) affected by alcoholic drink or other intoxicants.
醉酒的

undue influence—unfair pressure which may invalidate a contract.
不正当压力；不正当影响

不正当影响是英国衡平法本着公平正义的原则发展而来的一种确认合同效力的制度。所谓不当影响是指一方当事人利用其优越的地位、意志或思想在精神或其他方面向另一方当事人施加非正当的间接压力，从而迫使

unencumbered

> 对方签订合同的一种非法行为。施加这种影响的人,往往滥用自己的被信任地位,或者利用对方薄弱的意志、懦弱的体质以及精神上的痛楚而影响对方当事人进行自主的抉择,以致迫使对方与自己签订在自由状态下绝不会同意的合同。这种影响虽然没有完全摧毁对方的自由意志,但却压制了对方的自由意志,使之产生了一定程度的偏向。在此情形下,当事人所表达出来的意思就偏离了其内心的效果意思,形成了有瑕疵的意思表示。不正当影响不同于胁迫。

unencumbered—not having any burden or impediment.
没有负担的;不受妨碍的

unenforceable—(esp. of an obligation or law) impossible to enforce.
不可强行的;无强制力的

unenforceable contract—a valid contract is unenforceable when some defense exists that is extraneous to the formation of the contract, such as when the contract violates the Statute of Frauds or the Statute of Limitations has passed.
不可强制执行的合同

unicameral—(of a legislative body) having a single legislative chamber.
一院的;单院的

Uniform Interstate Family Support Act/UIFSA—statutes governing support actions that involve parents living in different states or on tribal lands.
统一州际家庭抚养法

unjust enrichment—profit unjustly obtain by a wrongdoer. To obtain reimbursement, the plaintiff must show an actual benefit to the defendant, a corresponding loss to the plaintiff and the absence of a legal reason for the defendant's enrichment.
不当得利

> 不当得利指没有合法根据,或事后丧失了合法根据而被确认为是因致他人遭受损失而获得的利益。如售货时多收货款、拾得遗失物据为己有等。

> 取得利益的人称受益人,遭受损害的人称受害人。不当得利的取得,不是由于受益人针对受害人而为的违法行为;而是由于受害人或第三人的疏忽、误解或过错所造成的。受益人与受害人之间因此形成债的关系,受益人为债务人,受害人为债权人。

unlawful—not conforming to, permitted by, or recognized by law or rules.
非法的

unlawful detainer—a detention of real estate without the consent of the owner or other person entitled to its possession.
非法扣押

unlawful search—examination or inspection of premises or persons without authority of the law and in violation of the immunity from unreasonable search and seizure under the Fourth Amendment to the U.S. Constitution and Article II, Section 10 of the New Mexico Constitution.
非法搜查

> 美国宪法第四修正案规定,任何人的人身、住宅、文件和财产不受无理搜查和查封,没有合理事实依据,不得签发搜查令和逮捕令,搜查令必须具体描述清楚要搜查的地点、需要搜查和查封的具体文件和物品,逮捕令必须具体描述清楚要逮捕的人。

unliquidated—(of a debt) not cleared or paid off.
未清算的

unsecured—in collection or bankruptcy proceedings, a debt or a claim is unsecured if there is no collateral, or to the extent the value of collateral is less than the amount of the debt.
无担保的;无抵押的

unserved—(of a writ or summons) not officially delivered to a person.
(文书、传票)未送达的

unsworn—(of testimony or evidence) not given under oath.
未宣誓的证言

untried—(of an accused person) not yet subjected to a trial in court.
未经审讯的

unwritten—(esp. of a law) resting originally on custom or judicial decision rather than on statute.
不成文的；口头的；没有记录的

user—the continued use or enjoyment of a right.
权利的实际享有

usurer—a person who lends money at unreasonably high rates of interest.
高利贷者

usurious—of or relating to the practice of usury.
高利贷的；放高利贷的

usury—excessive or illegal interest rate.
高利贷

utter—put (forged money) into circulation.
假币流通；使用（伪造物品，尤指假币）

V

v—versus

对(指诉讼、比赛等中);相对

vacant—(of premises) having no fixtures, furniture or inhabitants; empty.

空的;空白的

vacate—

1. leave (a place that one previously occupied).

离职;退位

2. cancel or annul (a judgment, contract, or charge).

取消或废除(判决、合同、收费)

valid—legally binding due to having been executed in compliance with the law.

有效的

valuable consideration—legal consideration having some economic value, in order to make a contract enforceable

有值对价;有值约因

variance—a discrepancy between two statements or documents.
不一致；分歧

vend—sell (something).
出售

vendee—a buyer; a person to whom something is sold.
买方

vendor—a seller; a person who sells something.
卖方

venire—technically, a writ summoning prospective jurors; popularly refers to the group of jurors summoned.
陪审员召集令

venireman—a member of a jury panel.
陪审员

venue—the jurisdiction in which court proceedings may be instituted.
审判地；管辖地

verbatim—the recording of the exact word-for-word proceedings of a trial court, as prepared in transcript format.
详细记录

verdict—a decision by a judge or jury on the issues submitted to the court for determination.
（陪审团的）裁决；判决；判断；结论

verification—a person's statement under oath or penalty of perjury that certain statements of fact in a document or court paper are true.
诉状结尾的举证声明

verified statement—

1. a statement (e.g., in a court paper) that contains verification by the party submitting it.
属实证明

2. a confidential statement that must be provided to the Friend of the Court and attached to the complaint in a domestic relations action involving a minor or requesting child or spousal support.

保密说明

versus—against.

对（指诉讼、比赛等中）；相对

vested—fixed; accrued; settled; absolute.

既定的；绝对的

vested interest—an interest (usually in land or money held in trust) recognized as belonging to a particular person.

特权阶级；既得权利

veto—

1. a constitutional right to reject a decision or proposal made by a lawmaking body.

否决权

2. exercise a veto against (a decision or proposal made by a lawmaking body).

否决；行使否决权

vexatious—denoting an action or the bringer of an action that is brought without sufficient grounds for winning, purely to cause annoyance to the defendant.

缠讼；无理上诉

vice chancellor—

1. a deputy chancellor, esp. one of a British university who discharges most of its administrative duties.

（英国分管行政事务的）大学副校长

2. a judge appointed to assist a chancellor, esp. in chancery court or court of equity.

大法官（协助首席大法官工作）

vice crimes—activities such as gambling, prostitution and pornography which are illegal because they offend the moral standards of the community.

妨害社会风气罪行

vicinage—the area from which cases may be brought to a court.

附近的地区

view—(in court proceedings) a formal inspection by the judge and jury of the scene of a crime or property mentioned in evidence.

检查

violence—the unlawful exercise of physical force.

暴力

violent—involving an unlawful exercise of force.

暴力的

visitation—a person's right to spend time with their children who are in the custody of the other parent, a foster parent, or other legal guardian.

探望权

visitation order—see *parenting time*.

探望令

vis major—a greater force, superior force; it is used in the civil law to mean act of god.

不可抗力

vitiate—to void or render a nullity; to impair.

破坏;使无效;可撤销

void—

1. not valid or legally binding.

无效的

2. declare that (something) is not valid or legally binding.

宣告无效

voidable contract—a valid contract that a party may cancel upon request. For example, a contract made by a minor is voidable by the minor or his or her legal guardian.

可撤销的合同

void contract—a contract that does not have any legal effect and cannot be enforced under any circumstances. For example, a contract to commit an illegal act is void.

无效合同

voir dire—a preliminary examination of a witness or a juror by a judge or counsel.

挑选陪审员

voir dire exam—the preliminary examination into the qualifications and potential biases of prospective witnesses or jurors.

对方对被传讯证人预先所作的讯问；对陪审员是否适合参加陪审所进行的调查

volenti non fit injuria—This is a Latin phrase which can be translated "For a willing person, there is no harm." It is used as a defense in civil cases. Someone who attempts to sue because he or she knowingly engaged in dangerous activities and was injured may not be able to recover damages, under the argument that the person knew the risks and consented. However, volenti non fit injuria is not a blanket defense which excuses people of all potential suits. In a simple example of this type of defense, an American football player takes to the field with the understanding that she or he may be involved in tackles and other sports maneuvers which could result in personal injury or even death, because of the nature of the game. As a result, if someone is tackled and sustains a head injury, that person cannot sue, because the player willingly participated, being aware of the risks. On the other hand, if a player beans another player over the head with a stick, the injured player has grounds for suit because being hit on the head with a stick is not a known and accepted risk of playing American football.

自愿承担风险（在美国侵权法中，受损害人明知且明确同意了活动中可能存在的风险，他就不得在事后就该活动导致的损害要求赔偿。）

voting trust—the accumulation in a single hand, or in a few hands, of shares of corporate stock belonging to many owners in order thereby to control the business of the company.

委托表决权；委托股票权

voucher—a small printed piece of paper that entitles the holder to a discount or that may be exchanged for goods or services.

优惠券

W

wade hearing—a pretrial hearing to test the fairness of a lineup. The issue at such a hearing is whether to admit or suppress the identification of the accused that resulted from the lineup.

公正指认听证；辨认嫌犯听证

waive—to give up a right, claim, or privilege.

放弃（权利、声明、特权）

waiver—the act of waiving or giving up a right, privilege, or claim.

自动放弃；弃权

waiver hearing—where a juvenile is charged with a felony, a two-phase hearing on a motion requesting that the family division of circuit court waive its jurisdiction and transfer the case to the criminal division of the circuit court. Waiver hearings are only held in cases involving "traditional waiver". See *waiver of jurisdiction*.

弃权听证

waiver of immunity—a means authorized by statute by which a witness, before testifying or producing evidence, may relinquish the right to refuse to testify against himself or herself, thereby making it possible for his or her testimony to be used against him or her in future proceedings.

放弃豁免权

waiver of jurisdiction—the process through which the family division of the circuit court relinquishes its jurisdiction over a juvenile who has committed a criminal offense, and transfers the case to the criminal division of the circuit court.

放弃(少年犯罪)司法管辖权

> 在美国,少年犯罪法律程序与正常的刑事法律程序不同,因为它们根据少年(未满18岁)的特点而设计。每个州都有不同类型的制度来处理它们的青少年事务。一些州还设有实际的少年法庭,而其他州将少年事务放在家庭或遗嘱法庭里处理。不过,当被控的犯罪非常严重时,拥有就少年事务进行聆讯的司法管辖权的大多数法庭可能将案件转入审判法庭。转移少年犯罪案件的过程被称为放弃司法管辖权。

There are two types of waivers:

1. *automatic waiver*: If a juvenile between ages 14 and 17 is charged with certain violations specified in statute (e.g., murder, armed robbery, first degree criminal sexual conduct), the prosecutor may file a complaint charging the juvenile as an adult. Such cases automatically come under the jurisdiction of the criminal division of the circuit court. Automatic waivers are sometimes referred to as "prosecutorial waivers".

自动放弃

2. *traditional waiver*: If a juvenile between ages 14 and 17 is charged with any felony, the prosecutor may file a motion requesting the family division of the circuit court to waive jurisdiction. If the prosecutor's motion is granted, the case is transferred to the criminal division of the circuit court, and the juvenile is tried as an adult.

传统放弃

walker hearing—a court proceeding to determine whether the police officer advised the defendant of his or her Miranda rights prior to giving a statement and whether the defendant voluntarily gave the statement.

沃克听证(法庭主要审查警察在抓捕嫌犯的过程中是否违规,比如是否明确告知嫌犯有米兰达权利、是否嫌犯自愿作的供词等。)

wanton—grossly negligent or careless; extremely reckless, etc.; virtually synonymous with reckless.

恶意的;漠不关心的;不道德的

ward—under the Michigan Revised Probate Code, a minor or legally incapacitated person who has been placed under the care of a guardian.

被监护人

warrant—a writ or paper issued by a judge or magistrate that allows the police to arrest a person or search a place. See also *arrest warrant*, *bench warrant*, *fugitive warrant*, *search warrant*.

批捕令;搜查令

warrantee—a person to whom a warranty is given.

被保证人;被担保人

warrantless search—examination of a person or premises without first obtaining a warrant, which may be lawful under such limited circumstances as a domestic violence situation, emergency, hot pursuit, consent, or threat of immediate removal of contraband.

无证搜查;未经批准搜查

warrant of arrest—a writ issued by a magistrate, justice, or other competent authority, to a sheriff or other officer, requiring him to arrest a person therein named and bring him before the magistrate or court to answer to a specific charge.

逮捕令

warrantor—a person or company that provides a warranty.

保证人;担保人

warrant recall—a procedure for removing from Department of State and State Police computers information concerning canceled warrants in order to avoid repeated or mistaken arrests.

撤销批捕令或搜查令

warranty—a written guarantee, issued to the purchaser of an article by its manufacturer, promising to repair or replace it if necessary within a specified period of time.

保修卡;保修单

waste—damage to an estate caused by an act or by neglect, esp. by a life-tenant.

（由终生受益人的行为或疏忽造成的）产业价值降低

watered stock—in corporate law, shares of stock that have been issued by the corporation for less than full lawful consideration.

（公司法中）虚股;掺水股票

weight of evidence—the balance or preponderance of evidence; the inclination of the greater amount of credible evidence, offered in a trial, to support one side of the issue rather than the other.

证据充分;大量证据证明

whereas—(esp. in legal preambles) taking into consideration the fact that.

鉴于

widow—a woman whose husband is dead, and who has not remarried. A man whose wife is dead is called a "widower".

寡妇

widow's election—a widow's choice whether she will inherit under the will or under statute; that is whether she will accept the provision made for her in the will, and acquiesce in her husband's disposition of his property, or disregard it and claim what the law allows her.

寡妇取得丈夫遗产的选择权

wildcat strike—an unauthorized strike.

自发的罢工;未经批准的罢工

will—a written instrument whereby a person makes a disposition of his or her property to take effect after his or her death. A will includes any codicil.

遗嘱（包括遗嘱附件）

willful /wilful—in civil proceedings, denotes an act that is intentional, or knowing, or voluntary, as distinguished from accidental.

故意的

winding up—the process of liquidating a corporation or partnership. It involves the process of collecting the assets, paying the expenses involved, satisfying the creditor's claims and distributing whatever is left—the net assets, usually in cash but possibly in kind, first to any preferred shareholders according to their liquidation preferences and rights, then to any other shareholders with more than normal liquidation rights, and finally pro rata among the rest of the shareholders.

停业清理

wiretap—the acquisition of the contents of any wire or oral communication through the use of any electronic, mechanical, or other device.

窃听

without prejudice—A dismissal "without prejudice" means that the plaintiff in a civil case or the prosecution in a criminal case may bring the case or claim again.

不影响将来的(权利或法律地位);可以再起诉

with prejudice—A dismissal "with prejudice" means that the plaintiff in a civil case or the prosecution in a criminal case is forever barred from bringing the case or claim again.

影响将来的(权利或法律地位);永远不得再起诉

witness—one who testifies to what he or she has seen, heard or otherwise observed.

证人

witness stand—the place in a court from which a witness gives evidence.

证人席

words of limitation—words used in an instrument conveying an interest in property which seem to indicate the party to whom a conveyance is made but which actually indicate the type of estate taken by the grantee.

限制用语

words of purchase—words in a property transfer that indicate who takes the estate. The term designates the nature of the estate granted, while words of limitation define the property rights given to the grantee.

财产转让中表明谁受让的用语

writ—a court order giving the authority to require the performance of a specific act.

正式文件；书面命令

writ of attachment—a writ of the court ordering the sheriff to seize or hold a debtor's property and bring the property before the court.

扣押令

writ of certiorari—see *certiorari*.

诉讼文件移送令

writ of error coram nobis—a common-law writ, the purpose of which is to correct a judgment in the same court in which it was rendered, on the ground of error of fact.

纠正有事实上错误的判决令

writ of execution—a judicial order that a judgment be enforced.

执行令状

writ of mandamus—a writ to compel performance of one's responsibilities as set forth by law.

（上级法院向下级法院发出的）书面命令；履行职责令

writ of prohibition—a writ used by a superior court to prevent an inferior court from exceeding its jurisdiction.

（上级法院向下级法院发出的不能越权的）禁令

writ of superintending control—a writ issued to prevent a gross miscarriage of justice by correcting the erroneous ruling of a lower court that is acting within its jurisdiction but is making mistakes of law or is acting in willful disregard of the law. The writ is issued when there is no appeal or when an appeal cannot provide adequate relief.

（对下级法院的）监管控制令

written instrument—anything reduced to writing; the agreement or contract the writing contains; a document or writing that gives formal expression to some act.

书证;书面证明

wrong—a breach, by commission or omission, of one's legal duty.
违反法律职责

wrongful—constituting a wrong; not fair, just, or legal.
违反法律职责的;不公的,非正义的,非法的

X

X—a mark that may be used as signature by one who is unable to write his or her name. The mark may be placed wherever the signature could be placed and does not have to be attested unless so required by statute.

"X"式签名(不写出某人的名字)

xoanon—primitive, usually wooden image of deity supposed to have fallen from Heaven; seldom found in Irish courtrooms.

木雕的神像

Y

year—when used without any other qualification, a 12 month period beginning on January 1.
一年时间;一个年度

year-and-a-day-rule—in criminal law, the common law rule that a death must occur within one year and one day of the act alleged to cause the death, for the death to constitute murder. The rule was not incorporated into the Model Penal Code and has been abandoned by most states.
一年零一天规则

yellow dog contract—an employment contract expressly prohibiting the named employee from joining labor unions under pain of dismissal.
以不加入工会为条件的雇佣合同

yield—the current return as a percentage of the price of a stock or bond.
利润;红利;利益

yield to maturity—a calculation of yield on a bond that takes into account the capital gain on a discount bond or capital loss on a premium bond.
到期收益

young person—person under 16, whose regular, fulltime employment is forbidden by the 1996 Protection of Young Persons (Employment) Act. A child over 14 may do light work during school holidays, but a child under 14 cannot be employed at all.

(14—17岁的)未成年人

youthful offender—term generally designating one who is for purposes of sentencing, older than a juvenile but younger than an adult.

未成年犯;未成年违法者

Z

zealous witness—a witness who displays undue favouritism towards one party in the case.

有偏见之证人；偏袒一方的证人

zero hours—If an employee is available for work but there is no work for him to do, the zero hours provision of the Organization of Working Time Act 1997 requires the employer to compensate him for one quarter of the time for which he had to be available.

零时条款

zoning—legislative action, usually on the municipal level, which separates or divides municipalities into districts for the purpose of regulating, controlling, or in some way limiting the use of private property, and the construction and/or structural nature of buildings erected within the zones or districts established.

分区规划；分区制

附录一　常见美国法引证缩写

Abbreviation	Title	Contents
A., A.2d	*Atlantic Reporter*, 1st and 2nd series	cases from Connecticut, Delaware, District of Columbia, Maine, Maryland, New Hampshire, New Jersey, Pennsylvania, Rhode Island,
A. L. R., A. L. R. 2d, A. L. R. 3d, A. L. R. 4th, A. L. R. 5th, A.L.R. Fed.	*American Law Reports*, 1st, 2nd, 3rd, 4th, 5th, Federal series	cases from Connecticut, Delaware, District of Columbia, Maine, Maryland, New Hampshire, New Jersey, Pennsylvania, Rhode Island,
Am. Jur. 2d	*American Jurisprudence*, Second	encyclopedia
B.R.	*United States Bankruptcy*	United States Bankruptcy Courts cases
C.F.R.	*Code of Federal Regulations*	federal regulations arranged by subject
Cal. Rptr., Cal. Rptr. 2d	*California Reporter*, 1st and 2nd series	cases from California Supreme Court; California Court of Appeal; and California Superior Court, Appellate
C.J.S.	*Corpus Juris Secundum*	encyclopedia
Ct. Int'l Trade or Ct. Intl. Trade	*Court of International Trade Reports*	cases from the United States Court of International Trade

(续表)

Abbreviation	Title	Contents
F., F. 2d, F. 3d	*Federal Reporter*, 1st, 2d, and 3d series	cases from all United States Courts of Appeals
F. Appx	*Federal Appendix* (*Bluebook* citations)	"unpublished" cases from all United States Courts of Appeals
F. Supp., F. Supp. 2d	*Federal Supplement*, 1st and 2d series	cases from all United States District Courts
F. R. D.	*Federal Rules Decisions*	rulings involving procedural rules, from all United States District Courts
Fed. Appx.	*Federal Appendix* (*ALWD Manual* citations)	"unpublished" cases from all United States Courts of Appeals
Fed. Cl.	*Federal Claims Reporter*	cases from the United States Court of Federal Claims
Fed. R. Civ. P.	*Federal Rules of Civil*	court rules
Fed. R. Crim. P.	*Federal Rules of Criminal*	court rules
Fed. R. Evid.	*Federal Rules of Evidence*	court rules
Fed. Reg.	*Federal Register*	federal regulations by date
ILCS	*Illinois Compiled Statutes*	Illinois statutes arranged by subject
Ill., Ill. 2d	*Illinois Reports*, 1st and 2d series	Illinois Supreme Court cases
Ill. Admin. Code	*Illinois Administrative Code*	Illinois regulations arranged by subject
Ill. App., Ill. App. 2d, Ill. App. 3d	*Illinois Appellate Court Reports*, 1st, 2d, and 3d series	Illinois Appellate Court cases
Ill. Cl.	*Illinois Court of Claims Reports*	Illinois Court of Claims cases
Ill. Comp. Stat.	*Illinois Compiled Statutes*	Illinois statutes arranged by subject
Ill. Comp. Stat. Ann.	*West's Smith-Hurd Illinois Compiled Statutes Annotated*	Illinois statutes arranged by subject
Ill. Dec.	*West's Illinois Decisions*	cases from Illinois Supreme Court and Illinois Appellate Court
Ill. Laws	*Laws of Illinois*	Illinois statutes by date
Ill. Reg.	*Illinois Register*	Illinois regulations by date
Ill. Rev. Stat.	*Illinois Revised Statutes*	Illinois statutes arranged by subject (previous code)
L. Ed., L. Ed. 2d	*United States Supreme Court Reports*, Lawyers' Edition, 1st and 2d series	United States Supreme Court cases

(续表)

Abbreviation	Title	Contents
M.J.	*West's Military Justice Reporter*	cases from the United States Court of Appeals for the Armed Forces and Military Service Courts of Criminal
N.E., N.E.2d	*North Eastern Reporter*, 1st and 2d series	cases from Illinois, Indiana, Massachusetts, New York, Ohio
N.W., N.W.2d	*North Western Reporter*, 1st and 2d series	cases from Iowa, Michigan, Minnesota, Nebraska, North Dakota, South Dakota, Wisconsin
N.Y.S., N.Y.S.2d	*New York Supplement*, 1st and 2d series	cases from New York Court of Appeals and New York Supreme Court, Appellate Division
P., P.2d	*Pacific Reporter*, 1st and 2d series	cases from Alaska, Arizona, California, Colorado, Hawaii, Idaho, Kansas, Montana, Nevada, New Mexico, Oklahoma, Oregon, Utah, Washington, Wyoming
S., S.2d	*Southern Reporter*, 1st and 2d series (*ALWD Manual* citations)	cases from Alabama, Florida, Louisiana, Mississippi
S.Ct.	*Supreme Court Reporter*	United States Supreme Court cases
S.E., S.E.2d	*South Eastern Reporter*, 1st and 2d series	cases from Georgia, North Carolina, South Carolina, Virginia, West
S.W., S.W.2d, S.W.3d	*South Western Reporter*, 1st, 2nd, and 3d series	cases from Arkansas, Kentucky, Missouri, Tennessee, Texas
So., So.2d	*Southern Reporter*, 1st and 2d series (*Bluebook* citations)	cases from Alabama, Florida, Louisiana, Mississippi
Stat.	*United States Statutes at Large*	federal statutes arranged by date
T.C.	*United States Tax Court Reports*	cases from United States Tax Court
U.S.	*United States Reports*	United States Supreme Court cases
U.S.C.	*United States Code*	federal statutes arranged by subject
U.S.C.A.	*United States Code Annotated*	federal statutes arranged by subject
U.S.C.S.	*United States Code Service*	federal statutes arranged by subject
Vet. App.	*West's Veterans Appeals Reporter*	cases from the United States Court of Appeals for Veterans Claims

附录二 常用法律缩略语

A

A. Atlantic Reporter (USA)
ABA American Bar Association
A. B. L. R. Australian Business Law Review
A. C. Appeal cases (see Library guide no. 4 Finding Law Reports + Digests)
ACC Association of Corporate Counsel
A. J. C. L. American Journal of Comparative Law
A. J. F. L. Australian Journal of Family Law
A. J. I. L. American Journal of International Law
Ala. Admin. Code Alabama Administrative Code (unofficial text)
Ala. Code Code of Alabama 1975 (unofficial text)
Alaska Admin. Code Alaska Administrative Code (unofficial text)
Alaska Stat. Alaska Statutes (unofficial text)
A. L. J. Australian Law Journal
A. L. J. R. Australian Law Journal Reports
All E. R. All England Law Reports
All E. R. Rev All England Law Reports Annual Review
A. L. M. D. Australian Legal Monthly Digest
A. L. Q. Arab Law Quarterly

A. L. R. American Law Reports

A. L. R. American Law Reports **or** Australian Law Reports

A. L. R. Fed. American Law Reports，Federal

Am. Jur. American Jurisprudence

Am. Jur. 2d. American Jurisprudence，2nd Series

Anglo-Am. L. R. Anglo-American Law Review

Anor another

A. R. Alberta Reports（1977— ）

Arbitration Int. Arbitration International

Ariz. Admin. Code Arizona Administrative Code（unofficial text）

Ariz. Admin. Reg. Arizona Administrative Register（unofficial text）

Ariz. Rev. Stat. Arizona Revised Statutes（unofficial text）

Ark. Code Arkansas Code（unofficial text）

Art. article

Asap as soon as possible

A. T. R. Australian Tax Review

Atty attorney

B

B. A. P. Bankruptcy Appellate Panel

B. C. C. British company law cases

B. C. L. C. Butterworths company law cases

B. C. L. R. British Columbia Law Reports

BFP Bona fide purchaser

B. J. I. B. & F. L. Butterworths Journal of International Banking & Financial Law

B. L. Business Lawyer

B. L. R. Building Law Reports **or** Business Law Review

Bracton L. J. Bracton Law Journal

Brit. J. Criminol. British Journal of Criminology

BR or B/R Bankruptcy（also the abbreviation for the United States Bankruptcy Courts Reporter，West's Bankruptcy Reporter）

B. T. R. British Tax Review

Build. L. R. Building Law Reports

Bull. E. C. Bulletin of the European Communities

B. Y. I. L. British Yearbook of International Law

C

c. Chapter（of Act of Parliament）

CA class action

C. A. Court of Appeal

Cal. Code California Code (unofficial text)

Cal. Code Reg. California Code of Regulations (see: CCR below)

Cambrian L. R. Cambrian Law Review

Can. Bar J. Canadian Bar Journal

Can. B. R. Canadian Bar Review

CB casebook

CBJ California Bar Journal

C. B. L. J. Canadian Business Law Journal

C. B. R. Canadian Bar Review

CC Commerce Clause

C-C Counterclaim

C. C. L. T. Canadian cases on the law of torts (1976—)

CCR California Code of Regulations (official text?) (source: Thomson/West)

CE Collateral estoppel

C. E. C. European Community cases

C. F. I. L. R. Company Financial and Insolvency Law Review

CFR Call for Response (At the US Supreme Court, if the other side has stated it will not)

C. F. R. Code of Federal Regulations

Ch. Chancery Division (see Library guide no. 4 Finding Law Reports+Digests)

CIF coming into force

C. I. L. J. S. A. Comparative and International Law Journal of Southern Africa

C. J. Q. Civil Justice Quarterly

CJS Corpus Juris Secundum

CL common law

C. L. current law

C. L. B. Commonwealth Law Bulletin

C. L. E. A. Newsletter Commonwealth Legal Education Association. Newsletter

C. L. J. Cambridge Law Journal

C. L. P. Current Legal Problems

C. L. & P. Computer Law and Practice

C. L. Q. Civil Justice Quarterly

C. L. R. Commonwealth Law Reports (Australia)

C. L. S. R. Computer Law and Security Report

C. L. Y. Current Law Year Book

C. M. L. R. Common Market Law Reports

C. M. L. Rev. Common Market Law Review

CNeg contributory negligence

Co. law company lawyer

C. O. D. Crown Office Digest
Com. Cas. commercial cases
Com. Jud. J. Commonwealth Judicial Journal
Comp. & Law Computers and Law
Comp. L. & P. Computer Law and Practice
Cong. Rec. Congressional Record
Con. L. R. Construction Law Reports
Const. L. J. Construction Law Journal
Conv. (n. s.) Conveyancer and Property Lawyer (new series)
C. P. C. Carswell's practice cases
Cr. App. R. Criminal Appeal Reports
Cr. App. R. (S.) Criminal Appeal Reports (sentencing)
Crim. L. J. Criminal Law Journal
Crim. L. R. Criminal Law Review
Csl. counsel
C. & S. L. J. Company and Securities Law Journal
Ct. Cl. the United States Court of Federal Claims Reporter
C. T. & E. P. Q. Capital Taxes and Estates Planning Quarterly
C. T. L. R Computer and Telecommunications Law Review
Cx-C cross-claim
Cx constitution
Cxl constitutional

D

DA district attorney
DAC days after contract
DAR driving after revocation
DB dead body
DBD death by drowning
DC denied charges
DC district court
D. C. divisional court
Denning L. J. Denning Law Journal
DL driver's license
D. L. R. Dominion Law Reports
DOA date of accident
DOB do our best
DOD day of death
DOJ decree of justice

DOP division of prison

DOV date of violation

DP due process

DR delayed remedy

D. & R. decisions and reports of the European Court of human rights

DT direct transfer

DTF drug trance force

DWD drunk while driving

DWS driving while suspended

Δ (Greek letter delta) Defendant

E

E. B. L. R. European business law review

E. C. C. European commercial cases

E. C. L. European current law

E. C. L. R. European Competition Law Review

E. C. R. European Court Reports (the official series)

EE employee

E. G. Estates Gazette

E. G. C. S. Estates Gazette Case Summaries

E. G. L. R. Estates Gazette Law Reports

E. H. R. R. European Human Rights Reports

E. I. P. R. European Intellectual Property Review

E. J. I. L. European Journal of International Law

E. L. Q. Ecology Law Quarterly

E. L. R. European Law Review

E. M. L. R Entertainment and Media Law Reports

Ent. L. R. Entertainment Law Review

ER employer

E. R. English Reports

et al. Latin for "and others"

E. T. M. R. European Trade Mark Reports

Eur. Access European access

F

Fam Family Division (see Library guide no. 4 Finding Law Reports + Digests)

Fam. Law family law

F. App'x Federal Appendix

F. Cas. Federal Cases 1789—1880

F. C. R. Family Court Reporter **or** Federal Court Reports（Australia）**or** Federal Court Reports（Canada）

Fed. R. Bankr. P. Federal Rules of Bankruptcy Procedure

Fed. R. Civ. P. （sometimes FRCP）Federal Rules of Civil Procedure

Fed. R. Crim. P. Federal Rules of Criminal Procedure

Fed. Reg. （sometimes FR）Federal Register（see Federal Register for full text from 1994 to date）

Fed. R. Evid. （sometimes FRE）Federal Rules of Evidence

Fin. L. R. Financial Law Reports

F. L. R. Family Law Reports **or** Federal Law Reports（Australia）

F. S. R. Fleet Street Reports

F Supp. Federal Supplement（USA）

F. Supp. 2d Federal Supplement，2nd Series

F. T. L. R. Financial Times Law Reports

G

GAC guilty as charged

GAS gang anti-social

GATT General Agreement on Tariffs and Trade

GB gun broker

GC General Counsel

GC grandfather clause

GCR general court rules

GFA grounds for assault

GI general inquiry

GL government and laws

GSW gun shot wound

GTI getting teenagers involved

GVR Grant，Vacate，and Remand

G. W. D. Green's weekly digest

H

Harv. L. R. Harvard Law Review

HBC hit by car

HBD has been drinking

HDC holder in due course

H. L. R. Housing Law Reports

Howard Journal Howard Journal of Criminal Justice

H. R. J. Human Rights Journal（shelved as Revue des droits de l'homme）

H. R. L. J. Human Rights Law Journal

H. R. Q. Human Rights Quarterly

HS home search

I

IALS Bull. Institute of Advanced Legal Studies. Bulletin

I. B. L. International business lawyer

I. Bull. Interights Bulletin

I. C. C. L. R. International Company and Commercial Law Review

I. C. J. International Court of Justice. Reports of judgments.

I. C. L. Q. International and Comparative Law Quarterly

I. C. L. R. International Construction Law Review

I. C. R. Industrial Cases Reports (see Library guide no. 4 Finding Law Reports + Digests)

I. F. L. Rev. International Financial Law Review

I. I. C. International Review of Industrial Property and Copyright Law

I. J. E. C. L. International Journal of Estuarine and Coastal Law

I. L. J. Industrial Law Journal

I. L. M. International Legal Materials

I. L. P. International Legal Practitioner

I. L. & P. Insolvency Law and Practice

I. L. R. International Labour Review or International Law Reports

I. L. R. M. Irish Law Reports Monthly

I. L. T. Irish Law Times

I. M. L. International Media Law

Imm. and Nat. L. & P. Immigration and Nationality Law and Practice

Imm. A. R. Immigration Appeals Reports

Ind. Sol. independent solicitor

Ins. L. & P. Insolvency Law and Practice or Insurance Law and Practice

Int. J. Comp. L. L. I. R. International Journal of Comparative Law and Industrial Relations

Int. J. Law & Fam. International Journal of Law and the Family

Int. J. Soc. L. International Journal of the Sociology of Law

Int. Rel. International Relations

I. P. D. Intellectual Property Decisions

I. P. Q. Intellectual Property Quarterly

I. P. R. Intellectual Property Reports

I. R. Irish Reports (Eire)

Ir. Jur. Irish Jurist

Ir. Jur. Rep. Irish Jurist Reports
I. R. L. I. B. Industrial Relations Legal Information Bulletin
I. R. L. R. Industrial Relations Law Reports
I. T. E. L. R. International Trust and Estate Law Reports
I. T. R. Industrial Tribunal Reports

J

J judge **or** justice，according to jurisdiction
J. A. L. Journal of African Law
J. B. L. Journal of Business Law
J. Ch. L. Journal of Child Law
J. C. L. Journal of Child Law **or** Journal of Contract Law **or** Journal of Criminal Law
J. C. L. & Crim. Journal of Criminal Law and Criminology
J. C. M. S. Journal of Common Market Studies
J. Env. L. Journal of Environmental Law
J. E. R. L. Journal of Energy and Natural Resources Law
J. I. B. L. Journal of International Banking Law
J. I. F. D. L. Journal of International Franchising and Distribution Law
J. J. Jersey Judgments
J. Law & Soc. Journal of Law and Society
J. Leg. Hist. Journal of Legal History
J. L. H. Journal of Legal History
J. L. I. S. Journal of Law and Information Science
J. L. S. S. Journal of the Law Society of Scotland
J. M. L. C. Journal of Maritime Law and Commerce
J. M. L. & P. Journal of Media Law and Practice
JMOL judgment as a matter of law
JNOV judgment notwithstanding verdict
J. P. Justice of the Peace Reports
J. P. L. Journal of Planning and Environment Law
J. P. N. Justice of the Peace Journal
J. R. Juridical Review
J. W. T. Journal of World Trade
Jx jurisdiction

K

K contract
K. B. King's bench (see Library guide no. 4 Finding Law Reports + Digests)
K. C. L. J. Kings College Law Journal

Kingston L. R. Kingston Law Review
K. I. R. Knight's Industrial Reports
KOS kill on sight
KP kidnap and ransom
KS kill stealing
KT kid toucher

L

Law & Just. Law and Justice
Law Lib. Law Librarian
Law & Pol. Law and Policy
L/C letter of credit
L. C. lord chancellor
L. C. News Law Centres News
L. C. P. law and contemporary problems
L. Ed. United States Supreme Court Reports (Lawyers' Edition)
L. Exec. legal executive
L. G. Rev. Local Government Review
L. I. E. I. Legal Issues of European Integration
Lit. Litigation
Liverpool L. R. Liverpool Law Review
L. J. Law Journal (each vol. divided into Ch., Ex., K. B. etc.)
L. J. R. Law Journal Reports
LLC limited liability company
Lloyd's Rep. Lloyd's List Reports (after 1951)
LLP limited liability partnership
Ll. Rep. Lloyd's List Reports (before 1951)
L. M. C. L. Q. Lloyds Maritime and Commercial Law Quarterly
L. Q. R. Law Quarterly Review
L. R. R. P. Reports of Restrictive Practices Cases
L. S. Legal Studies
L. S. Gaz. Law Society's Gazette
L. T. Law Times
L. Teach. Law Teacher

M

Mal. L. R. Malaya Law Review
McGill L. J. McGill Law Journal
Med. Leg. J. Medico-legal Journal

Med. Sci. Law Medicine, Science and Law
Mel. L. J. Melanesian Law Journal
M. L. B. Manx Law Bulletin
M. L. J. Malayan Law Journal
M. L. R. Modern Law Review
MOU Memorandum of Understanding
MPC Model Penal Code

N

N. D. new directions in the law of the sea
NDA Non-Disclosure Agreement
N. E. North Eastern Reporter (USA)
New L. J. New Iaw Journal
NGO non government organization
Nig. L. J. Nigerian Law Journal
N. I. J. B. Northern Ireland Law Reports
N. I. L. Q. Northern Ireland Legal Quarterly
No. Number
N. W. North Western Reporter (USA)
N. Y. S. New York Supplement
N. Z. C. L. C. New Zealand company law cases
N. Z. L. R. New Zealand Law Reports

O

OBJ objection
O. D. I. L. ocean development and international law
OFA order for arrest
O. F. L. R. Offshore Financial Law Reports
O. G. L. T. R. Oil and Gas Law and Taxation Review
O. J. Official Journal of the European Communities
O. J. L. S. Oxford Journal of Legal Studies
OOB out on bail
OOC out of control
OOJ order of justice
OPN opinion
Ors other
OTD on the docket
OWO only way out

P

P. Pacific Reporter

p. page

P. Probate Division (see Library guide no 4 Finding Law Reports + Digests) **or** Pacific Reporter (USA)

PA power of attorney

PA public act

P. A. D. planning appeal decisions

Parl. Aff. parliamentary affairs

P. C. C. Palmer's company cases

P. & C. R. Property and Compensation Reports

PL public Law

P. L. R. Planning Law Reports

P. N. professional negligence

Pol. J. Police Journal

pp. pages

Prison Serv. J. Prison Service Journal

Probat. J. Probation Journal

Proc A. S. I. L. Proceedings of the American Society of International Law

PSV probably stealing vehicles

PT police training

PTO pretrial order

PTR pretrial release

Pub. L. Public law

Π (Greek letter Pi) Plaintiff

Q

Q. B. Queen's bench

QCD quickclaim deed

QDRO qualified domestic relations order

QEW qualified expert witness

QLU quarterly legal update

QPD qualified public depository

R

R Rex **or** Regina

R. A. rating appeals

R. A. D. I. C. African Journal of International and Comparative Law

R. C. A. D. I. Recueil des cours. Hague Academy of International Law

R. E. or R/E real estate

Res. B. Home Office Research Bulletin

Rev. Proc. Revenue Procedure (published in IRB)

Rev. Rul. Revenue Ruling (published in IRB)

R. F. D. A. Revue francaise de droit aérien et spatial

R. I. A. A. Reports of International Arbitral Awards

R. I. D. A. Revue internationale du droit d'auteur

R J Recurring Judgement (published in All In Reports)

R. M. C. Revue du Marché commun

R. P. C. Reports of Patent, Design and Trade Mark Cases

R. P. R. Real Property Reports (Canada)

R. T. R. Road Traffic Reports

R. V. R. Rating and Valuation Reporter

S

s. or § section

S. Southern Reporter (USA)

S. A. L. J. South African Law Journal

S. A. L. R. South African Law Reports

S. A. S. R. South Australian State Reports

S. C. C. R. Scottish Criminal Case Reports

S. C. L. R. Scottish Civil Law Reports

SCOTUS Supreme Court of the United States (Supreme Court of the United States)

S. C. Session Cases (Scotland)

S. C. R. (or SCR) Supreme Court Reports (Supreme Court of Canada)

S. C. R. Supreme Court Reports (Canada)

S. Ct. Supreme Court Reporter (Supreme Court of the United States)

sd said

S. E. South Eastern Reporter

S. E. South Eastern Reporter (USA)

S. E. 2d South Eastern Reporter, 2nd Series

SI statutory instruments

S. I. statutory instrument

S. J or Sol. J Solicitors' Journal

S/J summary judgment

S. L. G. Scottish Law Gazette

S. L. T. Scots Law Times

SMJ subject-matter jurisdiction

So. Southern Reporter

So. 2d Southern Reporter, 2nd Series

Sol. L. Socialist Lawyer

SOL Statute of Limitations

SOR Statutory Orders and Regulations

S. P. L. P. Scottish Planning Law and Practice

ss. or §§ sections

Stat. United States Statutes at Large (See United States Code)

Stat. L. R. Statute Law Review

S. T. C. Simon's Tax Cases

S. W. South Western Reporter (USA)

T

Tas. S. R. Tasmanian State Reports

Tax taxation

Tax. Int. Taxation International

T. D. treasury decision

T. L. R. Times Law Reports (the published series 1884—1952). Since 1971, reports from the Times are in the Short Loan Collection or Trading Law Reports.

TM Trademark (such as a word or phrase identifying a company or product)

Top. L. topical law

Trent L. J. Trent Law Journal

Tr. & Est. Trusts and Estates

Tr. L. trading law

Tru. L. I. Trust Law International

U

UCC Uniform Commercial Code

UCMJ Uniform Code of Military Justice (Laws of the U.S. military)

U. G. L. J. University of Ghana Law Journal

U. L. R. Utilities Law Review

UPC Uniform Probate Code

USC United States Code. It is a compilation and codification of all the general and permanent Federal laws of the United States.

USCA United States Code Annotated

USCCAN United States Code Congressional and Administrative News

USCS United States Code Service

UST United States Treaties and Other International Agreements (See Treaty series.)

U. T. L. J. University of Toronto Law Journal

V

VA verbal abuse
V. A. T. T. R. Value Added Tax Tribunal Reports
VAW violence against women
VIO violence
V. L. R. Victorian Law Reports
VOC victim of corruption
VOCA victims of crime act
VOL volume
VOP violation of parole
VOV victory over violence
VR violent rage

W

WA with attitude
WB wife beater
WCK weapons check
WCO weapons control officer
WDR world domain rights
Web. J. C. L. I. Web Journal of Current Legal Issues
Welf. R. Bull. Welfare Rights Bulletin
W. I. R. West Indian Reports
W. L. R. Weekly Law Reports
W. N. Weekly Notes
WTNS witnesses
WTO World Trade Organization
WTTL where the truth lies
W. Va. Code West Virginia Code (unofficial text)
W. W. R. Western Weekly Reports

X

XIP execute in place
XN examination in chief
XXN cross examination

Y

YA young arrest
Y. B. Eur. L. Yearbook of European Law

Yb. Int'l. Env. L. Yearbook of International Environmental Law
Y. B. W. A. Yearbook of World Affairs
YC youth court
YJ youth justice
Y. L. C. T. Yearbook of Law, Computers and Technology
Y\N yes or no
YSP youth smoking prevention

Z

ZD zero dignity
ZH zero hum
ZI zero intelligence
ZR zero restriction
ZRM zero releasing module
ZTZ zero tolerance zone